SMASHING THE GATES OF HELL

IN THE LAST DAYS

Cover photo: Scene at Banias, Israel. At the foot of Mount Hermon lies the deserted village of Banias. Here stood the mighty Roman city of Caesarea Philippi in Christ's time. It was here that Jesus came to make His pronouncement of the ultimate victory of the Church (see chapter 13).

Dr. Amos Millard has written: "From an archaeological, geographical and topographical point of view, Jesus' prophecy concerning the Church being planted at the gates of hell (hades) could hardly have been more dramatic. This city was built by Philip the Tetrarch and dedicated and named for Caesar Augustus, and for himself. Josephus describes a huge temple of whitish stone built by Philip and dedicated to the worship of Augustus Caesar.

"The temple was near the Greek cave dedicated to the worship of Pan. The face of the cliff is covered with niches in which idols were placed. From the cave of Pan flowed the stream that is one of the principle sources of the Jordan River. The cave was considered to be the entrance to the Nether World, Hades or Hell."

As the Romans worshipped Caesar in Christ's time, humanity is today turning to the worship of man as the deity. We see this as the core teaching both of humanism and the New Age Movement. The deity of man has always been a great challenge to the unique Lordship of Jesus.

Jesus stood at the gate of hell to announce the ultimate victory of His Church (Matthew 16). Within one generation the Church had launched a spiritual thrust that penetrated the very household of Caesar in Rome and shook the foundations of the Imperial throne.

Millard comments, "The river shifted and no longer comes out of the mouth of the cave, but from an opening somewhat below. The decaying niches and caves (cover picture) to the right of the main cave testify to the decadent power and glory of self deistical man."

In this last day generation the Church must once again advance and smash the very gates of hell—before the return of our Lord Jesus Christ.

Dr. John Wilson of Pepperdine College will soon excavate Caesarea Philippi and will undoubtedly unearth some of Israel's most marvelous treasures of Biblical significance. This is one of the most important geographical cities for Christendom, for here Jesus said, "Upon this rock I will build my church and the gates of hell shall not prevail against it."

(Photo reversed for visual effect on cover design)

SMASHING THE GATES OF HELL

IN THE LAST DAYS

DAVID ALLEN LEWIS

New Leaf Press

FIFTH EDITION
November 1992

Library of Congress Catalog Number: 86-63887
ISBN: 0-89221-143-1

Typesetting: Type-O-Graphics, Springfield, MO.

TABLE OF CONTENTS

DEDICATION

To Ramona, my loving wife and dedicated co-laborer in all aspects of our ministry and calling.

To my mother Verda Lewis for her guidance in my early Christian life.

To my daughters Rebecca and Cassandra, still involved in our work in the Kingdom of God.

PUBLISHER'S PREFACE

Finally, here is a book that presents the positive side of prophecy...a perspective of victory and triumph rather than doom and gloom. After reading this revolutionary book, believers will understand the true reasons why God chose to end His Word with the Book of Revelation—for in it we can discover secrets that will revolutionize our spiritual lives.

This is a book about Bible prophecy, but the theme of it is "Worship God, for the testimony of Jesus is the Spirit of Prophecy" (Rev. 19:10). What excites us about *Smashing The Gates Of Hell* is that the emphasis is on Jesus Christ—the author and finisher of our faith. Dr. Lewis is careful to point out that the last Book of the Bible is not a doomsday book—but a message of the hope, triumph and victory of Jesus Christ over the Antichrist and all the powers of darkness. There is no need to fear, for we will share the victory with our Lord!

As host of "The Prophecy Digest" television program, Dr. Lewis has shared the excitement of his biblical research with millions of viewers. His research and interpretation of God's Word have helped piece together the end-time prophecy puzzle and have helped Christians understand the "total picture" of final victory outlined in God's Word.

Dr. Lewis's purpose in this book is to present the full scope of God's plan and purpose for His Church and to challenge believers to work diligently to advance those purposes until the return of Jesus Christ. Dr. Lewis outlines an agenda for end-time victory and presents challenges to last us until the trumpet sounds!

In a day when the secular media pounds the doomsday drum, here is a clear, prophetic message of faith, courage and victory. Here, truly, is a word of hope for modern man.

This book is a must for every believer.

The Publisher

INTRODUCTION

The premise of this book is that it is possible for the Church to maintain powerful, high-level victory as we approach the end of the age. This concept flies in the face of the doomsayers who see no hope for the Church as anything other than an underground remnant of the faithful few.

The victory we speak of is potential, not predetermined. It is available, but not inevitable. We, the Church, must awaken from slumber with a will to cooperate with God. We must begin to implement His purposes as revealed in His Word. We must be "doers of the word and not hearers only."

In order to attain the greatest manifestation of victory in these end times we must operate through knowledge (Colossians 1:9), intercession and faith-action, or good works. This is the threefold path to realized victory. The "if clauses" of the Bible, as we shall point out, show us that we have alternatives set before us. Oh yes, there are predetermined events. The whole scheme of end-time, prophetic events as declared in the Bible is fixed by the forecouncils of God; but passages such as Jeremiah 18:7,8 indicate that there is a flexibility in God's dealing with man on the short-term basis for the immediate future. Should we be concerned about the quality of life in the time frame before us—from now until the trumpet sounds? Is there anything we can do to affect the quality of life, the degree of liberty, the level of victory the Church experiences in the last days? Is it important? Should we be fatalists and "accept what comes" as inevitable, or is there something God wants us to do about our situation in this present world?

I believe in a *literal* rapture of the Church, a tribulation time, a *literal* 1000-year Millennium. I believe the coming of Christ is potentially imminent, but I have believed that for over 40 years—since I was a small child. I still believe it, but realize that what is "soon" to one is not "soon" to another. Soon is a relative term. I cannot say that Jesus is coming soon, for without knowing what soon means to you I could be misleading you. I believe He could come today, but that we should make every preparation for future life right here on this earth. "Ready to go, ready to stay, ready oh, Lord, thy will to do." Buy life insurance. Go to college. Get married. Have a family. Build a house. Prepare for life here on earth. Witness for the gospel's sake. Win souls. Occupy until He comes.

The task before us is enormous, but not impossible. We undertake nothing without the help and guidance of our Lord. There is no desire to *change* His will, but to *understand* and implement His will, remembering that "faith without works is dead."

Here is a brand new journey into the great, old truths of Bible prophecy, for we seek to see the *positive* side of prophecy. If you want a doomsday message all you have to do is watch the evening news on your television. God's prophetic Word is a message of courage and hope to His children. Further, it is a mandate to action. God is looking for participants, not spectators, in the end-time drama.

Everyone senses that something is truly different about this age in which we live. A great polarization of humanity is taking place. There is no neutrality possible. Jesus said, "He that is not with me is against me." Secular humanists, eastern mystics, the New Age Movement, and a host of others are strangely drawn together in a bond of agreement. Like the church of the born-again ones, they too have an invisible head. Our head is Christ, and all born-again believers are united in Him (regardless of our divisions). Even so, all outside of Christ have an invisible head to whom Jesus says, "Ye are of your father the devil." Satan is the invisible spiritual head of all lost souls.

Our task is to win Satan's followers to our Lord and His cause. Our purpose is furthered by bringing new prophetic, visionary hope to the Church so that we may be best equipped to wage the end-time spiritual warfare.

We will not stop the end-time apostasy, but we will not participate in it. We will enlighten many who would have succumbed to Satan's final deception. It is a deception so vast, so enormous, so devious that it staggers the mind to contemplate its scope and effect; but we will not be deceived, and we will rescue many souls from the last apostasy. Even now leaders of the New Age Movement are coming to Jesus and renouncing the lies of the devil—and that is a fact.

No, we will not put the devil out of business, but we will not surrender to him. We can deal him some heavy blows. God is bigger than the devil. Fatalism and hopeless doomsaying play into the devil's hands. How Satan would like for the Church to believe in and preach nothing but defeat. That is faith in reverse.

Rise up, men and women of God! Charge the enemy's citadels! The gates of hell shall not prevail! There is "strength for today and bright hope for tomorrow."

How some people can read the book of Revelation and see more Antichrist than Jesus Christ is hard to understand. How can you see more devil than God in the *Revelation of Jesus Christ?* It is a sorry state when many prophetic systems center more on evil than on the triumph of righteousness.

It must be admitted that this is a strange book. There is probably not another like it. This is a message about the *positive side of prophecy.* How unfortunate that some Christians fear the study of prophecy. They are afraid of a doomsday message. How sad that they do not realize that for the believer *there is no doomsday message.* The message of the Bible is triumph, not doom.

Have you read the book of *Revelations* lately? If you have, you didn't read it in the Bible. My Bible has no book of *Revelations* (plural) in it. The last book in your Bible is "The Revelation (singular) of Jesus Christ" (Revelation 1:1). The last book of the Bible is the unique message of Christ's victory over the beast, his kingdom, and his diabolical cohorts. The star of the end-time drama is *not* the Antichrist. The star of the end-time drama is Jesus Christ our Lord. Antichrist will reign but a short time. He is a failure. He is slated for defeat. Jesus will reign forever and forever, hallelujah! We shall reign with Him, not only in the 1000-year Millennium, but in the continuing eternal Kingdom of God.

An old-time song by William Grum proclaims, there is "Victory Ahead!"

> Victory Ahead! Victory Ahead!
> Through the blood of Jesus, victory ahead;
> Trusting in the Lord, I hear the conqu'ror's tread,
> By faith I see the victory ahead.

Make no mistake, the conqueror is not Satan, it is Jesus. Our God is marching on. His truth is marching on. We have read the last page of The Book, and we win.

Yes, victory *ahead*—but what about now? Is defeat for the Church the only prospect in an apostate age? We face formidable foes. We are not blind to the problems of our times. We are asked, will there be end-time revival or apostasy? There will be both. It is not an either/or proposition. There will definitely be final rebellion against God. Satan will not quit until he is defeated at the hand of our Lord. Revival will come if we call out to God in faith. God uses human instrumentality, and basically *intervenes in human affairs only when He is invited to do so.* That is why intercession in prayer is so vitally important. It is true that there are certain specific circumstances that demand the intervention of God whether anyone prays or not. He will not allow the total destruction of the Church, for He assures us that "the gates of hell shall not prevail against the church" (Matthew 16). He will not allow the total destruction of Israel, the physical seed of Jacob, for He has a plan to fulfill that involves Israel. He will not allow the total destruction of the human race, for He has a plan for this earth that cannot be denied. Beyond that, I find the premise true that God intervenes when He is invited to do so. I am not limiting God. I am simply listening to what I hear Him saying in the Word. He ever seeks "for a man among them, that should make up the hedge, and stand in the gap before me for the land, that I should not destroy it: but I found none" (Ezekiel 22:30). In that dark and bitter hour of Israel's history we hear God lamenting, "I found none." Destruction came upon the land and upon the people. What will it be in our day? The choice is up to you. We have choices. The ultimate and eternal victory is secured. The end-time, prophetic events will not be altered; but for the time directly ahead of us it is essential that we be well informed, pray and take the right course of action. This book describes the reasons for intercessory prayer, examines the teaching of the Bible doctrines relating to end-time events such as the rapture of the Church and the Millennium. It is a call to active involvement in and implementation of the end-time purposes of God.

When the ten spies brought the bad report to Moses, and the two spies returned with a report that victory was possible, the children of Israel had a choice. When they stood between Mount Ebal and Mount Gerizim at a later date they were given a choice. We too have choices to make. Predicated on how you and I respond to these choices, the quality of our victory in the near future will be determined.

Ignore the whole thing or live in apathy and, believe me, Satan will make your choices for you. How he would love to shape the face of your future! How he longs to silence the Church. Listen! The darkest dreams and doom-visions of modern day "Jonah" prophets will be fulfilled if we do nothing. Have no doubt of that, but as Nineveh found the way to avert the God-inspired, prophet-pronounced judgment, so can we. Are you ready for a new challenge? Are you ready for a refreshing look at the old truths about end-time prophecy? Here it is: *Smashing the Gates of Hell in the Last Days.*

CHAPTER 1

THE DANIEL FACTOR

This is not a commentary on the book of Daniel. This chapter reveals some things normally overlooked in the life and activity of the prophet Daniel.

No prophet could have finer credentials than Daniel. Ezekiel speaks of three men as the highest illustration of righteousness. They are Noah, Job and Daniel (Ezekiel 14:14,20). Beyond that, and of far higher importance, Jesus himself places His seal of approbation upon Daniel when He says, "When ye therefore shall see the abomination of desolation, spoken of by Daniel the prophet..." (Matthew 24:15).

Daniel is a prime example of what prophecy should accomplish in and through the life of a believer. He is the role model for this chapter and a couple other chapters that tell of the Daniel Factor.

WHAT PROPHECY IS NOT

Bible prophecy is not a doomsday message. It should not promote fear in the life of a believer. Probably more nonsense has been promoted in the name of Bible prophecy than any other single religious subject. Eschatological literature today abounds with wild schemes for identifying the Antichrist and with questionable systems for fixing a date for the Second Coming of Christ. Prophecy is not a game.

Prophecy parlor games have done nothing but disgrace the noble message of the Bible. Many are deeply disillusioned when the fantasies fail to be fulfilled. Prophecy has been hurt by some of its professed friends more than by all of its enemies put together.

The critical element missing in a lot of modern Bible prophecy teaching is what we call the Daniel Factor. Daniel ranks with John the Revelator as one of the greatest eschatologists of all time, other than Jesus Himself. (Eschatology means teaching of end-time events.)

BIBLE PROPHECY CONFERENCE

The Bible teacher has a big chart covering the front of the church. It is a road map through the Scripture to eternity. It shows us where we are going. He outlines seven dispensations and fourteen end-time events. Some of the people in the audience are frightened by the seals, trumpets and vials of wrath. The thundering hoofbeats of the four horsemen of the apocalypse drum their doom message home to trembling hearts. Perhaps others are thrilled with the prospect that God is finally going to wind this mess up and get us out of here. This approach is not entirely without results. Thousands of people have been saved by reading Hal Lindsay's *Late Great Planet Earth*. Most of the people glance at their watches as the prophetic Bible teacher walks to the right hand side of the chart saying, "And in conclusion...." Ho, hum, well that's over. Let's stop for a pizza on the way home, but let's be quick about it. I have to get an early start to work in the morning.

Something is missing here. We call it the Daniel Factor. Prophecy is more than a mind trip. It is more than mere intellectual exercise. It should be a powerful motivational force in the believer's life. But how do you relate the future to the present? What does the rapture or the millennium have to do with practical, everyday Christian living?

MORE THAN A MIND TRIP

Daniel did more than study and transmit prophecy. He got involved with God's predicted plans through intercessory prayer. That in itself raises a question which we will deal with later. Further, Daniel was a man of action. He implemented what he saw to be God's purposes through his good works. There are the three elements of the *Daniel Factor*: knowledge, intercession, and action. All three are necessary if we are to attain end-time victory for the Church on the highest plane possible. We must *know* God's plan for the Church. We must intercede for the present benefit of the Church and all mankind. We must *act positively* to implement the purposes of God for this present time-season. God is looking for participants, not mere spectators in the end-time drama. Are you ready to get involved in the dynamics of Kingdom-living as we move through the process of time toward the day of the trumpet's sounding and the dawning of the millennial age? If so, you are ready for the Daniel Factor. We are not just going to a prophecy conference to look at yet another chart of future events. We will start there, but we will not treat prophecy as a mere set of mental gymnastics. Those who do will get trapped in the sensationalist "can-you-top-this" syndrome, and then you might as well read science fiction. It will do about as much good. We repudiate the fantasy approach to end-time prophecy. Prophecy properly understood encourages faith, courage, and hope. It is the highest motivational factor to get us involved in God's work right here and now. Believing in the Rapture does not make one an escapist. Rapture believers have been at the forefront of evangelism and foreign missions. Most who believe in the Rapture are responsible, hard workers in the Kingdom of God. Don't look at the bad examples, the escapists—look at those who are active in the work of the Kingdom of God.

DANIEL, MAN OF DREAMS AND VISIONS

Ten horned monsters... images of gold, silver, brass, iron and clay, rams and he goats, mystic dreams, esoteric visions, angelic visitors—these are the things most commonly associated with the prophet Daniel; but there is another dimension of the life and ministry of Daniel. It is an almost unknown quantity. We call it the *Daniel Factor*. A strong clue to the way in which Daniel is different from the image most people have of him is found in chapter nine of the little pamphlet he wrote, which is ambitiously called the *book* of Daniel in your King James Version. It is actually more of a tract, or pamphlet, than it is a book. Most of the study devoted to the ninth chapter of Daniel has been centered in the last few verses of the chapter—those relating to the celebrated and very important "seventy weeks vision." When the late Sir Robert Anderson of England set out to write a tract on the seventy weeks vision (Daniel 9:24-27), he ended up writing a volume of over 250 pages: *The Coming Prince* (reprinted and distributed by Kregel Publishing House: Grand Rapids, Michigan). However, our attention will fix on what preceded the vision in chapter nine.

BEFORE THE VISION

Preceding the seventy weeks vision, there are monumental truths for us in this ninth chapter of Daniel:

> In the first year of Darius the son of Ahasuerus, of the seed

---

15

of the Medes, which was made king over the realm of the Chaldeans; In the first year of his reign I Daniel understood by books the number of the years, where of the word of the Lord came to Jeremiah the prophet, that he would accomplish seventy years in the desolations of Jerusalem.

Daniel 9:1,2

Chronologically this chapter falls between chapter five, which marks the end of the Babylonian Empire, and chapter six which is into the reign of Darius, the Medo-Persian Empire (which conquered and succeeded Babylon).

The passages in Jeremiah that would have led Daniel to his astounding conclusion that the seventy years of the desolations of Jerusalem were about over would include Jeremiah 24:5-10; Jeremiah 25:11,12; and Jeremiah 29:10. Dark the night for Israel when Jeremiah's prophecy of the bondage of Israel was fulfilled!

And this whole land shall be a desolation, and an astonishment; and these nations shall serve the king of Babylon seventy years. And it shall come to pass when seventy years are accomplished, that I will punish the king of Babylon.

Jeremiah 25:11,12

As a young man Daniel had witnessed the fall of Judah and of Jerusalem. The temple had been destroyed in 586 B.C. He and his young friends were carried away as slaves to faraway Babylon. Now, by studying the prophecies of Jeremiah, Daniel realizes that it is about over. He has already seen the "signs of the times." He was a witness to the punishment of Belshazzar, King of Babylon (Daniel, chapter 5).

IT'S ABOUT TO HAPPEN!

The very atmosphere is charged with an electrical excitement! Oppressed Israel is about to go free. Prophecy is on the verge of being fulfilled. The seventy years of bitter bondage are about over. Daniel is almost overwhelmed with the enormity of his discovery. The long, dark night of Israel's slavery will end. It's coming soon.

If Daniel had reacted like many prophecy students, the mere discovery of this great truth with its thrilling element of anticipation would have ended the matter right then and there. It's wonderful. So, Lord, I'll just wait until it happens. Meantime, I've got to get to work in the practical world. See you at the next prophecy seminar, Lord. Even so, come Lord! Daniel glances at the sundial as he goes out the door—can't be late for work.

Yes, knowledge of the future is satisfying, and it is valuable. Knowing God has a plan assures me that what I am doing now is not merely "muddling through." Life has a purpose. There are real goals. Daniel thrilled to know that another exodus of the Jews will take place. What satisfaction! Yes, throngs of Jews will trek out over the shining Arabian sands and make their way back to the Holy Land, to the Holy City, to the task of rebuilding the sacred Temple of God. What is decreed by the Almighty will be done, no doubt of that, but for Daniel that does not end the matter. There is something for him to do.

One of the strangest revelations of truth now unfolds. Daniel is moved to do something about the prophetic illumination he has received, but what can one *do* about prophecy? If God predicted it, after all, "What will be, will be." What could mere mortals add to the Divine plan?

IT'S NOT ALL IN YOUR MIND

But it STARTS there. You cannot be a fulfilled Christian without some knowledge of Bible prophecy. Over a third of the Bible is cast in the mold of prophecy. How can we ignore such a major portion of what God has to say to us? Before you can get into phase two and three (intercession and works) of the *Daniel Factor* some knowledge is required.

Daniel was a scholar. Appreciation, application and implementation of Bible prophecy begins with knowledge of the subject. I am not saying that you must become an expert eschatologist to get involved in God's prophetic purposes, nor do you have to be an intellectual to understand prophecy; but you do have to use your mind. You do have to study the Word. Paul exhorts young pastor Timothy: "Meditate on these things...Take heed unto thyself, and unto the doctrine..." (1 Timothy 4:15,16). "Study to shew thyself approved unto God; a workman that needeth not to be ashamed, rightly dividing the word of truth" (2 Timothy 2:15).

One who is not studying the Word of God is not approved. You *should* be ashamed if you are neglecting God's Word. The remedy is simple: begin today to read your Bible. Three chapters daily and five on Sunday takes you through the Bible in a year's time. Eight hours a day for seven days takes you completely through the Bible. Listen to the Bible (not commentary on the Bible) on cassette tapes. Saturate yourself with the Word. Strive for mastery in the Word of God.

Daniel perceived by studying the prophecy of Jeremiah that the awful captivity of the Jews in Babylon was almost over. Most students of prophecy would have stopped there. The intellect has been satisfied. It is comforting to know that God has a plan and that He is in control. It is stimulating to realize that a partial fulfillment of the overall scheme of things is going to unfold very soon. But prophecy is more than knowledge. It is more than a mind-trip. God's program is not a table game nor a spectator sport. He wants us to get involved in His works. James McKnight comments:

> The study of prophecy has a marked effect on our service. The Scriptures with their promises and prospects of His return furnish the greatest stimulus to service. (Matthew 24:45-52; Luke 19:13; 2 Corinthians 5:10,11; 1 Corinthians 3:8-15.) In them is disclosed to us the divine purpose and program of service. (Acts 1:8; 15:13-18; Romans 11:22-32.) The truth constitutes the basis for the most effective consecrating of our life to God. We have shared extensive evidence from the Scriptures as to the importance of this doctrine. We need to ask the Holy Spirit to make it real in our hearts as we study it. It must become more than a mental concept! It must affect our lives! (*Eschatology*: Pastor James McKnight. Unpublished notes for class use, Bethel Temple; Ottawa, Ontario, Canada. Rev. McKnight is now the General Superintendent of the Pentecostal Assemblies of Canada.)

James points out to the Church of all ages that we are to be "doers of the Word and not hearers only." But what can be *done* about prophecy? Is it presumption to touch that which is predestined, or is there something we have missed?

INVOLVEMENT THROUGH INTERCESSION

Here is a great mystery. Daniel learns of the plan of God and then proceeds to get involved through intercessory prayer. "I set my face unto the Lord God, to seek by prayer and supplications, with fasting and sackcloth..." (Daniel 9:3). Most of chapter nine consists of the prophet's prayer, confession of national sins, and a plea to God that He will fulfill the announced plan for the release of Israel from Babylonian captivity. (See especially Daniel 9:17,19,20.)

Why did Daniel feel it necessary to pray about something that would be accomplished anyway, since God had prophesied it through Jeremiah? The destination is clearly marked, but is it possible that there is more than one route that can be travelled in reaching the final goal?

IS THERE FLEXIBILITY IN THE FUTURE?

God has predestined certain events. These events are described in Bible prophecy. They will not be changed—this much of the future is rigid. There will be a rapture of the Church, a tribulation time, the Millennium, etc. The exact day of Jesus' return is clearly known to God, though unknowable to man. (See Matthew 24:36; Mark 13:33.) My Heavenly Father *knows* the very day and hour—but I am not to even inquire into it.

Not everything in your future is predestined, however. That is where free will comes into the picture. It is predestined that there will be an election (of the saved ones) and a damnation (of the lost ones) but you will choose which you will be in.

It is predestined that Christ will return, but our prayers and good works will determine many details of the future from now until the trumpet sounds. The occultist tries to use magical, supernatural forces to manipulate, or create, a future scenario. The Christian, quite the opposite, endeavors to find out what the will of God is and then to cooperate with the will of God, fully knowing that the will of God is frequently not done in this rebellious world. The trumpet will sound one day and then it's "take over Jesus" from then on out. Our new assignments will be revealed to us then. In the meantime He has put us in a stewardship role of responsibility in this present world. We are not working against His will. We do not want to change His will. We want to know and cooperate with His will. We are partners. We are not working *for* God, but *with* Him. Satan would like for the Church to be passive and not get involved in intercession and works. Then he could have a field day.

As we approach the end of this age either your faith-works, or lack of them, will determine the quality of life and degree of liberty you will experience to fulfill God's will in our time. We cannot fail now. Too much is at stake.

IF CLAUSES IN THE BIBLE

In many passages God shows that alternate futures lie before His people. Not alternate in the ultimate sense, but alternate on the short-term basis— that is from now until the trumpet sounds. Unless you are a totally selfish person, you will recognize how important this is; for contingent on our exercising control over evil rests the destiny of millions of souls who will be either saved or lost for all eternity. How the evil one would love to drive us underground, stop us from using the media, close the doors of our churches, and cripple our missionary outreach to the world. We cannot let it happen.

> If my people which are called by my name, shall humble
> themselves, and pray, and seek my face, and turn from their
> wicked ways; then will I hear from heaven, and will forgive
> their sin, and will heal their land.
>
> 2 Chronicles 7:14

IF! IF! IF!

That word "if" loudly commands our attention. It shouts at us, saying that we have choices before us. If we enter into God's creative activities through prayer, then healing will be promoted in the land. If we don't, we lose by default. It's either one or the other. That is what the "if" means.

When we transform our spiritual energy into prayer, we help to produce a spiritual channel that God can use to intervene on our own behalf and that of others. It is vitally important that we enter into intercession to accomplish His purposes. It has been suggested that whenever any true, God-anointed prayer is made, that a spiritual power is formed that never goes out of existence and never ceases to operate in our behalf. Consider the following statement found on a bookmark:

> Based on psychological tests it is believed that prayers continue to have latent power. A basic law of physics is that energy can be changed in form, but cannot be destroyed. Once it was taught that this law applied only to physical energy; but now it appears that this same law applies to spiritual energy.
>
> (author unknown)

Not only is there "psychological" evidence for this concept; there is Scriptural evidence as well. A dramatic illustration of this is found in the book of Revelation:

> And when he had opened the seventh seal there was silence in heaven, about the space of half an hour. And I saw the seven angels which stood before God, and to them were given seven trumpets. And another angel came and stood at the altar, having a golden censer: and there was given unto him much incense, that he should offer it with the prayers of all saints upon the golden altar which was before the throne. And the smoke of the incense, which came with the prayers of the saints ascended up before God out of the angel's hand. And the angel took the censer, and filled it with fire of the altar, and cast it into the earth: and there were voices, and thunderings, and lightnings, and an earthquake.
>
> Revelation 8:1-6

Think of it—the prayers of *all* saints are before God. The prayers offered by the angel call for justice and God's judgments are then poured out on the earth. Commentators agree that there is a connection.

INTERVENTION BY INVITATION

"That he should offer it with the prayers of all saints." This heavenly scene reveals that once you pray, a spiritual power is released that never ceases to have an influence. The power produced by every sincere, God-directed prayer is still in existence before God right now. This fascinating concept is further explored in a booklet, *Canopy of Prayer*, written by my dear friend Guy Bongiovanni, the General Overseer and Superintendent of the Christian Churches of North America. (P.O. Box 208; Farrell, Pennsylvania. To order send $4.00. Includes postage.)

CAN GOD DO ANYTHING

Fasten your seatbelts. I believe that God is God. There is none other beside Him. He is not the creation, He is the Creator of all things. He stands independent and separate from the creation. He is all powerful. He knows all. He is everywhere present at all times in every state of relativity and reality—He is Omnipresent. *But He has limitations.* Before you close the book in disgust take note that we know this because He told us so in the Bible. There is no doubt of this and it is important for you to know. There is a little worship chorus that goes like this:

> God can do anything,
> anything.
> God can do anything
> but fail.

It's a lovely chorus, so don't stop using it; but understand that technically it is not correct. God cannot just do *anything*. The Bible says so. God is all powerful, and to be correct the chorus should say, "God can do anything that is consistent with His Divine nature and does not violate reality." I do not refer to our perception of reality, but His perception of ultimate reality cannot be violated. That would be a little hard to put to music, so go ahead and sing the chorus as it is, but remember that God can only do those things that are consistent with His own nature. For example, *God cannot lie.*

> In hope of eternal life, which God, that cannot lie, promised before the world began.
> Titus 1:2
> That by two immutable things, in which it was impossible for God to lie, we might have strong consolation...
> Hebrews 6:18
> If we believe not, yet he abideth faithful: *He cannot deny Himself.*
> 2 Timothy 2:13

21

There it is as plain as can be! God who is all powerful has limitations. They are limitations because if He *lied* then He would not be God. He either would not exist or He would be something else. He could not lie and still be the God we find revealed in the Bible. God cannot deny Himself. He cannot do anything that violates His own reality. It is prayer that gives God the moral and legal right to intervene in human affairs. God does not break His own laws or agreements. You can trust Him. He keeps His word. The devil may lie and man may lie but never God. Basically we can say (with certain exceptions which have been noted) that God intervenes in human affairs by invitation.

A bit later we will look at phase three of the *Daniel Factor*—the realm of our good works, or implementation through action. First it is necessary to take another look at the matter of the nature of God's laws and His relationship to them. For some reason the concept that there are laws (conceived of and emanating from God) that govern the universe, and that God Himself does not deny or violate this reality, has become very controversial. We need to set the record straight. We are *not in agreement* with the occult or New Age treatment of the concept of universal law. They are simply counterfeiting and distorting these truths to their own ends which are anti-God. We seek to *know* God and His Divine will and cooperate with the Lord.

CHAPTER 2

THE LAWS OF GOD

The law of God is not a set of codes designed to "spoil all our fun." Everything in this harmonious universe is governed by law. We describe lesser parts of the law as the laws of science, physical laws, moral laws, spiritual laws, etc. Actually all law is part of a whole. Since God is the Creator, all law proceeds from Him. What is the nature of law?

LAW IS NOT CAPRICIOUS

The laws of the universe are constant. They do not change. We are very thankful that the law of gravity, for example, always works the same. If you drop an object such as your ballpoint pen, you know that it will not go floating off into the air. You *know* that it will fall to the floor. The same is true of all laws in every realm. Our lives would have absolutely no stability if the laws of all realms were not dependable. Sometimes we see an example of the law in a certain case seemingly not working the same. This is due to faulty perception. Let's continue using the example of gravity. There is a situation in which a ballpoint pen might not return to the earth. If it were placed inside a rocket probe and sent out into space, never to return, it would seem that the law of gravity had been nullified, as far as the casual observer would be concerned; however, the simple truth is that there are laws and forces that operate and are capable of overcoming the earth's gravitational pull. The law of gravity is still in effect, but other forces not previously understood come into the picture—and gravity is overcome, not eliminated. We live in a universe governed by law, and so does God, who originated all law. How did He do this, and to what extent is He obligated to obey His own laws?

LAW DESCRIBES REALITY

The best way to understand the concept of the law of God as it permeates every part of reality is to comprehend that law simply describes reality. Rather than being arbitrary rules to be obeyed or suffer the consequences, all the laws of God describe what things are and how they function. It is true that if you go against the law there is a consequence to be borne. If you try to defy gravity by jumping off the roof of your house you will suffer the consequence. Still, you are thankful that gravity works and is constant, unchanging. If it were not we would lose the atmosphere of our earth and all die. Things would drunkenly go flying off into space. Earth would be a chaos, if indeed it could exist at all.

Everything works a certain way. Defy the laws of the universe and harmony is disrupted.

ASK AND RECEIVE

Jesus said, "Ask, and it shall be given you; seek and ye shall find; knock, and it shall be opened unto you. For every one that asketh receiveth; and he that seeketh findeth; and to him that knocketh it shall be opened" (Luke 11:9-10).

"Ask, and it shall be given...." Either that is true or it is not. If it is true then it is a law or principle that you can count on. Jesus did not lie to us. Ask and ye shall receive.

What about those who already asked and did not receive? All laws or principles stated in the Bible interreact to other laws. Asking and not receiving is understood in the light of Jesus teaching on faith. When you ask, you must ask believing. You must have faith. The writer of Hebrews says, "But without faith it is impossible to please him: for he that cometh to God must believe that he is, and that he is a rewarder of them that diligently seek him" (Hebrews 11:6). Further we are told in the Epistle of James that "ye have not because ye ask not" (James 4:2b). James recognizes the law of asking and receiving. He then elaborates: "Ye ask, and receive not, because ye ask amiss, that ye may consume it upon your lusts." When the disciples pressed Jesus for a promise of special privilege and position in the Kingdom, Jesus told them that "Ye know not what ye ask" (Mark 10:38).

That is why phase one of the *Daniel Factor* is so important. We should seek *knowledge* of God's plan and purposes as revealed in the Word of God. Our asking should be within a framework of God's revelation. There is no use asking in unbelief or outside the framework of His Divine will. Hosea cautions that God's people can be destroyed for a lack of knowledge.

Beyond knowledge we enter into the realm of intercession to bring God's will to pass in our present realm, both for personal needs, for the needs of the Church, and of the whole world. We do not bypass knowledge—we begin there, fully realizing that knowledge in itself is not enough. Knowledge must be linked with prayer and action.

GOD'S RELATIONSHIP TO HIS OWN LAWS

As noted previously, God is limited by His own Divine nature. He *cannot* lie and He *cannot* deny Himself. (See Titus 1:2; 2 Timothy 2:13; Hebrews 6;18.) The Hebrews passage tells us that it is *"impossible* for God to lie." God cannot be both good and evil. He may use evil when it exists, but He cannot do evil.

Hostile unbelievers have asked questions that are supposed to shut the mouths of Christians because they are thought to be unanswerable. An example is the question, "Could God make a rock so big He could not move it?" No matter which way you answer the skeptic, it will make you look bad. Never fear! It is a stupid question based on a false premise. The answer is clear and plain. The answer is, *No, God cannot make a rock so big He cannot move it because by definition such a rock could not exist.* The Bible plainly shows us that far from hereby disproving the omnipotence of God we simply recognize that God works within the framework of reality. God does not violate reality.

A number of authors have dealt with the concept of God's limitations from time to time:

> God is all powerful but that does not mean that he can do anything. He cannot make $2 + 2 = 5$, and He cannot make it raining and not-raining at the same moment in the same place. These are not, as some have argued, limitations on God's power as though some Platonic arithmetic were forcing its will on to Him. It is simply that He is rational....When we say God is all-powerful we mean He can do all things that can be done which includes many things that are impossinble to man. But we do not mean that He can give a hydrogen atom and a helium atom the

same atomic structure. Even God could not create free men without at the same time creating men who were able to rebel. (Hugh Silvester, *Arguing With God.* Downers Grove, IL: InterVarsity Press, pp. 60-61.)

Truly God obeys His own laws, which is simply to say He does not distort reality. Obviously we know only a little about the laws of God. We have only fragmentary knowledge. That is where the element of the miraculous comes in. A miracle is when a higher, unknown law takes over and cancels out the effects of those laws we are familiar with. We noted this truth in the discussion on asking and receiving earlier in this chapter. The concept of a miracle is from our viewpoint only. To God nothing is miraculous. He is Omnipotent and Omniscient. He understands all of reality and the principles governing reality. To God nothing is supernatural.

Because God works in the framework of reality, because He cannot lie, because He obeys His own laws we can have faith in Him. That is why we can have confidence in His Word. God does not break the laws of the universe. To do so would be to rip apart the fabric of reality and introduce chaos into the universe. The Scripture says that God is not the author of confusion. He created everything and set it in order. He does not disrupt that order.

WHAT HAS GONE WRONG WITH THE WORLD?

We inhabit an area of God's creation where His laws have been defied. Chaos and confusion reign. Satan is the "god" of this world (1 Corinthians 4:4). Jesus called the devil the "prince of this world" (John 12:31; 14:30; 16:11). It was not by accident that Satan gained such a position of power in our world. Since nothing happens without God's permission, it is implied that Satan enjoys his position because God has granted it to him.

Marshall Fishwick, an Episcopal minister, has made some interesting comments. Note especially the last two sentences of this quotation:

> The enemy of God is dynamic: Evil on the move...His doings and disguises have occupied the fears and fancies of mankind more than any other character, historical or mythical, except for the very God whom he opposes. Evil isn't merely embodied in matter; it has a vigor and vitality of its own.
>
> Because he has defied the authority under which we must live, we envy the Black Prince who has ventured into unknown seas, employed new stratagems, defied omnipotence itself. He it is who dices for destiny, and

schemes for our souls. He covers bets on struggling souls, warring nations, and crumbling civilizations. He maintains recruiting stations everywhere; they are always open. No one chooses evil for evil's sake; but many can be deceived into thinking bad is good—that circumstances justify a deviation. Whenever we plead the exception to the rule we are at Satan's mercy. God made the rules and will not himself break them. When we do, we forsake Him. (Marshall Fishwick, *Faust Revisited—Some Thoughts on Satan.* New York: Seabury Press, 1963, p. 27.)

When our father, Adam, abdicated his kingship over the earth by rebelling against the command of God, Lucifer (Satan) was allowed to take over. God had to give His approval to this, or it could not have happened. It implies that there is a "contract," or understanding, between God and the devil. In essence God said, "All right Satan, you can have a time of dominion over the world. I reserve the right to interfere in the affairs of men whenever one of your servants decides to change his allegiance and leave your kingdom of darkness. I will translate those who call on Me for redemption into the Kingdom of Heaven. They will be born again by My Spirit and will be My subjects." War was declared, but that war is waged within the bounds of the laws of the universe and within the bounds of reality. Now we see prayer taking on a new significance. When I pray I am giving God the legal right to intervene in the world. I am defying the world system under Satan's control and I am inviting God to step in and take action.

In my personal library there is a rare and precious volume printed and bound in 1865. It is a set of Bibliotheca Sacra for that year. Let me share a quotation from its pages:

We seem to be driven, then, to the only remaining conclusion, that right and wrong are distinctions immutable, and inherent in the nature of things...they are eternal as the throne of Deity; they are immutable, as God himself....Law does not make them, but they make law. They are the source and spring of all law and obligation. Reason points out these distinctions; the moral nature recognizes and approves them. God's law, and will, and nature are in conformity to these distinctions....

There is a sense in which Deity himself is subject to this eternal and immutable law of right. There are things which it would not be right for even Deity to do. So fully does his moral nature approve the right and abhor the wrong, that the Scriptures declare it impossible for him to do evil....This his moral nature is to him a law, the highest possible and conceivable, placing him under obligation, not indeed to another, but to himself, to adhere ever to the eternal principles of right, and truth, and justice. (Joseph Haven, Bibliotheca Sacra. Article: "The Moral Faculty;" London: Trubner and Co., 1865, pp. 261-262.)

Prayer gives God the moral and legal right to act on your behalf. Prayer is important not only to you, but to God as well. He ever seeks a man to stand in the gap. God is a moral being. He has structured a moral and legal universe. His laws simply state the realities of existence—the way things work. There are natural, spiritual and moral laws that govern all things. God does not break His own laws. The word law appears in the Bible over two hundred times. The Hebrew word for law is "torah" and it simply means teaching or instruction. God's laws are not merely arbitrary rules dreamed up as Divine whims. They are statements of eternal, immutable truth. They are instructional. They describe the way things function. God works within the framework of reality as it is described by these laws, some of which we are probably not even aware at this time.

It is essential in the idea of law that it be universal and unchangeable, the law for all things and all places....Hence law requires conformity to the fundamental realities in the constitution of things. (Samuel Harris, *The Philosophical Basis of Theism*. New York: Charles Scribners & Sons, 1893, pp. 190,191.)

INTERVENTION BY INVITATION

Basically God intervenes when He is invited to do so. There are three notable exceptions to this rule. Three circumstances call for God's intervention whether anyone invites Him to do so or not. Without lengthy commentary I will simply mention these areas: First of all, God will not allow the final extinction of the natural seed of Jacob, the people of Israel. Secondly, He will not allow the final destruction of the Church. Thirdly, He will not allow the total destruction of the human race. God has a plan for this planet and that plan will not be disrupted as far as its final outcome is concerned. There are many roads we can travel to reach the final destination. The quality of life can be drastically altered by our actions and prayers, or lack thereof, but the final outcome will not be foiled by any satanic plot or action. As far as I can tell, in all other areas of our lives and the destiny of the nations God intervenes when He is invited to do so. That is why prayer is so important. When I pray I am working with God to implement His will for mankind. It is true that God may answer before we call on Him. He affords miraculous deliverance for His children in some cases where there is no time to call on Him; however, it must be recognized that those who enjoy such benefits have already been calling on Him and committing their ways to Him. They are simply drawing on "funds already in the heavenly bank of deliverance."

God will intervene when His ultimate plan is threatened. Satan would like to sabotage the grand design of God's eternal purposes and make God out to be a liar before all intelligent beings. This God will never allow. His predestined plan will never be thwarted.

As we move on toward that grand finale of the ages there are a thousand, thousand details of our lives that are not rigidly predestined. God places a great deal of control over these areas of future development into our own hands. That is why He ever seeks the cooperation of humanity—for our own good. By intercession and good works we mold the very face of the future as we move into it. It is time to stop treating prophecy like a parlor game, or a childish curiosity. It is time to discover the grandeur of being a part of the ongoing plan of God. If you believe that prayer changes things then you believe that prayer shapes the future. The past is forever immutable. Only the future is flexible and subject to change. We will not change anything that God has predestined, but there are things that can be changed. Let us discover what they are and how this change may best be effected for the good of the Kingdom of our Lord.

GOD NEEDS YOU

I have often heard ministers say, "God doesn't need your money. God doesn't need your good works. You must give and work and pray because you need God." This is a half truth. Yes, we need God more than He will ever need us, but the rest of the truth is that *God does need you* . He does need your money. He does need your good works. He does need your prayers. God uses human instrumentality to bring His purposes to pass. He cannot work miracles without you. If God worked a miracle in the middle of an empty desert there would be no miracle. There would be no one there to observe or partake of the miracle. To God nothing is miraculous, so there would be no miracle without a human presence.

One day Jesus told His disciples to go and bring Him a certain donkey. He would ride it through the Eastern Gate in the triumphant entry to the city

East of Eden

of Jerusalem. He told the disciples that if anyone asked them what they were doing with the donkey they were to reply, "The Lord hath need of him" (Luke 19:31). God *needed* that donkey. God needs people to intercede that the land should not be destroyed. (See Ezekiel 22:30.) God needs your donkey! God needs and uses human instrumentality. *God needs you for things He wants done in this world.*

When you pray you are providing a legal channel through which God can intervene in this world (for He will not violate His agreement with Satan, regardless of how dishonest or crooked the devil may be). Also when you pray you are converting your spiritual energy into power that God can use to bring His purposes to pass in this world. God's will is normally *not* done in this world unless one of His children implements His will through prayer and positive good works.

Why must we pray? Simply because God does not answer prayers that are not prayed. He intervenes in human affairs when He is invited to do so.

CHAPTER 3

HOLY SPIRIT MOVEMENT VS. NEW AGE MOVEMENT
Supernatural End-Time Victory

It is necessary to write a short chapter to make it perfectly clear that we have no sympathy nor association with the so-called New Age Movement. The New Agers' teachings are based on Eastern mysticism and Hinduism. Their purposes are exactly the opposite of ours. They herald the coming of a New Christ which is clearly not Jesus. Their Avatar, or New Christ, is described as being the same as the Buddhist's Bodisattva, the Hindu's Krishna, the Moslem's anticipated Imam Mahdi, the Lord Matreya, etc.

We herald the coming of the true Jesus. The chapter on the rapture of the Church will clarify beyond doubt where we stand.

The New Agers promote the manipulation of the world through the use of recognized universal laws (and a few they invent) to bring to pass their own desired globalist government, religion, and the new world economy (including the mark of the beast, though they would not use this terminology).

We promote the recognition of *Biblical laws* and principles that reveal the will of God for mankind. We seek to know His will and to implement His will through intercessory prayer and our good works. Obedient submission to God is the keynote of our prayer and action. Resistance against Satan is our method of warfare in the Holy Spirit. Liberation (salvation) of souls is our desired goal.

Just because the New Age Movement distorts the truth about God's laws, let us not reject the laws of God altogether. Don't throw out the baby with the bath water. Some study the cultist New Age Movement closely, then look at the Evangelicals, Pentecostals, and Charismatics to see if there is any comparison. That is getting it backwards. The New Age copied us, not vice-versa. Theirs is a poor, cheap, shoddy counterfeit; filled with lies and distortion. Both the New Age and the Holy Spirit Movements operate in the realm of the supernatural. There are two sources of supernatural power, God and the devil. You cannot have both. It must be understood that if we are going to defeat the devil and his hosts in this supernatural war (Ephesians 6:12) we need the power of God and the gifts of the Holy Spirit (1 Corinthians 12). You cannot defeat the devil's activities just by embracing fundamentalist Christian doctrine. A mind trip is not enough. We must move in the Spirit. The Word is, indeed, of primary importance. It shows us where we are, where to go, and how to get there. Biblical prophecy is of vital importance to motivate us to prayer and action in the Kingdom of God in this present time.

NEW AGE PENETRATION OF THE HOLY SPIRIT MOVEMENT

Because of misunderstanding, some exposers of the New Age Movement have accused brethren in the Holy Spirit Movement (Charismatics, Pentecostals, Evangelicals, Word of Faith teachers) of being part of the New Age Movement, or at least in sympathy with the New Age. Many have been falsely accused.

This is not to say that the New Age is not trying to penetrate our ranks. They are. They may have met with some degree of success. Some in our midst are teaching errors similar to New Age concepts.

Because I have made this declaration, because I have written in various publications exposing the New Age, and further because I have refused to name those in our ranks who might be involved in erroneous teaching, I have been attacked and misunderstood by my own brethren. They want me to name the personalities involved. I do not hesitate to name the openly declared New Age cultists, and have freely done so. They make no profession of being born-again Christians, but when a man clearly states that he is a born-again Christian and a follower of Jesus the Christ, I am hesitant to say that he is anything less than he claims. I may have suspicions, but I will not expose him. Let the wheat grow up with the tares in the Kingdom. God will separate them. I could too easily make mistakes.

ERROR MUST BE EXPOSED

On the other hand error must be exposed. We will teach concerning concepts and doctrines. We will expose error, but we will not enter into personality warfare within the body of Christ. If you steep yourself in the Word of God, if you have an awareness of errors that are being taught (even in the church) you will not need for me to tell you who is the promoter of those errors. You will spot it yourself. Don't witch hunt, but measure all teachings by the Word of God. Beware of any man's revelation if he proclaims it to be equal to the Bible. All revelations and visions must be measured by the Bible. Bear in mind that every person teaching error is not necessarily a part of the New Age Movement.

NEW AGE DISTORTION

The New Age seizes upon the fact that laws exist, and then proceeds into distortion of truth and into proclamation of lies. They try to use the laws of God's creation to manipulate the creation for their own antichrist "plan" or for their own selfish desires. They confuse the Creator with His creation. The end of their distortion is self-worship. They "hold the truth in unrighteousness" (Romans 1:18). Paul's letter to the Romans well describes the New Age Movement:

> For the invisible things of him from the creation of the world are clearly seen, being understood by the things that are made, even his eternal power and godhead; so that they are without excuse: Because that, when they knew God, they glorified him not as God, neither were thankful; but became vain in their imaginations, and their foolish heart was darkened. Professing themselves to be wise they became fools...Who changed the truth of God into a lie and worshipped and served the creature more than the Creator, who is blessed forever...And even as they did not like to retain God in their knowledge, God gave them over to a reprobate mind, to do those things which are not convenient.
>
> Romans 1:18,20-22a; 25,28

The New Age does not recognize the God of the Bible. Their method is to descend into the lower depths of human consciousness and there find God. The Bible teaches that every person is born in sin and separate from God. You do not find God within. You come to God and repent of sin, find salvation, and then Christ enters your heart. Only the Christian can claim that Christ dwells within. God does not dwell in the heart of the unregenerate. Jesus said that they are of "their father the devil." The New Age teaches that all is God and God is all. Creation is God. You are God, the sky is God. The grass is God. Everything is God.

The Bible teaches that God is the Creator and existed before the creation, and even now stands as distinct from the creation which is upheld by the word of His power.

The New Age teaches that Christ is the same person known by other names such as Avatar, Lord Matreya, Bodisattva, Imam Mahdi and Krishna. No! A thousand times no! Jesus is not just one of the boys. Jesus is not part of the gang of gurus. Jesus is unique. He is the *only begotten son of God.* He is the only way by which men come to the Father.

THE LAWS OF GOD

As examined in the last chapter, we know that there are laws that govern this universe, God's creation. They are very real and they always work. That is why you can depend on God, because He is the "same yesterday, today and forever."

"...the soul that sinneth, it shall die" (Ezekiel 18:4,20). That is a fact. It is a law, and the Bible states it over and over. It is a law of God. You can count on it. This law of sin and death can, however, be superceded by the working of other laws which describe the working of the grace of God. Salvation from sin is predicated upon certain things God has done (atonement) to satisfy the demands of the law. It is also based upon our response to the grace of God, and it always works. "Whosoever calleth upon the name of the Lord shall be saved." We count on these principles, or laws, to be reliable, otherwise there would be no assurance of salvation.

NEW AGE COUNTERFEITS

The New Ager seeks a paradigm shift of perception whereby he may alter reality. We Christians seek to find and know reality and work with God within the framework of His revealed will. The fact that the cultists perceive that laws exist and proceed to distort the truth should not make us back off from the truth. They are counterfeiters. I have never seen a counterfeit fifty-three dollar bill. There are counterfeit fifty dollar bills, because there are real fifty dollar bills. Only reality gets counterfeited. We must not allow New Age distortion to rob the Church of its power to work with God in controlling events, according to His will (which is usually not done in this evil world unless we do work with Him). According to His will—that is the key. "Not my will but thine be done, Lord." This does not imply a passive role for the believer. It is a call for us to cooperate with God in bringing His will to pass in our present world. In the future He will intervene personally, visibly, dramatically. It is all in His hands from then on. We will get further instructions then as to what we will be doing in ruling and reigning with Christ in the Kingdom. For now, the Bible is our instruction book and we must seek to know and implement its commands.

Some are looking at the cultic counterfeiters and thinking that because the cultist speaks of laws, and since the cultist is a deceiver, therefore there are no absolute laws which govern the universe. That is incorrect and circuitous thinking. We need to see the truth of God's Word in this area, then discern where the New Age distorts the truth in defiance of the laws of God.

There may sometimes be a fine line of difference between the real and the counterfeit as far as man's perception of that difference is concerned, but that dividing line is all-important. I cannot afford to reject the exercise of supernatural power, nor can I afford to be on the wrong side. It cannot be over-emphasized: We do not seek to use the laws of God to manipulate God. We seek to understand His Divine will and purpose, and then to cooperate through the implementation of intercessory prayer and by our good works. God calls us to action, not mere observation in these end times.

TWO MAJOR SUPERNATURAL MOVEMENTS

God promised to pour out His Spirit in the last days. We are seeing a mighty move of His Holy Spirit today. The Holy Spirit Movement is known as the Pentecostal, or Charismatic, or Full Gospel Movement. There may be other designations. It crosses all denominational boundaries. It is a manifestation of the true spiritual unity of the Body of Christ (not organizational ecumenicity).

I have heard Demos Shakarian, founder of the Full Gospel Businessmen International, speak of the early outpouring of the Holy Spirit and of the Pentecostal revival in Russia and Armenia in the mid-1800's. Many indicate that this was when the end-time moving of the Spirit began. Most Pentecostals think that the Holy Spirit revival started around the beginning of the twentieth century.

AN INTERESTING OBSERVATION

In the 1930's *The Communist Party Manual of Instructions on Psychopolitical Warfare* made a heavy attack on the Pentecostalists. Why, at that time, should the Russians have such an awareness of the Pentecostal movement? Where had they observed this phenomena? Why did they have such a strong reaction to it? An English translation of the manual is in our possession.

The manual begins with an address by Beria, head of the Russian Secret

Police, who states: "...Pentecostal Bible faith healers amongst your misguided people must be swept aside. They must be discredited, defamed, arrested, stamped upon even by their own government...." While Beria attacks other religious groups as well, no group is so consistently and vehemently slandered as the Pentecostalists. Where did he get such an awareness of the Pentecostals? Did he somehow know, perhaps by Satanic revelation, that this is where the real power lies within the Church—in the end-time Holy Spirit Movement?

Lavrenti Pavlovich Beria rose to prominence in the Cheka (secret police—predecessor to the present KGB) in the Georgian province of Russia (now the Georgian Soviet Socialist Republic, part of the U.S.S.R.). In both Georgia and in the Transcaucasus he became party secretary of these areas. It was those very areas where the Pentecostal outpouring of the 1800's took place in Russia. Hundreds of thousands of Christians received the infilling of the Holy Spirit in Russia in the 1800's. They prayed in unknown languages and demonstrated the miracle working power of God.

Beria's Manual on Psychopolitics for party workers and organizers states: "Among Fundamentalist and Pentecostal groups healing campaigns are conducted, which, because of their results, win many to the cult of Christianity...All these must be swept aside. They must be ridiculed and defamed and every cure they advertise must be asserted as a hoax. A full fifth of the psychopolitician's time should be devoted to smashing these threats. Just as in Russia we had to destroy, after many, many years of the most arduous work, the Church, so we must destroy all faiths in nations marked for conquest."

We have noted that the Holy Spirit Movement actually did not begin in America in the 1900's. It began much earlier than that in Russia. Demos Shakarian tells how Russian Christians came over the mountains to Armenia in the early 1840's bringing a wondrous message about the miraculous moving of the Holy Spirit in Russia. Demos says, "They listened to the tales of what the Russians called 'the outpouring of the Holy Spirit' upon *hundreds of thousands of Russian Orthodox Christians* [emphasis added]...everything the Russians were talking about was Scriptural." (*The Happiest People on Earth*, Demos Shakarian. Chosen Books—Zondervan; 1975, pp. 13-19.)

Brother Shakarian tells the wondrous story of how his grandfather and grandmother received the infilling of the Holy Spirit in Armenia: "Grandfather knelt and the old Russian laid his work-gnarled hands on his head. Immediately Grandfather burst into joyous prayer in a language neither he nor anyone present could understand. The Russians called this kind of ecstatic utterance "tongues" and regarded it as a sign that the Holy Spirit was present with the speaker. That night Grandmother, too, received this 'Baptism in the Spirit.' " (*The Happiest People*, p. 19.) That took place in

1900, after the Russian Pentecostal revival had been going on for sixty years or more.

It was a revolutionary thing that God was doing in the Church. The Holy Spirit Movement did not get a start in America until in the early 1900's.

SATAN'S COUNTERREVOLUTION

The New Age end-time occultic and globalist activity is a Satanic counterrevolution designed to compete with the true supernatural move of God's Holy Spirit. It is interesting to note that the New Age Movement got its start in Russia. Madam Helena Petrovna Blavatsky, a Russian woman, founded the movement known as Theosophy. Theosophy is the grandmother of the present New Age Movement. Blavatsky clearly rejected Christianity although she taught there would be a coming of a new Christ (not Jesus). In Blavatsky's abridged *Key to Theosophy* there is a chapter titled "The Fundamental Teachings of Theosophy." The question is asked: "Do you believe in God?" The answer: "That depends what you mean by the term." The next question is: "I mean the God of the Christians, the Father of Jesus, and the Creator: the Biblical God of Moses, in short." The answer to this second inquiry is: "In such a God we do not believe. We reject the idea of a personal, or extra-cosmic and anthropomorphic God, who is but the gigantic shadow of man, and not of man at his best, either. The God of theology, we say is a bundle of contradictions and a logical impossibility. Therefore we will have nothing to do with him."

MAN IS GOD?

The questioner continues: "Then you make of man a God?" The answer is the very heart of the New Age Movement: "Please say 'God' and not *a* God. In our sense, the inner man is the only God we can have cognizance of. And how can this be otherwise?" (*The Key to Theosophy*, H. P. Blavatsky, Theosophical Society: Wheaton, Illinois, pp. 35,39.) It is interesting to note that Blavatsky's teaching came on the heels of the Holy Spirit outpouring in Russia. Is it not possible that this Satanic movement was designed to offer a confusing counterfeit for the true supernaturalism of God, as based on sound Biblical concepts? *Encyclopedia Brittanica* rightly comments, "The influence of the Theosophical Society has been rather significant...The movement has been a catalytic force in the 20th century Asian revival of Buddhism and Hinduism and a pioneering agency in the promotion of greater Western acquaintance with Eastern Thought. In the United States it has influenced a whole series of religious movements, including the Mighty I Am Movement, Rosacrucianism, the Liberal Catholic Church, Psychiana, Unity, and sections of the New Thought Movement. In the estimation of some scholars, no other single organization has done more to popularize Asian religious and philosophical ideas in the West than the Theosophical Society." (*Encyclopedia Britannica*, 1981 Edition. See entries on H. P. Blavatsky and Theosophy.)

H. P. Blavatsky died in 1891. Her co-founder of the movement, an American lawyer, Henry Steel Olcott, dominated Theosophy until 1907 when, upon his death, the leadership was taken over by Annie Besant, an Englishwoman with a dynamic personality.

One of the disciples of the Theosophical Movement, Alice Bailey, founded the Lucifer Publishing Company in the early 1920's. The name of the organization was changed to Lucis Trust and is one of the more powerful of the New Age organizations. It is located in prestigious quarters at 866 United Nations Plaza in New York City. One of the principle teachings of Lucis Trust is that there will be a coming of a New Christ (not Jesus). He is the same person as the Imam Mahdi of the Moslems, the Bodisattva of the Buddhists, Krishna of the Hindus, etc. The New Age New Christ is not the Lord Jesus I am looking for.

NEW AGE MOVEMENT NOT NEW

According to *Encyclopedia Brittanica*, which I refer to frequently in this chapter because of its easy availability, "Theosophy is a religious philosophy with definite mystical concerns that can be traced to the ancient world but is of catalytic significance in the religious thought in the 19th and 20th centuries...refers to a certain strain of mystical thought to be found in such thinkers as the Greek philosophers Pythagoras (6th Century B.C.) and Plato (4th-5th Century B.C.); the Gnostic teachers...Modern theosophists follow Madame Blavatsky in claiming to have revived this ancient tradition in this modern era." (*Encyclopedia Brittanica*; entry on Theosophy.)

CONTRAST BETWEEN THE HOLY SPIRIT MOVEMENT AND THE NEW AGE MOVEMENT

Both the Holy Spirit Movement and the New Age Movement emphasize the supernatural. We cannot say that "here all similarity ends," for even here there is no true similarity. The Holy Spirit Movement glorifies Jesus, declares the need for each person to admit that he or she is a lost sinner, and the need to accept Jesus as personal Saviour and Lord. The Holy Spirit Movement teaches that the gifts of the Spirit (1 Corinthians 12) are in operation *in the Church today*.

The New Age (Theosophist) Movement teaches that man is divine, and produces miracles through a paradigm shift in perception, and thus controls events "supernaturally." We conclude that it is demonic since there are only two sources of supernatural power.

ONE WORLD

Adherents of the New Age Movement are calling for global government, one world religion, and a one world economic system.

The Holy Spirit Movement believes there will be a New World Order, brought to pass by the personal return of Jesus Christ. It is called the Millennium.

AMAZING GROWTH OF THE TWO MOVEMENTS

We can, from our own files, document the existence of over four thousand organizations in America that are loosely linked into the New Age Network. This is only the tip of the iceberg. There are probably over ten thousand such organizations.

The true Holy Spirit Movement has grown phenomenally as well. The Pentecostalist branch of the Holy Spirit Movement began in America in the early 1900's. Some historians trace the beginning to Topeka, Kansas, where at God's Bible College in 1901 Agnes N. Ozman received the Baptism in the Holy Spirit and spoke in tongues. The fact, however, is that similar occurrences were taking place all over the world. Around 1907 there was a great Holy Spirit revival at 312 Azusa in Los Angeles. It swept from there like a blazing flame to spread all over the world. Some people do not know how extensive the Holy Spirit Movement is today. While some oldline traditional denominations are losing membership, the Pentecostalist, the Charismatics and Full Gospel Churches are growing. "Pentecostals with 51 million members worldwide, *now constitute the largest family of Protestants,*" according to David Barratt, editor of the World Christian Encyclopedia, which appeared in May 1982. This did not include the 11 million Charismatic Pentecostals in the traditional churches. (*Encyclopedia Britannia Yearbook.* 1983, p. 595. Emphasis is added.) These figures are out of date at the time of this writing. I understand that at present there are about 60 million Pentecostals and about 20 million Charismatics. Some of the brethren in Hong Kong told me that there are also from 50 to 75 million Spirit-filled believers in Red China, mostly in underground home church movements. There are a few million Spirit-filled believers in Russia and other oppressed nations. There is no way to verify the exact numbers in these areas. There may be as many as 100 million or more Spirit-filled believers living today!

FUNDAMENTALISTS EXPOSE THE NEW AGE

When a fundamentalist Christian believer begins to expose the New Age Movement he sometimes sees things in the Holy Spirit Movement that look similar. Well, we did not copy them. The New Age Movement copied us. All supernaturalism in the world that is not of God is a cheap, Satanic counterfeit. The devil tries to sow confusion. He wants to get Christians to abandon the source and base of their own spiritual power so he can have the advantage. The answer is not to look at the occult and then reject all supernaturalism. The answer is to have the true power of God in operation in your life. Fundanegativism is not the answer. Mere exposé of the error of the New Age is not enough. We must have the true supernatural power of Jesus Christ at work in the Church. How the devil would like to trick us into rejecting God's power in our lives by creating fear of the supernatural! If you are seeking God for the Holy Spirit's influence in your life, make sure your understanding of the Word is correct. If you are a sincere person and you stay in the Word, and really want God in your life, *never fear that you will get something false*. That just won't happen, and as a matter of fact, we have Jesus' assurance:

> And I say unto you, Ask, and it shall be given you; seek, and ye shall find; knock, and it shall be opened unto you. For every one that asketh receiveth; and he that seeketh findeth; and to him that knocketh it shall be opened. If a son shall ask bread of any of you that is a father, will he give him a stone? or if he ask a fish, will he for a fish give him a serpent? Or if he shall ask an egg, will he offer him a scorpion? If ye then, being evil, know how to give good gifts unto your children; how much more shall your Heavenly Father give the Holy Spirit to them that ask him?
>
> Luke 11:9-13

CONTRAST OR COMPARISON

Some would *compare* the New Age Movement and the Holy Spirit Movement. It is more accurate to *contrast* the two supernatural movements.

Both are looking for Christ, but the New Age heralds the coming of a Lord Matreya, a different Christ who is just "one of the boys"—one of the gang of gurus. Jesus warned of the coming of false Christs (Matthew 24). Spirit-filled and fundamentalist believers look for the coming back of the one and only real Jesus, the unique incarnation of God, the true Son of God who was here before, who is even now at the right hand of Father God in the Third Heaven. "This same Jesus" will come back (Acts 1:11). The chapter on the rapture of the Church explains how we will know the real Christ when He comes.

Another interesting contrast is that the New Age Movement is basically anti-Semitic. Even though some Jews are involved in the New Age Movement, the New Age is noted for its Jew hatred. Nazism was definitely part of the New Age philosophy. This has been well documented in numerous books on the subject of the Nazis' and Hitler's involvement in the occult, from Ostara to the inner circle of the Gesaltshaft Thule.

WHERE THE REAL POWER IS

The real power of God is being manifested in the Holy Spirit Movement. The New Age is a lie. It is not even new. It is ancient error. It began with the fall of Lucifer who rejected God's way as the old, outdated way. He decided to try something new. He would be God or His equal. (See Isaiah 14:12-15; Ezekiel 28:12-16. Note that the language here soars far beyond any description possible for the earthly kings of Babylon or Tyre.) The so-called New Age is Satan's last-ditch stand against God in these end times. It proclaims man the creature as the Deity, and endeavors to dethrone the true God, Jehovah, in the minds of mankind.

The Holy Spirit's indwelling of believers prepares them for the end-time spiritual warfare with the New Age counterrevolution against God's mighty end-time revival. The New Age is not innovative. It is reactionary. Do you want to know about the *real New Age*? It is when God Himself says, "Behold I make all things new" (Revelation 21:5). This is not the New Age today—we are in the old age of earth's tragic Satanic regime. We Holy Spirit-led people are the revolutionaries. We have declared war on hell's minions. King Jesus will come back to finish off the war and then the real New Age, the Millennium, will begin. First comes the Rapture of the Church. Can you resist turning and reading the Rapture chapter right now? It is one of the most thrilling truths God has revealed by His Word for our times. The Rapture is not for escape. It is to prove something very important to the Church. It guarantees that no New Age Christ will ever fool you. It is God's guarantee that you will know the real Jesus when He comes back.

CONSPIRACY!

I am now fifty-four years old. I first heard about the New Age Movement, the Network of Light, and Illuminism when I was seventeen years old. A Baptist minister was preaching in an Assembly of God church in Aberdeen, South Dakota, where I went to high school. He gave me my first introduction to this subject. Since then I have read hundreds of books on various conspiracy theories. Early in my studies I discovered that looking into conspiracies is like taking a journey into a world of fantasy and science fiction. You can work out almost any kind of scenario you want. There are book houses that sell nothing but conspiracy related literature, written from scores of points of view. Various authors will tell you that there is a world conspiracy, and each will assure you that he has it all figured out. One will tell you that it is a continuation of Adam Weishaupt's *Illuminati* founded in Bavaria in 1776. Note again a strange parallel. While Satan's political machinery was being set up by Weishaupt, a Satanist, men inspired by God were setting up a political system in America which would provide a climate of freedom where the Holy Spirit Movement could thrive in the last days.

Other authors will tell you that the conspiracy is Communism, Fascism, The Council on Foreign Relations, the Masons, the Jesuits, the Trilateral Commission, the Bildenbergers, the Oxford Circle, the Golden Dawn, the New Age Movement, and so forth. How can anyone make sense out of such a mass of contradictory data?—By recognizing that the New Age is a movement, not an organization.

WHAT IS A MOVEMENT?

The Holy Spirit Movement consists of scores of traditional Pentecostal denominations, Charismatics in the older churches of every kind, independent congregations, the Word of Faith churches, the Full Gospel Business Men International, and every Spirit-filled believer in the world, whether he even knows or not that there is a Holy Spirit *movement*. There is little or no organizational connection between these various parts of the movement. They are a movement because they have certain things in common. They believe the Bible is the Word of God. They believe in the unique character and nature of Jesus, the only begotten Son of God, who is the only incarnation of God there ever was or ever will be. I am not God. I am not the ongoing incarnation of God. I was a lost sinner until I found Jesus as my Savior. Jesus now dwells within me. God dwells within this human temple, but I am not God in the flesh. God is in my flesh, but I am not God in the flesh. The incarnation was a unique, one-time thing when God became flesh and dwelt among us in the person of Jesus. That is what the Holy Spirit Movement believes. Indeed, there is error in our midst that must be dealt with from time to time, but that does not mean that the error is what the majority believe. Even those in error are not to be seen as a part of the New Age Movement. We can deal with error in the brethren without casting them out. Any actual New Age corrupter and infiltrator will soon be identified and dealt with as an heretic. We are not blind to this possibility either, and we are ready and capable of handling such a situation.

The Holy Spirit Movement is not an organization. It is a movement and has a unifying influence because we have one Head, the Lord Jesus Christ (1 Corinthians 12:12-27).

The New Age conspirators are also united even though they may not know it. They are united because they too have a doctrine in common. They are all working for globalism and world religion. They herald the coming of a Christ (not Jesus). They believe in the essential divinity of man, or in pantheism. *They too have one spiritual, invisible head.* That head is the devil.

People who try to analyze political conspiracy from a purely political viewpoint seem ridiculous. There are too many conspiracies. Only the person taking the Biblical point of view can understand that the communists, the Nazis, the cultists, the New Age Movement are all connected because of their headship in Satan.

FINALLY

I don't want anyone to leave this chapter confused. Conspiracy studies can be confusing. Be sure you understand my meaning perfectly clearly. The Holy Spirit Movement and the New Age Movement have nothing in common. We have no common goals. We cannot join hands at any point. We are at war (spiritually) with each other. We can sign no peace treaty. Do you know which side will win? I have read the last page of the Bible, and I assure you the Holy Spirit anointed people win.

> Blessed are they that do his commandments, that they may have right to the tree of life, and may enter in through the gates into the city. For without are dogs, and sorcerers, and whoremongers, and murderers, and idolaters, and whosoever loveth and maketh a lie. I Jesus have sent mine angel to testify unto you these things in the churches. I am the root and the offspring of David, and the bright and morning star. And the Spirit and the bride say, Come. And let him that heareth say, Come. And let him that is athirst come. And whosoever will, let him take the water of life freely. For I testify unto every man that heareth the words of the prophecy of this book, If any man shall add unto these things, God shall add unto him the plagues that are written in this book: And if any man shall take away from the words of the book of this prophecy, God shall take away his part out of the book of life, and out of the holy city, and from the things which are written in this book. He which testifieth these things saith, Surely I come quickly:

Amen. Even so, come, Lord Jesus. The grace of our Lord Jesus Christ be with you all. Amen.

Revelation 22:14-21

CHAPTER 4

AGENDA FOR
END-TIME VICTORY

The world is full of doomsayers. In my personal library there is an entire shelf of books on doomsday subjects. The interesting thing is that the gloom books by secular futurologists seem to outnumber the religious prognosticators of dire coming events. Can it be that the world is waking up to the fact that it is in deep trouble, and the Church is waking to the fact that God is bigger than the devil? Could religious prophetic writers actually begin to realize that the message of King Jesus deserves more attention than that of Antichrist? To any degree that the latter is true, we are presented with significant good news! Prophecy is for winners! The good news is that God has an end-time victory program available to the Church (available, not inevitable).

WARN THE WICKED!

By no means are we indicating that the prophets in the Church should be silent when it comes to warning the wicked world of the consequences of rejecting God. But there is a need in the Church for a declaration of the positive side of prophecy. We need a greater emphasis on the *end-time victory message*. The Prophet Ezekiel declared:

> Again the word of the Lord came unto me, saying, Son

of man, speak to the children of thy people, and say unto them, When I bring the sword upon a land, if the people of the land take a man of their coasts, and set him for their watchman: If when he seeth the sword come upon the land, he blow the trumpet, and warn the people; Then whosoever heareth the sound of the trumpet, and taketh not warning; if the sword come, and take him away, his blood shall be upon his own head. He heard the sound of the trumpet, and took not warning: his blood shall be upon him. But he that taketh warning shall deliver his soul. But if the watchman see the sword come, and blow not the trumpet, and the people be not warned; if the sword come, and take any person from among them, he is taken away in his iniquity; but his blood will I require at the watchman's hand. So thou, O son of man, I have set thee a watchman unto the house of Israel; therefore thou shalt hear the word at my mouth, and warn them from me. When I say unto the wicked, O wicked man, thou shalt surely die; if thou dost not speak to warn the wicked from his way, that wicked man shall die in his iniquity; but his blood will I require at thine hand. Nevertheless, if thou warn the wicked of his way to turn from it; if he do not turn from his way, he shall die in his iniquity; but thou hast delivered thy soul. Therefore, O thou son of man, speak unto the house of Israel; Thus ye speak, saying, If our transgressions and our sins be upon us, and we pine away in them, how should we then live? Say unto them, As I live, saith the Lord God, I have no pleasure in the death of the wicked; but that the wicked turn from his way and live: turn ye, turn ye from your evil ways; for why will ye die, O house of Israel?

Ezekiel. 33:1-11

TWELVE INVESTIGATIVE REPORTERS

Commander Moses sent twelve investigative reporters into Canaan to bring back a report. Two versions of prevailing conditions were returned to him. Ten of the spies said, "It is a rich land, full of milk and honey, *but there are giants in the land and we cannot overcome them.*" Two of the spies, Joshua and Caleb declared, "It is a rich land, full of milk and honey. There are giants in the land, *but our God is greater and we shall overcome.*" Both groups agreed on everything except the conclusion of the matter. We need more Joshuas and Calebs in the Church today.

Many of God's servants are predicting judgment on the Church in North America and throughout the world. They paint dark scenarios of persecution and oppression. I grant that this is a possibility, *but it is not inevitable.* We have choices before us. Our reaction to these decisions will determine the quality of life we live, the freedom we will enjoy to continue preaching the Gospel, evangelizing the nations, lending our support and encouragement to Israel, and in general, the degree of liberty we will experience in these end times. Have you ever noticed that the Bible is full of "if" clauses? For example, Jeremiah says:

> At what instant I shall speak concerning a nation, and concerning a kingdom, to pluck up, and to pull down, and to destroy it; *if* that nation, against whom I have pronounced, turn from their evil, I will repent of the evil that I thought to do unto them. And at what instant I shall speak concerning a nation, and concerning a kingdom, to build and to plant it; If it do evil in my sight, that it obey not my voice, then I will repent of the good, wherewith I said I would benefit them.
>
> Jeremiah 18:7,10

The Prophet Joel speaks of multitudes in the valley of decision in the last days. We are surely in that valley today. Like Israel of old we stand in the valley between Mount Gerizim and Mount Ebal. From one mountainside comes thundering the voice of the priest speaking the curses that will befall the disobedient. From the other side we hear the voice of the priest speaking of the blessings that will come to those who are obedient to the Lord God. We have heard plenty from the mount of cursing, let's hear it from the blessing side!

END-TIME VICTORY PROGRAM

God's end-time victory program for the Church is on two levels. First of all, there is an absolute guarantee that the Church will finally prevail.

> When Jesus came into the coasts of Caesarea Philippi, he asked his disciples, saying, Whom do men say that I the Son of man am? And they said, some say that thou art John the Baptist: some, Elijah; and others, Jeremiah, or one of the prophets. He saith unto them, But whom say ye that I am? And Simon Peter answered and said, Thou art the Christ, the Son of the living God. And Jesus answered and said unto him, Blessed art thou, Simon Barjona: for flesh

and blood hath not revealed it unto thee, but my Father which is in heaven. And I say also unto thee, That thou art Peter, and upon this rock I will build my church; and the gates of hell shall not prevail against it. And I will give unto thee the keys of the kingdom of heaven: and whatsoever thou shalt bind on earth shall be bound in heaven: and whatsoever thou shalt loose on earth shall be loosed in heaven. Matthew 16:13-18

Before we reach the fulfillment of the eternal Kingdom, however, there are a thousand events that will affect our daily lives. In this latter realm there is great flexibility as to what the future holds. This is why there are "if clauses" in the Bible.

If my people, which are called by my name, shall humble themselves, and pray, and seek my face, and turn from their wicked ways; then will I hear from heaven, and will forgive their sin, and will heal their land.

2 Chronicles 7:14

FIVE IMPORTANT POINTS

Here is a program for the realization of *end-time victory for the Church*:

1. *Understanding*. You cannot realize full end-time victory without understanding the plan of God. You cannot be a fulfilled Christian without some understanding of prophecy. I don't mean that you will have to become an eschatological expert, but you must have a lively interest in interpreting the times we live in in the light of the Scripture. "Study to show thyself approved unto God, a workman that needeth not to be ashamed, rightly dividing the word of truth" (2 Timothy 2:15).

For a good guide to the study of prophecy I recommend *Until the Coming of Messiah and His Kingdom* by Dr. Robert Shank (Westcott Publishers); *Things to Come* by J. Dwight Pentecost, published by Zondervan; and *The Interpretation of Prophecy* by Paul Lee Tan (Assurance Publishers). All are available through your local Christian bookstore.

2. *Belief*. It is not enough to merely have intellectual comprehension of the victory provision. There must be an exercise of faith. You must believe that we can win victories over the dark powers, the servants of Antichrist.

Now faith is the substance of things hoped for, the evidence of things not seen. But without faith it is impossible to please him: for he that cometh to God must believe that he is, and that he is a rewarder of them that diligently seek him.

Hebrews 11:1,6

The apostle John writes: "This is the victory that overcometh the world, even our faith" (1 John 5:4).

3. *Confession.* It is not enough to know and believe. Here is the third step toward the appropriation of end-time victory: You must have a good confession.

God commands us to pray for the peace of Jerusalem. Some people can only think about Armageddon! Armageddon will come in its time, but God did not call you and me to be promoters of Armageddon. How tragic that some people study prophecy and it seems to make them bloodthirsty. We should be concerned for the quality of life here and now, as well as the future.

Stop talking defeat. Begin to confess that God is bigger than Antichrist. Realize that *His* mighty power is greater than all the dark forces put together.

"Pray for the peace of Jerusalem" (Psalm 122). Would God give us a command that could only frustrate us? Surely we can make a better confession than the doomsayers (like the ten spies) on the TV and in the newspapers. They can only see with carnal vision. We see beyond narrow human provincialism. We see by the revelation of the Word and the Spirit! The two spies who brought back the good report had the same empirical evidence the ten "bad news" spies had. They saw the same problems, but they proclaimed that God is greater than the enemy. Pray then, for the peace of Jerusalem, and *all her surrounding neighbors.* Let Armageddon come in its time. For now, follow the Prince of Peace.

PROCLAIM VICTORY!

Proclaim victory for the Church of our God. Impossible things are happening. After ministering in churches in Hong Kong and Kowloon we made a trip into Mainland (Communist) China as observers. We are happy to report that God is moving there, too. The Church is growing and revival is moving. I mentioned to the Rev. Thomas F. Zimmerman that the brothers in Hong Kong told me there are now about 50 million born-again Christians in Mainland China. A few years ago it was estimated that there were only about 25,000 Christians in China. Brother Zimmerman said that the estimate I gave was very conservative. He indicated that the missions department of the Assemblies of God estimates about 75 million Christians in China. The Church in China is oppressed but still experiencing victorious growth.

4. *Intercession.* We must implement the plan of God for end-time victory through intercessory prayer.

PASTORS SPEAK

I asked my pastor what was the most encouraging thing he was observing in the Church. He said that it is the remarkable fact that the Church is returning to a ministry of intercessory prayer. Many other pastors across America have told me the same thing.

We used to talk about "praying through" on a matter. Then, for a while, it seemed like people "got through praying" rather than praying through. Praying through means not to quit until you have the answer. That is true intercession.

A man in Virginia once told me that if you pray for the same thing ten times you have prayed nine times in unbelief. I cannot comprehend that, for it would mean that Jesus was an unbeliever! Once Jesus prayed for a blind man. The man was only partly healed. He said, "I see men walking as trees." Jesus prayed a second time for the blind man. Then he said, "I see all men clearly."

IMPORTUNITY OF PRAYER

In Luke 18 Jesus taught the importunity of prayer in the parable of the widow and the unjust judge. The judge did not answer the widow's cry because of any kindness of his heart. He did it just to get rid of her. Jesus then observed:

> And shall not God avenge his own elect, which cry day
> and night unto him, though he bear long with them? I tell
> you that he will avenge them speedily. Nevertheless when
> the Son of man cometh, shall he find faith on the earth?

5. *Good Works*. Following all the above, we must see the prophetic Word of God as a *call to action*. We must set out to defeat those four siblings of doom: Fatalism, Escapism, Irresponsibility, and Defeatism.

In our book about the Lebanese War, *Magog 1982, Canceled*, we share a new slogan: *"Belief without action is deception."* For some reason that statement seems to shock people, and yet it is just a paraphrase of James 1:22: "But be ye doers of the word, and not hearers only, deceiving your own selves."

DOES GOD HELP THOSE WHO HELP THEMSELVES?

The oft-abused saying, "God helps those who help themselves" (not in the Bible) has an element of truth in it. God does bless and aid those who put His plan in action. Of course, He also helps when no human works can avail, but He expects us to be active in His work.

Most evangelical Christians have a vague sympathy in their hearts for Israel. They know that God has predicted a return to the land and that prophecy is being fulfilled in their time, but what good are you to the kingdom and the cause if you are totally inactive? If you never intercede, never give, never work? You have deceived yourself.

Thank God there is a vast host of Christians who are now repudiating the old doomsday fatalism of the not-too-distant past.

Are you just a hearer of the Word, or are you a doer of the Word? Can there be peace in our time? Can there be a healing of the economy? Can the Church experience high-level victory? I sincerely believe that it is up to you. The question is, "Will we appropriate the end-time victory God makes available to us?" Note: Available...not inevitable.

PROPHECY AND VICTORY

This message is one of Christian victory. We are concerned for end-time victory for the Church in these last days before the visible coming of Jesus. New Age teachers are talking about the coming of a "New Christ," an Avatar, the Lord Matreya. They make sure that you know it is not Jesus they are talking about. The "New Christ" could deceive the very elect, but this book will show you God's absolute guarantee that you need not be deceived. This will involve an amazing new teaching relating to the Rapture of the Church. You will want to share this truth far and wide as an antidote to the final deception that is even now in the making. We do not plan to address the old argument of whether the Church goes through any part of the Tribulation. If that is important to you, you will have to find another forum for that discussion. It is time for all who believe in the Rapture (at any point) to join hands and stop fighting over minor issues. You will see clearly why this is necessary as we develop the theme of this book.

THE NEGLECTED EMPHASIS

Prophecy is a faith message. It is a message essential to end-time victory. Bible prophecy is not a message of fear, doom, and gloom. Here is the neglected emphasis. How unfortunate that many Christians ignore prophecy because they instinctively know that God is bigger than the Antichrist, yet they see a great deal of emphasis on end-time prophecy magnifying the antics of the Antichrist above the rulership and dominion of Jesus Christ our Lord.

Bible prophecy is given to us so we can understand the purposes of God. Once we understand those purposes we are called to live in such a manner that we implement the plan of God. God is looking for a people who want to get involved in what He is doing, now and in the future.

Fundanegativists won't be able to handle what we have to say. They see God working supernatural miracles in the past and in the remote future, but for now the only ones working miracles are the devil and the New Agers. Wrong! The devil is a cheap counterfeiter. He only copies and distorts what he sees God doing in the Church.

A study of prophecy should never promote escapism or irresponsibility. Quite the opposite, you will find that the more you learn of God's true nature and purposes the more active you will become in the work of the Kingdom here and now.

These are the end times. This is the final era. The existence of Israel as a nation is the one great proof of that fact. I cannot set any dates. All I know is that we are in the final era. I am not even sure what that will mean to you, but I know for sure that we are not to sit in a white bedsheet on a hillside waiting for the Lord to come.

> "Twiddle dee dee,
> Twiddle dee dum,
> We'll twiddle our thumbs
> Til Jesus comes."

That is the theme song of the escapists, and they have totally missed the reason why God has given us a message of end-time revelation.

Please do not confuse what we are writing with the weird New Agers and their Luciferian "plan" for a faked Second Coming to pacify "all those Christians" so they can get on with the "plan" for global government, economy, and the new religion based on the New Christ (not Jesus). Don't think that because we have preached Kingdom living and faith for the now season for three decades that we agree with any of the new wave of Christian teachers who are saying there will be no Rapture, Millennium, or seven-year Tribulation. Our interpretation of the Bible is based on literalism, not allegory. Symbols in the Bible have a literal meaning, and are all interpreted within the pages of the Bible. We believe the book of Revelation is a book of prophecy largely for these end times.

WE BELIEVE THE KINGDOM IS NOW

This book has been in the process of being written for the past twenty years. Even before that we have taught that the Kingdom of God is now, as well as future, because it is eternal. The Kingdom is presently "within you." It existed before the Church Age began.

The future 1000-year Millennium is not the totality of the Kingdom of God. There will be a millennium when Christ will literally reign on this earth from His throne in Jerusalem (even before there is a New Heaven, New Earth and New Jerusalem). The angel Gabriel spoke of this when he addressed the Virgin Mary:

And, behold, thou shalt conceive in thy womb, and bring forth a son, and shalt call his name Jesus. He shall be great, and shall be called the Son of the Highest: and the Lord God shall give unto him the throne of his father David: And he shall reign over the house of Jacob for ever; and of his kingdom there shall be no end.

Luke 1:31-33

In addition to ruling over Jacob (Israel), Jesus will reign over the nations with a rod of iron (Revelation 19 and 20). The Millennium is not the perfect age, it is but the inauguration to the eternal state which will be absolutely perfect. The 1000-year Millennium is the visible earthly demonstration of the Kingdom of God, but it is only a part of the Kingdom which is eternal. Kingdom living and principles should be put into practice right here and now as far as it lies within us. We will not usher in the visible manifestation of the Kingdom (the Millennium), for it will take Christ Himself to do that; but we will impact our world today with Kingdom living and the miracle-working power of God, and we will prepare ourselves for living and reigning with Christ in the future.

Satan is ever trying to introduce tribulation fury upon the world. Our response is to live as subjects of the Kingdom of God and exercise Kingdom principles and power in combating the dark powers of hell. God's revelation to mankind is complete in the Bible, but our illumination (understanding) of that revelation increases (Colossians 1:10; 2 Peter 3:18; John 14:29).

The 1000-year Millennium will finally be over and when it is past we will enter into the final phase of the eternal Kingdom of God. While we are in the end of this age of grace we must conduct ourselves as Kingdom subjects. We do not cower in fear before the antichrists of our time. I am hearing so many people say, "Don't you realize the threat of communism? Aren't you aware of the threat of secular humanism?" Listen! You and I are the real threat—to them. They last for a short season. What you and I are a part of never ends. Look out, devil, the Church is coming down the road, terrible with banners, a mighty army that will overcome in the name of Jesus!

What we have to add to the field of prophecy literature is not a radical departure from the great truths you have been taught about the end times, but rather the knowledge of how to apply that truth to life in the present. Prophecy is not a mere mind trip. It is more than an intellectual exercise. It is God's antidote to end-time defeatism and fatalism.

UNDERSTANDING OF PROPHECY IMPORTANT

You cannot be a truly fulfilled Christian without some knowledge and understanding of Bible prophecy. Over one-third of the Bible is prophecy. How could you possibly be balanced in your Christian walk while ignoring a third of what God has to say to us? Possibly you have been discouraged by the seeming complexity of prophecy, or by the disagreement of its proponents, or the radicalism of the date-setters and those who forever try to identify a living person as the Antichrist. Error on the part of others gives you no excuse for ignoring the true and noble message God is presenting to you in the prophetic Word.

Elsewhere we have recommended excellent books treating the basics of the prophetic word (Example: *Things to Come* by Dr. J. Dwight Pentecost; Zondervan). The purpose of this writing is to expose you to an element of end-time prophecy that has been tragically overlooked and that is far from promoting fatalism.

While fully aware that our efforts will not bring the Millennium, for that will take the personal coming and intervention of Jesus, we nevertheless strive to improve living conditions in our present world.

BLESSED HOPE

Paul encourages the believers as he writes to Titus, a young pastor. He says that we are:

> Looking for that blessed hope, and the glorious appearing
> of the great God and our Saviour Jesus Christ.
>
> Titus 2:13

Notice the interesting fashion in which Paul leads to this statement, instructing us that we must live a responsible lifestyle in and be concerned for "this present world."

> For the grace of God that bringeth salvation hath appeared
> to all men, Teaching us that, denying ungodliness and
> worldly lusts, we should live soberly, righteously, and
> godly, in this present world.
>
> Titus 2:11,12

Then comes the word of hope relating to our anticipation of the grand finale, the coming back of our Lord Jesus Christ (verse 13). Now take careful note of what Paul says after the blessed hope passage:

> ...Jesus Christ, Who gave himself for us, that he might
> redeem us from all iniquity, and purify unto himself a
> peculiar people, zealous of good works.
>
> Titus 2:13b-14

In the wisdom of God, Paul exhorts believers to watch for the coming of our Lord Jesus, but prefaces and follows the exhortation to future hope with a call for responsible living *in this present world*, a call to be *zealous of good works*. That does not sound like escapism to me, although some have seen Rapture teaching as the ultimate escapist theory. That simply is not true.

Bible prophecy is a powerful call and motivation to action for the Kingdom of God in the now season as we await its visible ushering in by Jesus Himself, following the Rapture and glorification of the believers. The importance of the Rapture to this whole end-time scenario will be examined in a later chapter. You have embarked on a journey into concepts that will give you a new appreciation for God's end-time victory provision for the Church.

At this point I want to make it clear that we believe the bickering among brethren over the timing of the Rapture is unfortunate. It should be stopped. Scholarly discussion of the matter in proper forums may continue, but the fighting over a minor position must cease. With formidable forces in the Church denying that there even will be a Rapture, that the coming of Christ is not even potentially imminent, it is time for those who believe in the Rapture to stop fighting and join hands in the outreach for truth in victory over the powers of darkness. The chapter on the Rapture in this book will show you vividly that it is not taught for escapism, but for an altogether newly revealed reason. Though newly revealed, it is *entirely Biblical*. We have shown the Rapture chapter to several leading Biblical scholars and it has met with universal approval. One outstanding theologian exclaimed, "David, the truth is so plain and evident in the scripture, it is a wonder that we have missed this powerful truth." I simply believe that it is God's time for the truth to be revealed. Jesus said that certain things were prophesied in advance so that when it is fulfilled our faith might be strengthened (John 14:29). We are coming to understand more and more of God's end-time truth that seemed obscure before, but nothing new is being added to the Word of God. No personal revelation takes any precedence over the Bible. All truth must harmonize with the Scripture. God is not writing new Scripture. The grand old revelation is complete, it is simply our comprehension that is increasing. In a later chapter we will deal with the question of doctrine, what is essential, and what is not for fellowship.

It is our observation that people who believe in the Rapture have been the most aggressive of soulwinners. They have been on the front lines for world missions. They have been active in promoting the true unity of the body of Christ. Of course, every doctrine suffers abuse at the hands of extremists, and we will deal with that in later chapters; but a concept cannot be condemned because of misuse at the hands of fanatics.

We who believe in the Rapture truly strive to improve living conditions in the now season. We intercede to bind the forces of darkness. We labor to keep the Church free and active. We get involved in a wide variety of social concerns.

There is no lust for Armageddon in our hearts. Armageddon will come in its time, but God did not call us to be promoters of Armageddon. I am a follower of the Prince of Peace. While I cannot join in with the communist dominated, phony "peace movement," I must nevertheless be a peacemaker in my own time, for "blessed are the peacemakers." Jesus, whom I follow, is the Prince of Peace.

Some note that Paul wrote, "When they shall say, Peace and safety; then sudden destruction cometh upon them, as travail upon a woman with child; and they shall not escape" (1 Thessalonians 5:3). Friends, Paul is talking about a specific era, the day of Antichrist deception (2 Thessalonians 2:3-12), the day of the Lord (tribulation period), about a specific time of false peace, when the Antichrist will usher in an era of seeming peace and prosperity. It does not mean that every effort man has made to achieve peace (treaties between nations, etc.) since the Thessalonian epistles were written was wrong or ill advised. Remember, Satan is the promoter of war. We must be strong as a nation to defend ourselves, but we must not be warmongers. I believe that is the role our nation has traditionally played. The Church in this nation should pray for and work for secure, defended peace.

CHAPTER 5

THE RAPTURE
OF THE CHURCH

VICTORY OVER END-TIME DECEPTION

The Biblical truth of the Rapture of the Church is God's ultimate assurance that you will not be fooled by the final "False Christ" or any of his forerunners. If you understand the Rapture concept you can never be fooled into thinking that any false Christ is the real One.

We who believe in the Rapture have been accused of preaching "escapism" for so long that we have been pushed into assuming a defensive posture. We have spent far too much energy defending our position as not being escapist. *Because of this distraction we have overlooked the real reason for the Rapture.* "Why," our critics ask, "would God yank the believers out of this world to take them to heaven, only to shortly return with Jesus to set up the visible Kingdom on earth?" It doesn't make sense until you learn of *the real reason for the Rapture.* Now we learn of the real necessity for the Rapture.

The potential for deception by Antichrist forces is greater than ever before. Mankind is being prepared for a fake "Second Coming" of a New Christ (not Jesus). It could be the worst deception ever perpetrated upon humanity.

The Rapture was not an invention of certain believers in the 1800's as our critics claim. The Rapture is a New Testament teaching that is vitally important for these end times. It may well be that in recent times the Holy Spirit has awakened interest in the Church in this truth.

You will find newly revealed information relating to the New Testament concept of the Rapture of the Church by reading this.

A WORD OF KNOWLEDGE FROM THE LORD

During Christmas week my family and I were at a conference where I was teaching seminars twice daily, and speaking for some of the night campmeetings. While teaching one day on the subject of the Rapture of the Church, I said, "The purpose of the Rapture is...." I paused for a moment as a powerful word of knowledge, a revelation of truth, flooded my being. I then began to pour out the truths contained in this chapter. Especially I am referring to the part about the coming false Christ and the ultimate deception wherein some of the very elect may be deceived. This may be the most important truth God has ever given me on the Rapture!

During the previous August I had written the following for our *Prophecy Intelligence Digest* (tabloid publication):

A serious problem must be considered. Since...(some)... people don't believe in the Rapture of the Church, nor in a literal Antichrist, how will they know when the anticipated one appears if it is Jesus or the Lord Maitreya or even the very Antichrist? Jesus said, "If any man shall say unto you, Lo, here is Christ or there; believe it not" (Matthew 24:23. Also see Matthew 24:24-27).

I wrote that few lines as a part of an article on New Age attempts to penetrate Neo-Pentecostal churches (as described by a New Age leader). The thought in seed form was planted in my mind, and frankly, I did not pursue it further. Then in December it blossomed in my spirit and came to fruition as a revelation gift from the Lord to the Church.

When the disciples asked Jesus, "What will be the sign of thy coming and of the end of the world (Greek: age)," He begins His lengthy answer with the warning: "Take heed that no man deceive you." The remaining portion of the Olivet discourse (Matthew 24,25) is replete with several more similar warnings. Jesus especially warns us to beware of false Christs and indicates that there is the possibility of the very elect being deceived. If not possible, why the warning? Indeed, many born-again believers have been deceived by false cultists in our own day.

THE REAL JESUS CHRIST

We are told that "The Lord Himself" shall descend from heaven to receive the Church (1 Thessalonians 4:16-18). Angels told the apostles that "This *same* Jesus...shall come in like manner..." (Acts 1:11). Jesus assured that He would "come again and receive you unto myself; that where I am there ye may be also" (John 14:3). With so many pretenders, how will the believers know when the real Jesus comes?

Just suppose that a powerful psychic, a miracle worker, would appear in Jerusalem soon. He has nail prints in his hands, thanks to plastic surgery. He wears a white robe and glows with an inner radiance. He is a miracle worker, just as the second beast of Revelation is described:

> And he doeth great wonders, so that he maketh fire come down from heaven on the earth in the sight of men, And deceiveth them that dwell on the earth by means of those miracles which he had power to do....
>
> Revelation 13:13,14

With modern technology he could even fake a "descent" from heaven. Suppose that this powerful man, with the T.V. cameras of the world trained on him, then proclaimed himself to be Christ. How would you know if he is the one? Jesus warns us not to go to the desert, nor to believe He is in "secret chambers," but here is a man in the right place, on the Mount of Olives as predicted by Zechariah (14:4).

I believe that something like this is going to happen. This may not be the exact scenario, but something like this will take place. It is an inescapable conclusion when you consider the acts of the two beasts of Revelation 13 (Antichrist and false prophet) and the fact that the man of sin will receive worship from masses of people on earth (2 Thessalonians 2:3,4 and Revelation 13:3,4,15).

Pre-tribulationists will want to know if this could take place before the Rapture of the Church. I cannot be sure, but I think it could. Jesus warns of false Christs (plural). God has given us insurance against deception. That is what this chapter is about. This is an important element in our end-time victory package. Proper understanding of the Rapture will make you "false Christ deception proof."

Surely God must have provided us some safeguard so that we can be sure to know the real Jesus when He comes. He has—and that safeguard is the Rapture of the Church. The Rapture of the Church will precede Christ's descent to the Mount of Olives with the glorified Church in His entourage. Upon this fact agree all who believe in the Rapture, whether they hold to a pre-, mid-, or post-tribulation Rapture. What do we mean by the Rapture, and is it a Biblical concept?

THE RAPTURE OF THE CHURCH

Many passages of Scripture teach that at the close of the Church Age, Christ Jesus will personally descend from heaven, bringing with Him the souls of all who have died in the faith. Their bodies will be resurrected. The believers who are alive on earth will be instantaneously transformed and glorified. We will rise to meet Christ, never more to die or feel pain, nor to suffer misunderstanding or disappointment. We will never be parted from our Lord Jesus Christ.

> But I would not have you to be ignorant, brethren, concerning them which are asleep, that ye sorrow not, even as others which have no hope. For if we believe that Jesus died and rose again, even so them also which sleep in Jesus will God bring with him. For this we say unto you by the word of the Lord, that we which are alive and remain unto the coming of the Lord shall not prevent them which are asleep. For the Lord himself shall descend from heaven with a shout, with the voice of the archangel, and with the trump of God: and the dead in Christ shall rise first: Then we which are alive and remain shall be caught up together with them in the clouds to meet the Lord in the air: and so shall we ever be with the Lord. Wherefore comfort one another with these words.
>
> 1 Thessalonians 4:13-18

This passage, along with a host of others, clearly defines the greatest event of the end of this age, relating to the Church. No one can deny the Rapture without ravaging the meaning of the Word of God. Those who reject the rapture concept admit that this rejection requires a non-literal interpretation of the Scriptures. That, in turn, introduces an anarchy into the science of Biblical interpretation which would allow you to make the Bible mean anything you want it to mean. If the Bible doesn't mean what it says, then one is faced with the possible conclusion that it might not mean anything at all. That is unacceptable. Literalism is best.

THE WORD "RAPTURE" NOT IN THE BIBLE?

There were two of them. Their colleagues had been at my door before, so I knew who and what they were. During our brief dialogue one of them said, "But the word 'rapture' does not appear in the Bible." Remembering a line written by H. L. Wilmington, I said, "It is true that of the 774,747 words comprising the King James Bible one of those words is *not* the word rapture. On the other hand, the words demon, grandfather, and trinity do not appear in the Bible, even though the concepts are clearly there." (They took strong exception to the latter). There are demons (evil spirits, devils, etc.), grandfathers exist, and there is a Trinity (the Divine Godhead), even though the specific words do not appear in the King James translation. At this point, my visitors nervously remembered that they were late for a very important meeting which they were required to attend.

Technically, the word "rapture" *does* appear in the original manuscript of the first Thessalonian letter. The word is "harpazo" in the Greek and is weakly translated "caught up" in 1 Thessalonians 4:17. It is better translated "caught or snatched up by forceful seizure." (See *Vine's Expository Dictionary of New Testament Words,* etc.) The context seems to allow a further amplification, "caught away forcefully in a state of ecstacy." In any case, the Latin-English word "rapture" is a perfect translation of the Greek "harpazo." It is this event that Paul refers to in the later Thessalonian letter as "our gathering together unto Him" (2 Thessalonians 2:1). Paul elaborates on the Rapture in the first letter to the Church at Corinth:

> Behold, I shew you a mystery; We shall not all sleep, but we shall all be changed, In a moment, in the twinkling of an eye, at the last trump: for the trumpet shall sound, and the dead shall be raised incorruptible, and we shall be changed. For this corruptible must put on incorruption, and this mortal must put on immortality. So when this corruptible shall have put on incorruption, and this mortal shall have put on immortality, then shall be brought to pass the saying that is written, Death is swallowed up in victory. O death, where is thy sting? O grave, where is thy victory? The sting of death is sin; and the strength of sin is the law.
>
> 1 Corinthians 15:51-56

What else could Jesus be talking about in His conversation with the disciples:

> Let not your heart be troubled: ye believe in God, believe also in me. In my Father's house are many mansions: if it were not so, I would have told you. I go to prepare a place for you. And if I go and prepare a place for you, I will come again, and receive you unto myself; that where I am, there ye may be also.
>
> John 14:1-3

ATTACK ON THE RAPTURE

It is no wonder that a wide variety of cultists, New Agers, false prophets, and false teachers attack the teaching of the Rapture so vehemently.

It is not the purpose of this book to get into the pre-tribulation, mid-tribulation, or post-tribulation Rapture argument. It is time for all who believe in the Rapture to close ranks, stop fighting each other, and see what others are trying to do. This anti-rapture teaching is even infiltrating the ranks of evangelical, fundamentalist, pentecostal, and charismatic churches.

Some teach there will be no thousand-year Millennium, Christ cannot return at any moment, Satan is already bound, Israel has no place in the end-time plan of God, and the Church must get rid of "that tired old doctrine of the Rapture." The apostle Peter was not writing to cultists, but to the true Church when he said: "But there were false prophets also among the people, even as there shall be false teachers among you" (2 Peter 2:1). I cannot accuse all those who teach these doctrines of being false prophets, but I must speak out on these grievous errors which can cripple the Church. The Rapture concept is vital to end-time victory over the ultimate deception—that of the false Christ.

FALSE CHRISTS

People who do not believe in the Rapture may be very puzzled by a false Christ. Already a number of these false Christs are on the scene. Many will remember a full-page advertisement in the *New York Times* proclaiming, "*The Christ Is Now Here.*" This advertisement appeared in major newspapers throughout the free world, at an estimated cost of over $500,000.00 The campaign was sponsored by the Tara Center, a New Age organization. We had referred to a New Age cultic movement in an article that appeared in the *Pentecostal Evangel* in 1966. The New Age is not new. It is a recent amplification of ancient error. The advertisement in the *New York Times* calls for world peace and an end to hunger and strife. Benjamin Creme of the Tara Foundation has lectured widely in the USA regarding the presence of the New Christ. In his book, *The Reappearance of the Christ and the Masters of Wisdom,* he makes it clear that the New Christ is not Jesus. Jesus is a mere disciple of the New Christ (p.46). The New Christ was a spirit meditating in the Himalaya Mountains until July 19, 1977, when he created a human body which he now inhabits (pp.30,36). Creme writes, "One day soon men and women all over the world will gather round their radio and television sets to hear and see the Christ; to see his face, and to hear his words dropping silently into their minds—in their own language. In this way they will know that he is truly the Christ..." (p.37).

Lucis Trust (originally Lucifer Publishing), located at 866 United Nations Plaza in New York, sponsored a full-page advertisement in the *Reader's Digest*. It was headlined, "The Great Invocation." I immediately recognized it as non-Biblical in nature, even though one line reads, "May Christ return to earth."

A recent mailing from Lucis Trust (a powerful New Age organization) contained the following line: "Today the reappearance of the World Teacher—the Christ, is expected by millions; not only by those of Christian faith but by those of every faith who expect the Avatar under other names— the Lord Maitreya, Krishna, Messiah, Imam Mahdi and the Bodhisattva." How amazed I was to see the prayer from the *Reader's Digest* pinned to the bulletin board of one of our churches. The pastor removed it as soon as I explained the nature and source of the invocation.

Hundreds of thousands today believe that Sun Myung Moon is the fulfillment of the Second Coming of Christ. Another evangelist, in Chicago, declares that he, himself is Christ. A pamphlet about the Chicago Christ is headlined: "The Lord Has Already Come—Jesus Has Returned and Is Walking On Earth In The Flesh." This piece of absurdity describes a man from India who was ministering in a church on July 20, 1969. The folder proclaims that he is a man "whose ancestry when it was traced showed that he is in the direct line of King David through Nathan, the brother of Solomon." Just before man first stepped on the moon, it is explained, "Jesus entered into the body of Brother ------ in the fullness. Just before man took that 'giant step for mankind' God came down to this earth and again became flesh in the person of Brother ------." This is a manifestation of one of the many false Christs Jesus warned about.

I SHALL KNOW HIM

When the real Jesus comes I will know Him—for sure! There will be no doubt about it. When Moses was withstood by the two magicians, Jannes and Jambres, in Pharaoh's court, they could duplicate some of the miracles; but the time came when their powers failed and God triumphed over evil, allowing the children of Israel to leave Egypt in triumph.

One of these days an event will take place that all the forces of hell cannot duplicate nor counterfeit, nor can they stop it. When the trumpet sounds and you are transformed into the likeness of Jesus Christ our Lord, and when you rise to meet Him along with millions of other believers, you will know beyond the shadow of a doubt who you are meeting. It is Jesus! It is the Rapture! Glory to God in the Highest! It is He and not another! This is the real Jesus!

JESUS ON TV?

If you ever hear that Jesus is going to be on television tomorrow at 3 p.m., that he will be seen "live" on the Mount of Olives, *don't believe it*. Don't watch it. It is deception. Listen! If your feet are flat on the ground, if you do not have a glorified body, if you have not risen to meet the Lord in the air, if you have to watch him on television *it is not the real Jesus*. It is an imposter.

Some think that "every eye beholding Him" means that the whole world will see the Second Coming on television. That is impossible since a few hundred million human beings do not have access to television sets, nor would the communist or Muslim world broadcast the coming of the real Jesus. How then will every eye behold Him? I don't know. I believe in God, His Word, and His supernatural powers. How He accomplishes it is His business, and I have full confidence the prophecy will be fulfilled. It is not my problem to figure out how. If I could humanize everything in the Bible in purely rational terms there would be no need for faith, would there? I accept it by faith.

RAPTURE TEACHING RESISTED

A leader in the New Age Movement who promotes the teachings of Alice Bailey (founder of the Lucis Trust) has written an essay titled "The Neo-Pentecostals and Their Amazing New Age Teachings." In it he expresses delight that some Pentecostals look upon the so-called rapture theory as absurd bunk...He proclaims these new Pentecostals as having a "more enlightened and spiritually substantial theology" than other Pentecostals. He notes that they do not take the Bible literally. Attention is called to the fact that the Neo-Pentecostals who teach the doctrine of the "Manifest Sons of God" are very close to the New Age Movement. The Manifest Sons believe that believers are *now* gradually receiving their glorified bodies and will be transformed *before* Christ returns. The most extreme form of this Manifest Sons teaching has a frightening element. Some are teaching that at a given point, when God gives the signal, the Manifest Sons will be the instruments of His wrath to slaughter the wicked ones. They will take up arms and kill their neighbors. The verse that says "one shall be taken and one shall be left" to the Manifest Sons indicates the removal of the wicked, not the rapture of the Church. They will be God's vengeful destroyers (killers of the unredeemed).

DANGEROUS DOCTRINE!

If this doctrine ever gets a foothold in the churches it will make the Jim

Jones—Guyana affair seem like a stroll in the park by comparison. May God deliver us from this madness. Jesus will destroy the Antichrist "with the brightness of His coming." I don't have to do it. The hosts who follow the beast will be destroyed supernaturally by Jesus Himself at the time of His Second Coming. Whether you see the Church being raptured and coming back with Jesus seven years later (Pre-tribulationism) or if you see the Church rising to meet the Lord in the air to return at once with Him (Post-tribulationism), the main thing is that *we will be raptured and transformed, and then return with Christ as witnesses of His victory over the Beast.* It is Jesus who will slay the rebels and not ourselves. Leave it to Him. He can handle it.

IS THE RAPTURE ESCAPISM?

I have heard it said that believing in the Rapture is escapism. I deny that. We who believe in the Rapture are not trying to escape our responsibilities in this present season. Rapture believers have been at the forefront of missions, church building, evangelization, and a host of other realms of responsible action. Of course you can find a few bad examples, but that is true of any group of people who embrace any concept.

There is a healthy escapism that has nothing to do with the charges leveled at us. We want a guaranteed escape from the deceivers and false Christs. This is important.

Furthermore, believing in the Rapture is no more escapism than is believing in salvation teaching that shows us how to escape eternal damnation. It is no more escapist teaching than divine healing is an escape from sickness. Everyone wants to "escape" evil. Environmentalists want to escape pollution. The peace movement wants to escape from war, and so on. My observation is that most of the people who believe in the Rapture are vigorously trying to work for God and mankind in the now season. True, there are abuses of any doctrine, but that does not prove the doctrine wrong.

I am not surprised that the enemy tries to discredit the Biblical doctrine of the Rapture. No one who believes in the Rapture will ever be fooled by any false Christ.

The word "rapture" (Greek: harpazo) implies that Jesus will use "force" to remove us from this world. This is because Satan and all the demons will try to prevent the resurrection of the believers and the Rapture of the living Church. But there is no doubt as to who will win in this struggle. It is all over in "the twinkling of an eye." When you get your brand new, disease-proof, transfigured, glorified, never-dying, fatigue-free body you will know that it is "this same Jesus." When you rise with millions of believers to meet

Him, when you leave earth behind, when you reach that golden shore, when you stand before the throne, you will *know* that it is "the Lord Himself" and no imposter.

PROOF OF JESUS' IDENTITY

The Rapture is the only possible proof of the true identity of Jesus. Modern psycho-technology, brain washing, subliminal influences, mood synthesizing generators, projected mood rays could produce a feeling of euphoria to people who still have their feet flat on the ground. They could be fooled into thinking they had been transformed simultaneously with the appearance of a false Christ. Or they could be told that the transformation promised will be gradual. (See the chapter on Psychotronic Warfare and Battle for the Mind.)

It won't fool the Rapture conscious believer! He knows that he will *rise to meet Jesus in the air.*

If your feet are flat on the ground and you have not been transformed, if you did not yet rise to meet Jesus *in the air,* and some "Christ" is presented on television, don't believe it—it isn't Him. It is not the real Jesus Christ we are watching for. Remember, the very end of the age is characterized by deception like the world has never known before. When psycho-science and demonic occultism are wedded it produces powerful tools for massive deception, but God has given us a safeguard against the ultimate deception.

A STRANGE ENCOUNTER

Now for the strangest part of this message on the Rapture. Just about three weeks after God gave me this insight at the conference, while teaching a seminar, I was giving the message in a church. Later I was talking to several people about it. One of them is a person who has done a lot of research on occultism and the New Age Movement. This person said to me, "Well, I can see you have been reading Peter Lemesurier's book, *The Armageddon Script.*" I replied that I had never so much as heard of Lemesurier. My inquirer responded, "You have to be kidding. He is an outstanding New Age leader and author. He is highly regarded in their ranks. What you have been talking about (false Christ) sounds like it is straight out of his book." Again I said that I had never heard of the author or the book, nor the concept, whereupon the speaker said, "This is truly awesome. I must bring you a copy of the book." Little did I realize how shocked I would actually be. At this point I was mildly curious.

I have Peter Lemesurier's book, *The Armageddon Script—Prophecy in Action,* before me at this very moment. Now I have read it and I am stunned at its contents. Here is a man who lumps the Bible along with Nostradamus,

Edgar Cayce, Jeane Dixon and other psychics. He indicates that Jesus failed in His mission. This is a long and complicated treatise. He says that prophecy is not so much for us to foretell the future as it is an instrument to create events in the future. He speaks of learning to manipulate the future through the use of self-willed and self-fulfilled prophecy. How is this different from the Christian view of prophecy? We believe that God has a predetermined, prophesied plan set before us. Nothing will change that. We understand that not every detail of the future is predestined. Human cooperation with (or on the other hand, apathy toward) the purposes of God will make a difference in how we pass through time on the way to eternity. Lemesurier indicates that the future can be *entirely* engineered to suit man. The Christian student of prophecy tries to find out the will of God through the Bible and then work in cooperative implementation of the will and purposes of God from now until the literal Second Coming of the real Jesus.

Lemesurier feels that there needs to be a manufactured Second Coming to fulfill the anticipations of millions of people. Then the New Agers can get on with the job of building a global society. He speaks of "Our basic plan of action" for an engineered "Second Coming." He believes that there is "every chance that we shall finally succeed in our task." He speaks of going to meet the Messiah. His six-point plan calls for: 1. Messiah appears on the Mount of Olives. 2. He will come dressed in white, from the East. 3. He will pose as the great King David returned. 4. He is crowned King of the "New Israel" on the Mount of the Temple in Jerusalem. 5. Divine fire and miraculous accompaniments attend his presence. 6. There will be a time of wrath.

I would note that this fits the scenario of either a false Christ or even the Antichrist himself. Only time will tell. Regardless of how powerful any coming one is, regardless of miracles, or claims, if you know the truth about the Rapture (which takes place *first* before any of the other things Jesus does in relation to the Church or the earth) then you will not be deceived.

Lemesurier's book indicates that "brief quotations" from his book may be used if "embodied in critical articles or reviews." (You can get a copy from St. Martin's Press, 175 Fifth Avenue, New York, NY 10010.)

This is a critical article, and here is a brief quote from the book by Lemesurier. The very last words of the book are: "It was the function of Jesus the Nazarene in his day, and will be the purpose, too, of the New David whose task it is to set the whole new, prophetic process in motion. Upon him and his associates much will therefore depend. Their script is now written, subject only to last-minute editing and stage-directions. The stage itself, albeit as yet in darkness, is almost ready. Down in the pit, the subterranean orchestra is already tuning up. The last-minute, walk-on parts are even now being filled.

Most of the main actors, one suspects, have already taken up their roles. Soon it will be time for them to come on stage, ready for the curtain to rise. The time for action will have come" (*The Armageddon Script*, p. 252).

Any coming of a new "Christ" as prophesied by Blavatsky, Basant, Bailey, Creme, Lemesurier and a host of other powerful New Agers (including a high official in the United Nations *who is saying the same thing*) will at best be a false Christ, and at worst the very Antichrist.

He will deceive the very elect if possible. We shudder when remembering that Jim Jones was a Pentecostal preacher (licensed by the Assemblies of God) before his total apostasy. We have seen too many of the elect of God deceived to scoff at the possibility. If one would say that the new Christ could be known by the gift of discerning of spirits, what about all the babes in Christ who have no operation of the gift? Further, who among us can honestly say we have never been fooled by a false "brother"? No, God has given us something much more sure. He has given us Bible truth about the Rapture. I will know the real Jesus when I "rise to meet him in the air," when I participate in the glorious Rapture of the Church, when I am "changed in the twinkling of an eye." I will shout in triumph, "Hello, Jesus, *I know it is really You.*"

The Lord brought the concept of "the Rapture as proof of the identity of the real Jesus" to me by a gift of the word of knowledge. All revelation gifts are to be tested by two criteria. First, does it measure up to the Word of God? Secondly, does it pass the approval of the elders of the church? Before publication I tested the concept in both ways. The manuscript was submitted to a number of brethren. I discussed it with a number of elders and pastors. All responded positively. Now I submit my thesis to the entire Church. Your comments are welcome.

CHAPTER 6

End-Time Victory Over Apathy in the Church

A great apostasy is prophesied for the last days. A great revival is prophesied for the last days. It is not an either/or situation. We will see both. There will be a crescendo of evil on one hand and a crescendo of God's power on the other. (See Daniel 12:9,10.)

What about all the apathetic Christians in the Church? How can God move in spite of apathy? Listen, it has always been that way. Humanity does not change that much. God always uses the dedicated minority.

MULTITUDES FOLLOWED JESUS

Draw five concentric circles around Jesus. It will illustrate a powerful concept.

In the outer ring you find the multitude that followed Jesus for the miracles, for the loaves and the fishes. He does not rebuke or drive them away. He heals their sick, casts out demons, works His mighty miracles. They come and go. Some are there because it looks entertaining. Their association with Jesus is tenuous, but "the common people heard Him gladly."

In the next ring find seventy people whom He commissioned to do His work in proclaiming the Gospel. These people were workers with some degree of motivation. Their brief story is told in the tenth chapter of the Gospel of Luke:

> After these things the Lord appointed other seventy also, and sent them two and two before his face into every city and place, whither he himself would come. Therefore said he unto them, The harvest truly is great, but the laborers are few: pray ye therefore the Lord of the harvest, that he would send forth laborers into his harvest. Go your ways: behold, I send you forth as lambs among wolves. Carry neither purse, nor scrip, nor shoes: and salute no man by the way. And into whatsoever house ye enter, first say, Peace be to this house. And if the son of peace be there, your peace shall rest upon it: if not, it shall turn to you again. And in the same house remain, eating and drinking such things as they give: for the laborer is worthy of his hire. Go not from house to house. And into whatsoever city ye enter, and they receive you, eat such things as are set before you: And heal the sick that are therein, and say unto them, The kingdom of God is come nigh unto you.
>
> And the seventy returned again with joy, saying, Lord, even the devils are subject unto us through thy name. And he said unto them, I beheld Satan as lightning fall from heaven. Behold, I give unto you power to tread on serpents and scorpions, and over all the power of the enemy: and nothing shall by any means hurt you. Notwithstanding in this rejoice not, that the spirits are subject unto you; but rather rejoice, because your names are written in heaven.
>
> Luke 10:1-9, 17-20

Now move to the next circle. There you find twelve men who were with Jesus most of the time. These men were very special to Him. They were His disciples and are known as the twelve apostles. He chose them, and they chose to follow and obey Him. Except for Judas, they all will play a special role in the coming manifestation of the Kingdom of God. The next "inner circle" narrows down to three men who were a bit closer to Jesus than the other twelve. Peter, James, and John went a bit further than the other nine. This is best illustrated in the Gospel account of the transfiguration of the Lord Jesus Christ (Mark 9; Matthew 17). Perhaps the nine were tired. The trip to Caesarea Phillipi was a rigorous journey. They tarried in the valley below the mount of the Transfiguration. In the absence of Jesus the nine disciples have suffered a humiliating defeat. They were unable (though they tried) to cast the evil spirit out of a suffering little boy. In the meantime, the three who put forth the extra effort, who stuck with Jesus all the way to the mountain top, saw the glory of the coming Kingdom. They saw Jesus transfigured before them. They saw two of the Old Testament prophets, Moses and Elijah, talking with the Son of God. What a moment! What a triumph!

Finally, stand right by Jesus in the very inner circle. It is the hour of His deepest agony. Nails pierce His hands. He hangs on the cross. Certain of the women who were His followers stand close to the cross. His mother, Mary, is there. Mother! What will happen to Mother? Who will take care of her? He looks for a strong person. All the disciples, save one, are hiding in the midst of the multitude. Fear grips their very souls, but there stands John. In the tenderest scene in the Bible Jesus looks down from the cross and says, "John, take care of Mother." Oh! I want to stand where John stood. God give me courage not to hide in the crowd in the crisis hour. Tradition tells us that John took Mary with him when he moved to Ephesus in Asia Minor (now Turkey) to become the pastor and founder of the church there. Today if you visit Ephesus you will be shown a little church built upon the foundations of the little house that John built for Mary. There she lived out her final days. My heart was deeply moved as I visited this traditional site a while ago. I fervently prayed that I might have the boldness to take a stand for Jesus, just like John did. Would Jesus entrust His mother to you? Where are you in the circles drawn around Jesus? You will be where you determine to be. He welcomes, but does not force you into a more intimate relationship with Him.

COMPASSION FOR THE CHURCH

Jesus lashed out at the crooked money changers in the Temple. He freely criticized religious hypocrites and false teachers, but the poor milling multitude He embraced. "A bruised reed He will not break and smoking flax He will not quench."

The Church is like that today. There is the multitude who come for a variety of reasons. They hurt, they fear, they are hungry, they need healing. Some Sundays they are there in the pew and sometimes not. There are critical

---

Christians who would like to lash the apathetic multitude. Scolding them won't help much. Just feed them, encourage them, and hope that they will move into the "inner circles." If they don't move according to your expectation don't give up. Just thank God that they are in the body and not "in the tents of the wicked."

Look around you. Not everyone in the church is lacking in motivation. Jesus still has His seventy, His twelve, the three, and even John. They are all represented in the Church of today. It has always been a minority that has had a priority on the power of God. It is always a highly motivated minority that gets the job done.

Just remember that initially you probably didn't come to God for lofty philosophical reasons. Most people come to God at first for selfish reasons. They come out of personal need. Jesus came to heal the sick, not the whole. We all start as babes in Christ. Now it is time to grow. It is time to advance, to move into the inner circles of relationship with our Lord and His end-time purposes. It is victory time for the Church, and Gideon's three hundred will still win the battle for the rest.

> Have your eyes caught the vision?
> Has your heart felt the thrill?
> To the call of the Master,
> do you answer, I will?
> For the conflict of the ages
> told by prophets and by sages
> In its fury is upon us, is upon us today.

God has called us to end-time victory through knowledge of His purposes and end-time plan. He has called us to involvement in the realm of intercessory prayer. He has called us to implement His will by our good works. One day we will all stand before Him for our evaluation. We want to hear Him say, "Well *done* (not well thought out) thou good and faithful servant, enter thou into the joy of thy Lord." It may seem like a mournful dirge, but it is true:

> Life's evening sun is sinking low
> Just a few more days and I must go
> To meet the deeds that I have done
> Where there will be no setting sun.

"To meet the deeds that I have done...." Can this be so? Yes, for Paul instructs us that all our works will be tried by fire. The third chapter of 1 Corinthians starts rather strangely. It seems that there *are* carnal Christians!

CARNAL CHRISTIANS AND THE JUDGMENT SEAT OF CHRIST

Harsh spirited Christians preach a "partial rapture theory." Only a select few "overcomers" will go in the Rapture. But here in Paul's letter I find "carnal brethren" in the body on earth (1 Corinthians 3:1-4). In the future evaluation judgment of believers I see some who are there "by the skin of their teeth," or as Paul says, "Saved, yet so as by fire." Some will just barely make it, by the grace of God. They are stripped of reward—but they are there. Everyone who is saved will go in the Rapture. We will have to let God decide who is saved and who is not. This is not to excuse carnality in the body. We deplore carnal living. We constantly challenge people to move into the inner circles of relationship with Jesus, but our eyes are not closed to reality. We remember the multitudes who followed Jesus for the loaves and the fishes. They are with us today. How many of them got saved in Christ's time? Only God knows that. We can leave it to Him.

GOOD WORKS ARE IMPORTANT

You are not saved by your works. But good works are important. You are saved by grace unto good works:

> For by grace are ye saved through faith; and that not of yourselves: it is the gift of God: Not of works lest any man should boast. For we are his workmanship, created in Christ Jesus unto good works, which God hath before ordained that we should walk in them.
>
> Ephesians 2:8-10

In a previous chapter we explored "The Daniel Factor." The third phase of attaining end-time victory is getting involved in the plan of God through our works. Not only is attainment of high level end-time victory contingent upon our involvement in the purposes of God, but our eternal reward will be determined by our works. Salvation is free, by the Grace of God, but reward is based on works. Some seemingly pious person might respond in a show of humility, "Oh, I am not interested in rewards, I just do whatever I do because I love the Lord." That sounds very nice, but I suggest you take it up with God. He set up the awards program, not man. It is not of our devising:

> For other foundation can no man lay than that is laid, which is Jesus Christ. Now if any man build upon this foundation gold, silver, precious stones, wood, hay, stubble; Every

man's work shall be made manifest: for the day shall declare it, because it shall be revealed by fire; and the fire shall try every man's work of what sort it is. If any man's work abide which he hath built thereupon, he shall receive a reward. If any man's work shall be burned, he shall suffer loss: but he himself shall be saved; yet so as by fire.

1 Corinthians 3:11-15

I can't argue with that. What you do for God in the Kingdom right now determines your status in the future manifestation of the Kingdom. Don't forget motivation behind the works is important too. We do work because we love Jesus and His Church, and we will be evaluated and rewarded accordingly.

CHAPTER 7

CHRISTIANS IN ACTION
The Daniel Factor—Phase III

God calls us to active participation in His on-going eschatological enterprise. We are to be participants and not merely spectators of the events of the last days. When we speak of the Daniel Factor we mean that Daniel was not just a student of the Word, although that is of basic importance. You *must* study to show yourself approved, but prophecy is more than a mind-trip. Daniel identified with the work of God in the realm of intercession. The Daniel Factor consists of three areas of involvement with God's plan. First, is the intellectual—understanding the plan. Secondly, is involvement through intercession. There is a third area to be considered.

PROPHECY, PRAYER AND POLITICS

What kind of man do you think Daniel was? What is your impression of this prophet of Israel? Daniel is best remembered for his mystic visions. His writings are filled with esoteric dreams of distant future scenes. His prophecy is like an encounter with surrealism. He paints word pictures that make one think of the art of Salvador Dali or Paul Fornier. One might tend to think of Daniel as being impractical. Perhaps if he were among us today some would accuse him of being so heavenly minded he is no earthly good. If that is our impression, we need to take a clearer look at Daniel. What did Daniel do for a living? What was his daily vocation?

Daniel was a politician. Because the word politician has become synonymous with "crook" in some people's minds we must give some definitions:

> "POLITICS: the art or science of government..."
> "POLITIC: Wise in promoting a policy (a statesman)."
> "POLITICIAN: A person actively engaged in government or politics."
>
> (Merriam-Webster Dictionary)

We have used the primary definitions here.

Daniel was no isolationist. He realized that if God's plan was worthy to be understood and worthy to be prayed over, then it was also worthy to be implemented by everyday good works. God has a plan for the nations. Daniel will penetrate his society so he can be in the place God can use him at any time for the working out of His purposes on a day-to-day basis. Daniel was a pragmatic participant in the field of national politics. Over and over again the excellence of Daniel's performance is noted, and recognition is made that this is due to the Spirit of God working in his life. This approbation came not only from the Lord, but from the earthly rulers under whom Daniel served. Daniel brought God's truth into the political arena.

> And the king communed with them; and among them all was none found like Daniel...And Daniel continued even unto the first year of King Cyrus.
>
> Daniel 1:19,21

> Then the king made Daniel a great man, and gave him many great gifts, and made him ruler over the whole province of Babylon, and chief of the governors over all the wise men of Babylon. Then Daniel requested of the king, and he set Shadrach, Meshech, and Abednego over the affairs of the province of Babylon: but Daniel sat in the gate of the king.
>
> Daniel 2:48,49

> It pleased Darius to set over the kingdom an hundred and twenty princes, which should be over the whole kingdom; And over these three presidents; of whom Daniel was first; that the princes might give accounts unto them, and the king should have no damage. Then this Daniel was preferred above the presidents and princes, because an excellent spirit

was in him; and the king thought to set him over the whole realm.

Daniel 6:1-3

Then King Darius wrote...I make a decree, That in every dominion of my kingdom men tremble and fear before the God of Daniel, for he is the living God, and steadfast forever, and his kingdom that which shall not be destroyed, and his dominion shall be even unto the end...So this Daniel prospered in the reign of Darius, and in the reign of Cyrus the Persian.

Daniel 6:25-28

And the vision of the evening and the morning which was told is true: wherefore shut thou up the vision; for it shall be for many days. And I Daniel fainted, and was sick certain days; afterward *I rose up and did the king's business:* and I was astonished at the vision, but none understood it. (Emphasis added.)

Daniel 8:26-27

In the midst of overwhelming visions Daniel still did the king's business! Prophetic ponderings did not displace practical daily work. Not everyone is called to be a politician, but everyone is called. You must understand the prophetic word as far as possible.

> Blessed is he that readeth, and they that hear the words of this prophecy, and keep those things which are written therein for the time is at hand.

Revelation 1:3

You are called to not only knowledge, but to good works, to penetrate your world and apply God's truth to the now season. Practical ways this can be done will be examined throughout this book. Concerning Daniel's involvement in Babylonian and Medo-Persian politics, Leon Woods comments:

> Apparently God wanted him in a place of influence to encourage and assist in the Jews' return to Judah, just as he had been in a position earlier to contribute to their welfare while in Babylonia.
> (*A Commentary on Daniel* by Leon Wood, Zondervan, Grand Rapids. 1973, p.154)

We are looking for the Second Coming of Christ. We strive to comprehend the prophetic scheme. Wise men admit with Paul, "We know in part, and we prophesy in part...For now we see through a glass, darkly..." (1 Corinthians 13:9,12). Those who see prophecy only as an intellectual exercise feel compelled to do better than Paul. They must have final, dogmatic, and finely detailed answers to every question about the future. Far be it from them to respond to a speculative question by humbly saying, "I don't know." Those three words belong in the vocabulary of every prophetic teacher, but they are seldom heard. Truly great understanding of Bible prophecy does not promote escapism or irresponsibility. It is a clarion call to involvement in the Divine plan. H. Edward Rowe leads seminars on "Effective Christian Citizenship." In his book *Save America!* he chides the Church:

> There is a noticeable trend toward Christianity without application. Millions of sincere Christians have been caught up in a certain pietistic withdrawal from reality. For them, Christianity is pretty much an individual and personal matter. The Bible is studied for the personal enjoyment which it brings, rather than for the purpose of discovering its applicability and doing something about it. Apathy prevails where action is needed.
>
> (*Save America!* by Edward Rowe; Fleming H. Revell Co., Old Tappen, N.J., 1976, p.39)

It is our hope that if this is the trend, it will be reversed. Perhaps we are even now beginning to see encouraging signs that believers are waking up to their true potential in God. The God who can heal a sinus headache can also heal a nation.

I have spent my whole life studying, preaching, and teaching Bible prophecy. My walls are lined with hundreds of books on prophecy. Sometimes they make me uncomfortable. As I peruse their pages I feel like I must be some kind of freak. Am I a minority of one? Now I know how Elijah felt when he said, "I even I only am left..." (1 Kings 19:10). Then I remember the words of God to the prophet: "I have left me seven thousand in Israel, all the knees which have not bowed unto Baal" (1 Kings 19:18). I hasten to add that this is no implication that our modern eschatological writers and teachers are prophets of Baal. On the contrary, most are sincere students of the Word. But too many of them have never gone beyond the study of prophecy. After all, what could one *do* about the future? Prophetic writers can be very dogmatic about details concerning the future but today's world is a lost cause and is fit only to be abandoned. To get involved in politics, the PTA, or any service organization would be a compromise. George Otis is a student of prophecy and has written a number of fine books. In *The Blueprint* Otis says:

> He (God) wants us to be involved with the nation in which He has placed us. Believers in each country which has already gone Communistic attended their churches on Sunday, then washed their hands of "unspiritual" government affairs. It has cost them all spiritual freedom. If God wanted His children isolated from the government aspects of society then why did He have Joseph man Pharaoh's government? Why would He have installed David as King? Why would God have prepared Daniel and Mordecai to be thrust into roles as politicians? Why would the parents of Jesus have responded to the government census process? Why would Jesus have said, "Render unto Caesar the things that are Caesar's"? Because Jesus has sent us into the world just as the Father sent Him. The natural and the spiritual are to work in harmony for a good society. We are to vote, work, and become involved with the affairs of our nation as well as to pray for it. We must be willing to act as God's "watchmen on the walls," and be a clear voice for righteousness.
>
> (*The Blueprint* by George Otis: Bible Voice, Inc.; Van Nuys, California, 1975, p. 122)

How in the world could my works have anything to do with Bible prophecy? Prophetic studies show us that a terrific spiritual struggle and deception precedes the reign of the Antichrist. That reign will inevitably come. We will not change that. In the meantime, Satan tries to rush the schedule. He wants oppressive tribulation conditions right now. He would like to destroy the Church. We may or may not see a great persecution of the Church in this nation before the trumpet sounds. That will depend on what the Christians do. The educational system is potentially the greatest brainwashing tool the friends of Antichrist could use to prepare a generation for the coming man of sin. If Christians do not get involved in the PTA, run for school board positions, and involve themselves in other organizations, who is to be blamed if anti-Christian forces dominate the field of education? Understanding the prophetic course of this age promotes involvement not only in education but in a host of activities—from zealous witnessing to individuals, to penetration of political parties, to drug rehabilitation work, etc.

WAR AND PEACE

The prophets of doom and gloom are so Armageddon conscious you would think that peace is a criminal offense. Arno Gaebelein's sentiment is typical:

> Then we see the attempts which are made to outlaw war, pacifism is advocated, in spite of the words of Christ who predicts the sword as well as wars and rumours of wars to the very end of this age.

Jesus also said, "Blessed are the peacemakers; for they shall be called the children of God" (Matthew 5:9). I am not a pacifist, for I believe my country has a right to defend itself. On the other hand, I thank God for every moment of peace which we have enjoyed since Gaebelein wrote his pessimistic words in 1933. I get no joyous thrills from the killing and suffering of endless wars. Often it is war that closes the doors to vast mission fields. Shall I take any comfort from this? Yes, Armageddon is coming, *but it is not my business to promote it.* It is my business to promote "peace on earth and good will to all men." When Jesus spoke of wars and rumors of wars He was not gloating over the misfortunes of mankind. He was weeping over the sad inability of mankind to solve their deepest problems. You may thirst for the day of "blood to the horses bridles" if you must, but as for me, I will do all I can to promote peace in my family, my nation, and my world. Men of evil will do the opposite, but can I agree with them? No! And furthermore, my God is bigger than their devil. We have bound the hands of the Lord through unbelief, prophetic game playing, misinterpretation of the Word, and just plain apathy. Watson Argue, Jr., makes a call for Christians who will get involved in their nation's life:

> Our founding fathers, God-fearing men, sought to establish a "nation under God, with liberty and justice for all." It should be obvious that this form of government cannot function efficiently and effectively if citizens are passive to its politics. If we ignore the responsibilities and obligations of our citizenship, we may lose our God-blessed freedoms and privileges. In Bible days the form of government called for Christians to be submissive and silent. Today it seems that our form of government, in order to be successful, requires its subjects to be active and involved...If Christians fail to support the government God has ordained, Christians may be forced to submit to the government God has allowed.
>
> (*Pentecostal Evangel,* Oct. 24, 1976; Article, "Should a Christian Be Involved in Politics?" p.7)

The prophets of Israel were as occupied with "forthtelling" as with "foretelling." Both are important. It is necessary to look to the future. It is also necessary to be concerned with the world of right-now. The Hebrew prophets saw visions of distant times, places, other dimensions. They pondered over dreams that would only be fulfilled millennia in the future. All of this they faithfully preserved for us, and thank God they did, for we are seeing much of it fulfilled right now. But read their words carefully, and you will find that these men of God were not neglectful of their own times and seasons. They were not escapists. Many were social reformers. They were concerned with the burning issues of their own times. Prophecy did not promote escapism:

> Perhaps the best way to describe the classical prophets is to show them to be the enigma that they were. They were men of vision but not impractical dreamers. Visions are not disjointed dreams but insights merged into pictures. Their visions projected them into the future yet they were wedded to the present. They were jealous for the integrity of each day, for the honesty of the next moment's decision. Their spiritual discernment enabled them to see cause-effect patterns of the past that could only bring one eventual result...The covenant was broken, yes, but life could be mended. The prophets alone were the genuine optimists ...The prophet became intoxicated with God, which is more sobering than sobriety itself.
>
> (*Prophet, Speak Now* by Robert McNeil. John Knox Press: Richmond, VA, 1961, pp. 18,19)

Where have we gotten off the track? I am truly interested in every detail of the Book of Revelation. I plan to write a verse-by-verse commentary on that apocalypse. The whole scheme of the end times fascinates me, but shouldn't that vast body of knowledge have some effect on life today? What is the intended purpose of prophecy for the body of Christ? What are we *doing* about the end-time message? What should we, what could we, do about prophecy? How should we be identifying with the purposes of God? We want to explore and try to find answers to these questions.

> God created man and put him in the garden of Eden and sent him for to "dress it and keep it." The Genesis account also tells us that God commanded man "to till the earth and subdue it..." When work is viewed in this way, the street sweeper and the space scientist alike have a part in

subduing and having dominion over God's creation. We are partners with each other and partners with God. God created the earth and gave us the responsibility of keeping it and using it for our own good and for His ultimate glory. We try to do the things that will bless our fellowmen and honor our Creator.

(*America It's Not Too Late,* by B. B. Baxter. Baker Book House: Grand Rapids, MI, 1974, pp. 98-99)

The Rapture of the Church will take place, but our future from now until the Rapture is not rigidly predestined. We do have some control over our own destiny. Our prayers and good works help influence the shape of tomorrow.

THE BLESSED HOPE

The Second Coming of Christ is the blessed hope. It is the hope that buoys us up in every time of distress. It is our ultimate comfort (1 Thessalonians 4:18b). We are "Looking for that blessed hope, and the glorious appearing of the great God and our Saviour Jesus Christ" (Titus 2:13). I first became interested in prophecy and the Book of Revelation when I was just eleven years old. From my childhood I have sung the song, "He's Coming Soon." Of course "soon" is a relative word and it means many things to many people. I am now fifty-five years old and Jesus has not come back yet. I no longer say "He's coming soon": rather I believe His coming is imminent, that is, He could come today; but He may not come for what to some people may seem like a long time. Paul told the Christians over nineteen centuries ago that the Second Coming was their blessed hope. He was careful to instruct them concerning current responsibilities.

For the grace of God that bringeth salvation hath appeared to all men. Teaching us that, denying ungodliness and worldly lusts, we should live soberly, righteously, and godly, *in this present world.* Looking for that blessed hope, and the glorious appearing of the great God and our Saviour Jesus Christ; Who gave himself for us, that he might redeem us from all iniquity, and purify unto himself a peculiar people, *zealous of good works.*

Titus 2:11-14

The announcement of the blessed hope is prefaced with instructions to Godly living "in this present world" and followed with an exhortation to be "zealous of good works."

Men tend to extremes. On one hand it is possible to be very interested in the prophetic scheme and yet to be very uninvolved in the works of God. At the other extreme is the reformer who has no time to look into the eternal plan of God. Instead of finding out the will of God and working in cooperation with it, he is continually inventing his own program and asking God for rubber stamp approval. God has no rubber stamps. He never asks for man's opinions, but He ever seeks the cooperation of humankind for the betterment of creation as we press on toward the final redemption, the ushering in of the theocratic Kingdom and all that it promises.

> We will work til Jesus comes.
> We will work til Jesus comes.
> And all be gathered home.

YOUR WILL AND HIS

We will all be gathered home. That is why what we do now is meaningful. Life has purpose. There is a great goal. Life is not existential, but eschatological. Life has meaning because eternity has meaning. We are not dominated by blind fate. We are led by a loving Heavenly Father into all truth. His Spirit "shows us things to come." We are moved to cooperate with Divine decrees. We press toward a goal set by the Almighty. The destination will not be changed, but He allows you to travel the route you choose in getting there. You can take the high road or the low. This is the real basis of prophecy. It goes beyond all consideration of pre-, mid-, or post-tribulation arguments. We proclaim that Jesus Christ is the *Lord of History.* Not just that He is historically the Lord, but He is the *Master of History.* All things will finally conform to His will. It will all come out all right. The highest form of wisdom is to cooperate with the One who has decreed the end from the beginning. Sometimes we get bogged down in inconsequential arguments.

I heard two brethren arguing vehemently over the pre-tribulation and the mid-tribulation positions. Frankly, they were angry with each other. They ended up calling each other heretics. How that must please the devil! Whether or not you agree with me on every fine point of prophecy, I will not call you an heretic. You are my brother, my sister in Christ. I may disagree with some of your details of interpretation, but I am convinced we can disagree without being disagreeable about it. We can discuss differences (or ignore them) without causing division in the body. Think of it—these two brethren agree on all eternity. They agree Christ is King of Kings and will reign forever and ever. They agree on the 1000-year Millennium. Because they disagree on a three-and-one-half-year period of time they become angry with each other. It is better to split atoms of spiritual power than to split hairs of dogmatism. If we do the latter, instead of releasing spiritual energy, we will sit and spin our wheels. If you fall out with a brother on the Tribulation issue you are missing the real purpose of prophecy. I am not saying that your position on the Tribulation is unimportant. I *am* saying that there are a lot of things that are more important. If we cannot get together on the exact moment of the Rapture in relationship to the seven years, then let's sing together:

> Ready to stay.
> Ready to go.
> Ready, Oh Lord,
> Thy will to do.

Let's make up our minds that regardless of what the future holds, we will pursue the will of God. We will live for *Him* regardless of circumstances. Whether it is good times or bad we will submit to God and resist the devil.

RESTRAINING EVIL

The Holy Spirit, working through the Church, is God's instrument of restraint against the "mystery of iniquity," the very spirit of Antichrist that now works in the children of disobedience. (See 2 Thessalonians 2:6-8.) It is the Holy Spirit working as restrainer that prevents the very Antichrist (man of sin) from being revealed before his season.

> And now you know what is holding him back, so that he
> may be revealed at the proper time. For the secret power
> of lawlessness is already at work; but the one who now
> holds it back will continue to do so till he is taken out of
> the way. And then the lawless one will be revealed, whom
> the Lord Jesus will overthrow with the breath of his mouth
> and destroy by the splendor of his coming.
>
> 2 Thessalonians 2:6-8, NIV

GIVE THE DEVIL HIS DUE—BUT NO MORE

The devil has power. He is a formidable enemy. We are not ignorant of his subtle wiles. But it would be a serious error to overestimate the devil's powers. God is bigger than the devil! Some of the Lord's fearful few act as if the devil were omnipotent and that God has limited power.

Today I talked to a very articulate Christian lady. She has been in the church since her childhood. Our discussion involved the world situation. When I expressed the idea that Christians could do something about world conditions through prayer-intercession and good works in cooperation with the plan of God her response was totally negative. In essense she said, "I believe the world is waxing worse and worse. There is nothing we can do about it. This is the day of apostacy. All we can do is draw closer to the Lord and be prepared to endure whatever comes. Jesus said there will be wars and rumors of wars. I don't believe there is one thing we can do to stop the trends toward an evil consummation of the age. The Rapture is our only hope. My hopes will be fulfilled in the Millennium, but conditions in the world must get worse and worse until Jesus comes." Her ideas are typical of a vast host of Christians. They believe God worked great miracles on a national scale for Israel. They believe that God will work great wonders internationally in the Millennium but they see no possibility that God could respond to the Church with His mighty power to work in our nation and world today. What ever happened to "yesterday, *today*, and forever"? Has the salt lost its savor? Is the light of the world hid under a bushel?

It is easy to recognize that God worked in the past, to hope for His works in the future, but for fatalists it seems dangerous to suggest that God's mighty works might be in operation *right now*. It it unthinkable that we might in some way be involved in the mighty acts of God to influence the world of the present.

ON THE WINNING SIDE

For every prophecy of apostasy in the Bible I will quote you several that speak of God "pouring out of His Spirit upon all flesh." I will speak to you of the army of God going forth terrible as an army with banners. I will call to your remembrance that "they shall do exploits" in the name of our God. Of course there will be apostasy, but you do not have to be part of it. Let the devil's crowd fulfill that prophecy. We must concentrate on cooperating with God's purposes for our generation. For nineteen centuries the devil has kept multitudes of Christians paralyzed with fatalistic hopelessness, for in every generation there have been those who believed that the end is almost upon us; therefore, it is useless to try to do anything about our world. They have given Satan a clear mandate to have his way in the affairs of men for their times. Thank God for men of rare insight like George Otis who wrote:

> Someone is continually saying, "But it's too late for America. Things are so hopeless." That's what Satan wants us to think. His strategy is to immobilize Christians by convincing them that resistance is futile. His lies are beginning to take root. Fear and despair are too widespread among the people of God. They must be healed. How can

we fall for such a lie when our God is so mighty?

(*The Blueprint,* George Otis, p. 91)

In Second Kings there is an account of some of the adventures of Elisha, the prophet of God. Elisha was living for a time in Dothan. The king of Syria was infuriated with Elisha because his spies had told him of the mysterious seer who was advising the king of Israel, thus effecting defeat after defeat for the Syrians. The king of Syria had his armies surround Dothan. The servant of Elisha discovered the threat early in the morning and brought the report to Elisha with the words, "Alas my master, how shall we do?" Elisha responded with words that must have seemed unbelievable to the servant: "And he answered, Fear not, for they that be with us are more than they that be with them." The prayer that Elisha prayed for the servant must be prayed for the Lord's dreading defeatists today:

> And Elisha prayed, and said, LORD, I pray thee, open his
> eyes, that he may see. And the Lord opened the eyes of
> the yong man and he saw: and behold the mountain was
> full of horses and chariots of fire round about Elisha.
> 2 Kings 6:17—read the entire chapter.

We are on the winning side. Final victory is ours. If God is so great, can we envision Him as being helpless to do anything right now? Elisha was not the only one to say "they that be with us are more than they that be with them." In an hour of extreme crisis for Israel, godly King Hezekiah challenged God's people:

> He...spake comfortably to them, saying: Be strong and
> courageous, be not afraid nor dismayed for the king of
> Assyria, nor for all the multitude that is with him: for there
> be more with us than with him: With him is an arm of flesh:
> but with us is the Lord our God to help us and to fight our
> battles...And the Lord sent an angel...Thus the Lord saved
> Hezekiah and the inhabitants of Jerusalem from the hand
> of Sennacherib the king of Assyria.
> 2 Chronicles 32:6,7,8,21,22

Our Father is limited only by our unbelief, apathy and inaction. God is greater than Satan. Never doubt that the final victory is God's, but the face of a thousand tomorrows will be molded by Father's children who are in this world as His ambassadors. If you do not work with God your apathy will allow Satan to determine the shape of the tomorrows that remain until the Lord returns. Oh, Church, awaken to the battle that rages today! Our liberty to preach the Gospel and openly witness will depend on our mobilizing the forces of righteousness to march forward boldly in the name of our Lord, to do battle with the minions of hell (Ephesians 6:12).

> Let's go forward for God and fight against the foe.
> Don't give in to the man of sin.
> Our God is mighty and we are bound to win.
> Satan has an evil force to fight against the Lord;
> So put on your armour,
> Take up your sword.
> We're going in the name of the Lord.
>
> (A gospel chorus—author unknown)

Let it be perfectly clear that our reason for wanting a victorious Church *now* is that we are concerned for a lost and dying world. We wish to maintain the freedom of worship and proclamation. We want to continue sending missionaries to the world. There are hateful Antichrist forces that want to stop us. They want to harass and oppress the Church. They are not idle, but working constantly, insidiously, to bring about our defeat. They will win many battles against us if we are careless, blind, and indifferent.

HEAD—HEART—HANDS

The Daniel Factor! That is the secret—Daniel studied prophecy—he got it into his head. The he identified with the plan of God in intercession—he got it into his heart. Finally, Daniel was a hard-working, practical, political figure in his nation—he got it in his hands. He did something about the plan of God for his time. In contrast, some people who are interested in prophecy today only get it in their heads. It goes no further. One day a prophecy expert was expounding why NATO is significant as a sign of the end times. He wondrously found Russia and the USA in the second Psalm. The host asked him what has to be the *key question*—here is the dialogue:

> **T.V. HOST:** What do you feel should be the position of the Christian today in the light of all this prophecy? How should we as Christians react? I feel like the Church should be victorious—and the Church is going out victorious. Some feel the Church should be defeated, but I see that God is going to have a Church of power, a Church of anointing, a glorious Church. How should the Church react to all this prophecy?
>
> **GUEST:** God is buying time for the Church to fulfill its last days mission to proclaim the return of Christ. God is

buying time for the Church through the American opposition and restraint of communism. That is the evangelical aspect of this prophecy. One meets with people who are scared of the military buildup of Soviet Russia. I say to them that one thousand years before the birth of Christ, God declared that He would deal with the communist menace. So therefore it doesn't matter what a nation may do, what attitude a nation may take, how much expansion communism may achieve. In the end God has declared what is the end of the story, and the end of the story is that God specifically wants Christ to deal with communism, because they are challenging the promise He gave to His Son in the second psalm: "I will give thee the nations for thine inheritance"—not communism—but "I will give thee the nations." Since communism is challenging that promise of God to Jesus Christ, it is fitting that communism be dealt with by Christ when He returns to take over the nations. The Christian church therefore should become aware of these prophecies which have already written the end of communism. In the Ezekiel passage the invasion of Israel by the communist bloc is prevented by God's intervention in the fire and brimstone—the great hailstones. If the Christian church were to become aware of these prophecies in which God certifies His intentions with communism, then they wouldn't be scared about communism, they wouldn't be nervous, apprehensive about the development and expansion of communism. They would be assured—God has the whole thing in His hand and will deal with it.

I find the host's question and comment stimulating and right to the heart of the issue: What should we do about the prophetic truth God has given us? While I do not wish to be "picky" nor take unfair advantage of the guest, I must confess that I was disappointed in the answer. I kept waiting for any indication of how a Christian could be involved in the works of God. There was no guidance along this line. The whole emphasis could be summed up: Be aware of the plan and what will finally take place. Aware, but no encouragement to be involved. Don't worry about the evils of this present world (communism being the thing stressed) for it will all turn out all right in the end.

I am uneasy about this answer. It is an answer that any prophecy teacher could have made in the early 1940's substituting Hitler and Nazism for communism. The answer would fit a lot of periods of history, and would be equally disastrous in all of them. Somehow I feel that the guest's answer to the question would delight the Communist Party. What could serve their purposes better than a do-nothing Church that is "aware" of God's plan but is not inclined to do anything about it. John Warwick Montgomery is an astute observer of the world scene. In *The Shaping of America* he wrote:

> When Christians abrogate their responsibilities in national life they present engraved invitations to non-Christians to enter the breach and impress their values on the nation. According to John 8 only Christians are "free indeed," because only they have been emancipated by Christ from debilitating slavery to sin: Christians, therefore, are just the indispensable people needed to articulate and implement the foundational American ideal of freedom...it does not follow that at any given point in history or in any given country there must be a uniform diminution of faith. To think so is the grossest defeatism and plays right into the devil's paws. National revival is a theoretical possibility at any time, and the essential precondition for it is the introduction of the Word of God into all spheres of national life by those committed to the scriptural Christ.
>
> Luther properly stressed not only the impossibility of our turning the kingdom of this world into the Kingdom of God (this requires the power of Christ's own Second Advent) but also the necessity of our personally serving as dynamic links between the two kingdoms in the present age. Christians are literally the connecting-point between God's kingdom and the world—the channel by which the living water of His revelation spills onto the parched landscape of a secular society.
>
> (*The Shaping of America* by John W. Montgomery. Bethany Fellowship Press: Minneapolis, MN, 1976, pp. 186,187)

THE TIME IS NOW

All about me I see Christians who are catching a vision for the work of God. When David Wilkerson caught the vision for a generation of lost inner city youth he left the comforts of a pastorate in rural Pennsylvania and went to the heart of New York. Quiet, unassuming David, whom I had known since Bible college days, became God's roaring lion in the city streets. Teen

Challenge, the world's most successful drug rehabilitation program, was born and continues to reach the "hooked" of our generation. The dramatic story is told in the best-selling book *The Cross and the Switchblade.*

Daniel did not rise from being a slaveboy in Babylon to the office of prime minister by sitting on the front porch reading comic books and watching the world go by. He was diligent in his good works, and both God and man honored him for it.

We can wring our hands in despair over the tragedy of hunger and poverty in the cities. It is easy to say, "Let the government take care of them." It is easy to say, "What could I do, I am just one person." A Hollywood TV actress friend talked to us on the phone for about an hour recently. She too was distressed by hunger and wanted to do something, personally, about it. Asking the Lord and nutritional experts about what to do, she came up with a plan that is nothing short of impressive. Each day she takes loaves of multigrain bread and spreads slices with a thick layer of crunchy peanut butter. Then on top of that raisins are added. The sandwiches, so nutritious, are individually wrapped. This lovely lady dresses herself very plainly and goes with a shopping bag of sandwiches into the Los Angeles inner city. She prays that God will guide her to the hungry people she is to minister to. While they eat the sandwich, they receive the Gospel and practical advice on what agencies could help them further. Just imagine if about ten thousand Christians did that tomorrow....

EASY TO COMPLAIN

How easy it is to complain about the corruption in politics and the government. Vern McLellan strongly believes that it is time for Christians to become more aware of the political process and to get involved in the political arena. This is not just for those who would seek office, but for everyone who is a caring Christian. Vern's book, *Christians in the Political Arena* is available in a new and updated edition, and should be read by every concerned person. It can be ordered from: Associates Press: P.O. Box 2021, Charlotte, NC 28211 ($6.95, postage incl.)

Some march in the streets to protest the abortion scandal. I have done that myself, but that is not enough. Thank God for men who start homes for the unwed mothers who wish to bring their pregnancies to a normal conclusion, rather than kill the unborn life within them.

For decades we heard pious teaching in the churches about Israel's place in prophecy. No one really got too excited about it. When we stood in front of the White House on August 2, 1975, with about one hundred people, we displayed a banner that read, "Christians United for the Biblical Right of

Israel to Its Land.'' The Christian "Zionist" Movement (as it was dubbed by the press) shifted into high gear. The "Christian" anti-Semitics came out of the woodwork and have been trying to shoot us down ever since. On the other hand, we see this work as implementing the purposes of God for Israel. Can you catch that vision? Words are not enough—God expects works as well.

WATCH, WORK, PRAY

The words of Jesus sum it up very nicely, showing that we are to ever be ready for His coming, but ever active in the work of the Kingdom here and now:

> Be ye therefore ready also: for the Son of man cometh at an hour when ye think not. Then Peter said unto him, Lord, speakest thou this parable unto us, or even to all? And the Lord said, Who then is that faithful and wise steward, whom his lord shall make ruler over his household, to give them their portion of meat in due season? Blessed is that servant, whom his lord when he cometh shall find so doing. Of a truth I say unto you, that he will make him ruler over all that he hath. But and if that servant say in his heart, My lord delayeth his coming; and shall begin to beat the menservants and maidens, and to eat and drink, and to be drunken; The lord of that servant will come in a day when he looketh not for him, and at an hour when he is not aware, and will cut him in sunder, and will appoint him his portion with the unbelievers. And that servant, which knew his lord's will, and prepared not himself, neither did according to his will, shall be beaten with many stripes.
>
> Luke 12:40-47

We are laborers together with God (1 Corinthians 3:9). We are helping to shape the future as we move into it. We are not all called to be politicians or statesmen (like Daniel), but we are all called. God has a place for you—not just in heaven, but here and now. His servants are to penetrate every strata of contemporary society, to better spread the Gospel and to promote the welfare of the members of the Kingdom of God.

> The Church of Applied Christianity is unique in that it carries Christianity into many areas of life which are not normally included within the vision and program of traditional churches. In fact, a requirement of membership is that the individual must be a "doer of the word." He

must assume a continuing responsibility, consistent with his gifts and interests, in some needy area of Christian application. He must also work with others in a serious effort to train and involve others in a grand Christian program designed to "do good to all men" (Galatians 6:10).

(*Save America!* by Ed Rowe, Fleming H. Revell: Old Tappen, N.J., 1976, p. 146)

You probably bought this book because you are interested in Bible prophecy. No doubt you have read many books on prophecy outlining future events like the Rapture of the Church, the Tribulation, the rise of the beast, Armageddon, etc. The question now is, what are you going to do about it? Can you get the prophecy out of your head, into your heart and hands? Can you apply the concept of the *Daniel Factor* to your own life? It may be that God is speaking to you right now. Is He calling you to prayer, to good works, to a special witness for the Kingdom of God? Will you respond to the call?

> Supreme in wisdom as in power
>> The Rock of Ages stands;
> Though Him thou canst not see, nor trace
>> The working of His hands.
>
> He gives the conquest to the weak,
>> Supports the fainting heart;
> And courage in the evil hour
>> His heavenly aids impart.
>
>> Isaac Watts

CHAPTER 8

WELCOME TO
THE FUTURE

Welcome to the future! This is the future you thought of, dreamed about, perhaps dreaded or hoped for. Today is yesterday's future. The present is but a 'vehicle' we are all riding in. Our journey ever moves out of the past and into the future. We are interested in the future, for that is where we will spend the rest of our lives—starting right *now*! Prophecy is important—it is for you!

This is the future ancient Hebrew seers foretold: "Knowledge shall be increased, and men shall run to and fro..." "I will pour out of my Spirit upon all flesh..." "The wicked shall do wickedly and none of the wicked shall understand, but the wise shall understand." (From Daniel and Joel).

Prophecy has to do not only with far tomorrows, but with this very day in which we live. The greatest flood-tide of fulfilled prophecy swirls about us in the stream of time—*now*! You are privileged to be not merely an anticipator of events, a spectator of the divine drama, but you can be a *participant* in the program of God as we journey through the process of time toward the fulfillment of the Kingdom of God.

HOPE—NOT DOOMSDAY

We are not looking for the end of the world. We are looking for the *beginning* of the new world under the reign of Christ. Prophecy is not a doomsday message. It is the greatest hope of mankind. The solid rock of our assurance is this: God has performed His prophetic plan thus far and He will complete it. Bible prophecy has proven one hundred percent accurate in its fulfillment so far. I read recently that there are over 2,700 prophecies in the Bible. Over 2,200 have already been fulfilled. "Faithful is He that calleth you, who also will do it" (1 Thessalonians 5:24). God will finish the book. History will not be left dangling. The last chapter will be penned. Humanity will end with neither a bang nor a whimper. It will not end. The purpose is eternal, and the story will turn out all right for evil shall not prevail. Truth crushed to the street shall rise again, and right shall triumph.

IS PROPHECY PRACTICAL?

God is not impractical. He has given us the Bible for guidance in all things. Thirty-seven percent of the Book He has given us is cast in the mold of prophecy. Jesus talked more about prophecy than any subject other than redemption. His primary emphasis was on salvation, and after that he emphasized the message of the future Kingdom. Far from being impractical, the study of prophecy is of the highest importance. The study of prophecy proves the authority of the Bible. It reveals the power and wisdom of God. It provides instructions for those who wish to intelligently promote the purposes of the Kingdom from now till eternity.

No one is more practical than the Swiss psychiatrist Paul Tournier. He teaches that a belief in the Second Coming of Christ promotes healing in the present:

> And the final return of Jesus Christ, which we await and expect because he promised it, will bring with it not only 'a new heaven' but also 'a new earth.' Even down to its final promises the Bible remains oriented upon the incarnation.

> Hence if today we wish to cure the world of its neurosis of defiance, if we believe that this is possible, if we mean to put an end to the deep disharmony of modern life, if we are to help men become whole in a broken world, if we are seeking the way to a culture in which all the disciplines are inspired by God, we do so because he himself is calling

us to this task. As in the days of the prophets his voice is raised above the ruins.

(*Whole Persons in a Broken World* by Paul Tournier)

WORKING WITH GOD

We are not hirelings, but partners in the great work of our Lord. We do not merely work *for* God—we work *with Him*, as Paul wrote to the Corinthian Church: "We are laborers together with God" (1 Corinthians 3:9).

A five-year-old boy wanted to do something nice for his daddy. One day when dad walked to the post office, Freddy found some paint cans in the garage. He located some brushes, pried the cans open, and gave the family car a coat of many colors. When dad came back he was greeted by a beaming boy, dripping paint brushes in his hands. Smiling, Freddy cried out, "Daddy, Daddy, just look what I did for you!"

How many Christians do you know who are busy, busy, busy with self-appointed tasks, but who have never inquired into God's plan for the day—and for tomorrow? Working *for* God—but not working *with* Him. This is the picture of the believer who cares nothing for the prophetic plan for the building of the Church.

Thank God we can see things from His point of view by studying the scriptures. We are delivered from narrow provincialism and the limited outlook of secular humanism.

One of the very important ministries of the Holy Spirit is mentioned by Jesus in John 16:13 as he describes the work of the Comforter:

> Howbeit when he, the Spirit of truth is come, he will guide you into all truth: for he shall not speak of himself; but whatsoever he shall hear, that shall he speak: *and he will shew you things to come*.
>
> John 16:13

NO ESCAPISM

Bible Prophecy never promotes escapism nor irresponsibility. Properly studying, understanding, and identifying with the plan of God promotes the highest Christian citizenship responsibility. Students of prophecy should never be escapists. Some fanatics misuse and twist prophecy and thus promote escapism, but correct understanding of God's word demands that one get involved with the work of God here and now. We are to occupy till He comes. While we anticipate a Kingdom of God on earth, we are also interested in solving the problems of our present world.

THE PROPER EMPHASIS

We are not surprised if some people are turned off on the whole idea of prophecy. Sadly, we admit that the worst enemies of the message have been some of its professed friends. It is too bad that when some people hear the word "prophecy" all they can think of is wild speculation, sensationalism, false reporting, doomsday scare tactics, fruitless arguments, date setting, hair splitting, and useless contention. Those who have been exposed to the proper emphasis of prophecy think in terms of hope, courage, confidence, purposeful living, motivation to good works, incentive to win souls, greater understanding of God and ourselves. We think in terms of love, worship, devotion, the courtship relationship of the Bride and the Heavenly Bridegroom.

Pastor, may I speak to you? Do not ignore the vital message of prophecy just become some fanatic has abused it. It is our task to reawaken a consciousness of the nobility of the message. We must restore confidence in the dignity of God's truth. If we ignore the message, people's hunger to know the future will drive them to the wrong source. Remember, all scripture is given by inspiration of God and is *profitable*. Pastor, you must be the source of truth for your flock as you give them the prophetic Word of the Lord.

CHAPTER 9

A VISION FOR TOMORROW

In the last days God will show many signs, wonders and revelations through dreams, visions, and expanded understanding of the Word of God. While God's prophetic revelation is complete in the Bible, our illumination and understanding of that revelation is growing. We understand more about prophecy today than we did a year ago. Jesus said that certain things were spoken (as prophecies) so that when they were fulfilled the believer's faith would be strengthened (John 14:29). The Amplified translation of Daniel 12:4 indicated a growth of understanding of the purpose of God in the latter times.

The great prophecies of the end of the age are not all negative! The prophet Joel speaks of the glories of the era preceding the establishing of Messiah's Kingdom:

> And it shall come to pass afterward, that I will pour out my spirit upon all flesh; and your sons and your daughters shall prophesy, your old men shall dream dreams, your young men shall see visions: And also upon the servants and upon the handmaids in those days will I pour out my spirit.
>
> Joel 2:38,29

97

This passage is quoted by the apostle Peter in his great sermon on the Day of Pentecost. He indicates a partial fulfillment at that time, and we can conclude that there will be a future fulfillment in the "end times." In the Millennial Kingdom the prophecy receives its ultimate fulfillment. At any rate, we are most certainly living in a day when God is revealing many things to his servants. It is important to understand the nature of visions and wherein their value lies.

Any personal revelation must be in agreement with the Bible. It will usually be a confirmation and/or an expansion of a truth revealed in the Holy Scriptures.

In the years from 1957 through 1960 God spoke to me in wondrous visions concerning the future destiny of the Church and of our nation. The Lord showed me that there *could be* a terrible persecution of the Church accompanied by a frightening loss of personal liberty. This was a matter of deep concern and I prayed for further information. What could be done to avert this destructive force from being unleashed on the Church and our free nation?

A REMARKABLE VISION

In August of 1973 Mrs. Lewis and I attended a church council in Miami, Florida. While there, we were approached by an old friend whom we had not seen for several years. Reverend O. Kenneth Brann said, "David, I have been trying to get a work going in a house in Elizabethtown, Kentucky. Could you come to our little church and help us?" Kenneth knew that my ministry involves holding teaching and evangelistic meetings in churches, colleges, etc. I told Brother Brann that after the council I did have a few days open, and could stop over in Elizabethtown for a few nights. It was while we were in that Kentucky town that God gave me one of the most unusual and powerful revelations I have ever received, outside the Bible itself. It changed the course of our lives and ministry. From that day on we began to emphasize *the positive side of Bible prophecy.*

In September of 1973, the Lord spoke to me by means of a vision in the night. It is clear and vivid in my mind right now as I write this. In the vision I was elevated high above the earth, looking down upon it. I saw many lights scattered over the land masses of the continents. The Spirit showed me that the symbol of the lights spoke of how the Gospel light is shining forth, throughout the whole world. There were more lights in Russia and China than I would have expected. Some areas had few lights shining (areas where the Gospel is not known or declared). I praised God for the wonder of His creation, for our beautiful earth, and I praised Him for the going forth of the Gospel. I felt very peaceful. I looked at the glaze of lights in the USA, Canada, some South American countries, and other areas. I felt a great thankfulness, and a sense of tranquility. I felt we could continue sending out the Gospel to the dark parts of the world, thus completing the task of fulfilling the Great Commission.

Suddenly my emotions changed. I was uneasy. Some dark forboding gripped my mind. Dark, thick, ugly clouds began to creep up around the horizons of the earth. They spread rapidly until they blanketed the whole world. Only a few lights feebly showed through. This symbolized a coming persecution of the Church. The Church was driven underground by the antigod forces that even now work in the world. No longer could the Church openly hold services, broadcast over TV and radio, and pass out literature. In horror I cried out, "Oh, God, must this be?" The Holy Spirit spoke in response to my tortured question and it was like thunder in my soul: *"No, it is not inevitable. This is what will happen to the Church if the Church fails in its mission and task.* If the Church is apathetic and continues in materialism and worldly pursuits, *this is what will happen, but it can be prevented. "* I began to rebuke this manifestation of Satan's power.

The clouds rolled back and I saw earth as at the beginning of the vision. I asked the Lord what we should do to prevent Satan's victory. The answer came, *"Let believers everywhere be united in prayer and faith. "* Suddenly all the lights on earth were interconnected by beams of light making a lacework of light over the earth: *The Church united in prayer!!!*

That was the end of the vision, but not the end of the time of anointed inspiration. I sat down and wrote out the prayer covenant concept (as explained in the next chapter, "Holy Spirit World Liberation").

You can now meet with a worldwide prayer meeting in the Spirit twice each week as indicated. Simultaneously believers will join together and generate Spiritual energies which can be directed as *thunderbolts of Holy Ghost power* against the citadels of hell. This all began in 1973—have you noticed the resurgence of evangelical Christianity in the last few years? Perhaps you are also aware of the intensification of Satan's resistance against the Church. God has raised up many other prayer ministries and emphasis similar to the Holy Spirit World Liberation Front. Study the next chapter carefully—look up every scripture reference. This will shake your very being. We cannot change events of the future that are predestined through God's prophecies in the Bible. But we can change many things that will affect the quality of your life, liberty, and witness for God in the end times. *Pray for the leaders of our nation* (Read 1 Timothy 2:1-6). Remember 2 Chronicles 7:14.

In Jeremiah 18:7-8 we are told that if God has pronounced a judgment (evil) upon a nation, to destroy it, if that nation repents then God will repent *(change his mind)* about the judgment He had planned to bring upon them! Also see Jonah 3:9 (better, read the entire book of Jonah). *We* will effect certain aspects of the future in cooperation with God if we identify with His plan and will, and enter into intercession. We stand at the crossroads. The fury of hell is mounting. Men of evil breathe threatenings against the Church. Satan wants to destroy us. *What you do about it is important.* God cannot answer prayers that are not prayed. Will you be content merely to study prophecy as a spectator—or will you be a participant in the on-going plan of God.?

Will He say to you one day *"Well done* (not just well "thought") thou good and faithful servant...?"

AN EXAMPLE OF PRAYER IN ACTION

On August 20, 1974, God gave me a revelation by the word of knowledge that there would be an assassination attempt on the life of President Gerald Ford. On August 21 we asked the congregation of Melrose Park Community Church (Chicago area) to join us in binding the spirit of murder, as it was going to be directed against the president. On August 22, the revelation came to me very clearly again. We have a statement signed (dated Aug. 22, 1974) by Rev. David Ulseth and Rev. Samuel Bush that the revelation was given at that time.

As Mrs. Lewis and I prayed over the matter we came to the conclusion that there would be two attempts to kill President Ford. The Lord had told us that if the people of God would pray, these attempts would fail. We shared this revelation with thousands of Christians in the year that followed. When the two attempts on President Ford's life failed (in Sacramento and San Francisco, California) we rejoiced to see prayer answered.

Lynette Fromm, one of the would-be assassins, was pictured on the front of *Time* magazine looking in amazement at the gun in her hand and crying, "It didn't go off!" When Billy Graham had a press conference in Texas, a few days later, he said, "It was angels of God that prevented the president's death." Later, former President Ford said in a news conference, "I am convinced that it was Divine intervention that prevented my death." He was recalling the two assassination attempts.

We believe God answers prayer. Write for more information which will help you to understand these prayer concepts. The literature will also help you to get involved in God's *end time victory program.* Request extra copies of the Holy Spirit World Liberation folder. The folder is available in English, Spanish and French. We distribute them free of charge all over the world.

CHAPTER 10

HOLY SPIRIT WORLD LIBERATION

It is true that Antichrist forces threaten. Many powerful persons and groups are actively working to bring suppression on the Church. Agencies of the government are on the attack. Many godly servants of Christ warn of impending persecution of believers. It is not a question of whether the bearers of dark tidings have heard from God or not. They have. *The question is what will we do about it?*

Judgmental warnings are given so the people of God can respond and avert the judgment. This raises an interesting question: Does God change His mind? The answer, clearly, is yes—no one can force God to change His mind, but if He chooses to do so He can, and in some cases He does. Judgmental warnings are given so the recipients can do something about it, thus stopping the calamity from falling. We are not victims of fate. God gives us a choice as to the quality of the future we will live in. Jeremiah shares this concept with us:

> At what instant I shall speak concerning a nation, and concerning a kingdom, to pluck up, to pull down, and to destroy it; If that nation, against whom I have pronounced, turn from their evil, I will repent of the evil that I thought

to do unto them. And at what instant I shall speak concerning a nation, and concerning a kingdom, to build and to plant it; If it do evil in my sight, that it obey not my voice, then I will repent of the good, wherewith I said I would benefit them.

Jeremiah 18:7-10

The "repentance" of God indicates a change in the Divine plan. I know this plays havock with some people's theology. Sorry about your doctrine, but I must go by what the Word of God says.

Please look up and carefully study the following scriptures: Exodus 32:1-14; 2 Kings 20:1-6; 1 Chronicles 21:15; Ezekiel 33:11; 2 Chronicles 7:14; Jeremiah 26:3, 12-13; and the entire book of Jonah, especially Jonah 3:9, 10.

I cannot say for sure what our future holds from now until the end of this age. Our anticipation of Christ's ultimate intervention is a blessed hope. There is hope for today as well, if we are willing to study the principles of prayer and prophecy, and then get involved in the end time Holy Spirit World Liberation Movement. You have the power, through the Spirit, to change the world of today!

WHAT NEXT?

Frequently I am asked, "What is the next great prophetic event? What is going to happen next?" I don't really know for sure. I know what I hope for, pray for, and work for. I can tell you what will happen ultimately, but what happens next may be up to you. God gives you the power to work with Him and produce a future of good quality and witness in this time-space capsule we will occupy from now until the trumpet sounds. He will also allow you to live in apathy if you choose. Then the devil will manipulate the quality of life you will live from now until the Rapture. The choice is yours. What happens *next* could well be up to you.

SOME THINGS ARE RIGIDLY PREDESTINED

The general plan of God is predestined. The Scripture reveals this. There will be a heaven and there will be a hell. You have a choice, however, as to where you will spend eternity. You can be part of the election or part of the damnation. God will not force you. You will make your own choice.

The very day and hour of the coming of Jesus is fixed (predestined) in the Father's mind. See Matthew 24:36. So there are things predestined. All the prayer in the world will not change that. But there are thousands of things that will determine the nature of our future, as far as the short term is concerned. These things are flexible. Prayer does change things. Intercession arranges the course of events. It brings the intervention of God. Otherwise, why pray other than in praise and worship? Why make requests? Why intercede? I know we will not put the devil out of business, but we can surely do him a lot of damage, binding the forces that would oppress the Church and rob us of our freedom to witness and preach the Gospel. There will be a crescendo of evil activity because the devil wills it and his servants work for it. God's servants must effect a crescendo of righteous action to resist the devil and hinder his activities.

Whatever the future holds, make up your mind that you are going to live for the Lord Jesus. We will serve Him whether there are good times or bad times. We hope that enough of God's people will take this message seriously, submitting to God and resisting the devil (James 4:7). If enough of us band together we will be undefeatable as we seek to implement the will of God.

A POSITIVE PLAN OF PRAYER-ACTION

Here is the prayer and resistance that God gave me in connection with the vision described in the previous chapter. Please read the prayer and resistance aloud at least once each day. Thousands of people are already involved. Write for a special card with the prayer/resistance printed on it for convenience. You will be joining with other committed Christians who are also yielding to God and resisting the enemy.

Note that the resistance *is not prayer*. We bind Satan, but we do not pray to him. We do not pray to the enemy, but just as Jesus did, we speak to him to command, bind, and rebuke him. Jesus spoke with authority to the devil during the wilderness temptation, but He did not pray to the devil. Here is our daily prayer for end time victory:

PRAYER

Almighty God we come to you in the mighty name of the Lord Jesus Christ. Grant to us the authority of believers to resist the powers of darkness. We plead the power of Jesus' shed blood as our covering. We claim the promise of Jesus that the gates of hell shall not prevail against the Church. We now join together in attacking the gates of hell and the powers of Antichrist. Let our liberties be preserved so that the Gospel may be freely declared.

RESISTANCE

Satan, I join my brothers and sisters in Christ to resist you in the name of our Lord Jesus Christ. The Lord rebuke you, Satan. You have no power over us. We come against the powers of Antichrist in the name of the Son of God. We resist the evil powers of darkness in the name of the Lord Jesus Christ. We come against you, Satan, in the power of Jesus' shed blood. You are a defeated foe and you must yield to our attack. Christ has conquered you.

We resist the power of Antichrist as it is manifested in government, communications, religion, education, economics, and all other realms.

Satan, we drive you back into a position of powerlessness and defeat. We restrain and rebuke the powers of Antichrist in other nations. We rebuke the demonic forces that try to hinder the work of missions. You must now free their hands in Jesus' name.

PRAYER

Heavenly Father, in the name of the Lord Jesus Christ protect the brothers and sisters who have joined the restraining force. Amen.

ANOTHER DIMENSION OF PRAYER ACTION

If you possibly can, in addition to a daily reading of the prayer, set aside some specific times to read the prayer, thus joining with thousands of others who will be doing the same thing at the same time. *Incredible spiritual power for the preservation of the Kingdom of God and the freedom of the Church will thus be loosed.* Here is a time schedule:

At a set time each Wednesday and Saturday believers everywhere will join in resisting the spirit of Antichrist. We join forces at specific times for strength. Standard time: 9 P.M. EST; 8 P.M. CST; 7 P.M. MST; 6 P.M. PST. Daylight time: 10 P.M. EDT; 9 P.M. CDT; 8 P.M. MDT; 7 P.M. PDT. Greenwich mean time: 2 A.M. Thursday and Sunday (one day ahead of USA and Canada). Adjust any place in the world with Greenwich mean time.

As Antichrist influence increases we choose to actively restrain Satan's powers. We do not use physical weapons. We war in the spiritual realm believing that the spirit is mightier than the gun (Ephesians 6:11-12; 2 Corinthians 10:3-5; James 4:7). We are linked with many other Christians in this outreach. We agree in a covenant of faith, for if two or three agree as touching any matter it shall be done!

The prayer and an accompanying study is also conveniently printed in a four-page folder. It is available in English, French and Spanish. There is no charge. Write to us for a free copy (or copies).

For the sake of our future, the future of the Church until Jesus comes, please help get others involved in *Holy Spirit World Liberation*. Encourage churches to get involved. We can win if we have the will to do so.

Since the Holy Spirit World Liberation was first published in 1973 we have received many questions. Here are answers to some of the questions most frequently asked.

1. Organization. The Holy Spirit World Liberation Movement is not an organization. The literature is provided by David A. Lewis Ministries, Inc. Membership is voluntary. There are no dues. There is no charge for the literature. David A. Lewis Ministries, Inc. is supported by contributions from friends and churches. Any donation is welcome and tax deductible, however no one is obligated to give to receive the literature. There is no formal membership.

2. Joining. One "joins" by entering into the prayer covenant: A. Read prayer and resistance aloud daily. B. Join simultaneously with thousands around the world at the set times, if possible.

3. Origin. God is raising up many prayer ministries as a part of His end time prayer army. In 1973 God gave a vision of how coming oppression of the Church could be prevented. He revealed that the concept would go around the world. It has. Awareness of it is constantly growing.

4. Why read the prayer? This seems formal to some, but it is similar to reading the Psalms aloud as prayer. Many do not know how to exercise spiritual authority and how to resist Satan and the spirit of Antichrist. You learn how as you read the covenant aloud. Add to it freely as led by the Holy Spirit.

5. Resistance. This is *not* prayer. You resist Satan (James 4:7) and wrestle against him (Ephesians 6:12), but it is not prayer any more than Jesus' spoken rebuke to Satan (Matthew 4) was prayer. Wrestling includes contact.

6. Rebuke. "The Lord rebuke thee (Satan)" Jude 9. "We rebuke" means you plus the Lord Jesus. The authority is His, not ours.

7. Why daily prayer reading? Read the prayer and resistance daily at any time. There are 1440 minutes in each day. As thousands worldwide agree in prayer, it is conceivable that two or more believers will be joining in the Spirit at any given moment. The Bible promises that *if two or three* agree—it shall be done (Matthew 18:19).

8. Why two set times weekly for worldwide united prayer? If two agree, what about when thousands agree? When we all join in at once it releases almost unbelievable spiritual power that can be hurled against the gates of hell (Matthew 16:18). "*They* overcame him by the blood of the Lamb and *by the word of their testimony*" (Revelation 12:11).

9. Not political. The Holy Spirit World Liberation Front is not political. We encourage each person to become involved in any realm of our society that he feels led to enter into by the Spirit. But the HSWLF is not political.

We resist the forces of Antichrist in all realms. "Not by might nor by power, but *by my spirit*, saith the Lord" (Zechariah 4:6).

10. Representatives. People have written from all over the world asking to represent the HSWLF in their area. Please do. Take it upon yourself. We appoint no representatives. Our task is to make the concept known. The Spirit of God must make it real to hearts. Please do the following: A. Distribute copies of the special folders, which are free on request. Some foreign languages are available. B. Translate into another language. Send us typed, double spaced copy. We will print the study in new languages. Be as accurate as possible. C. Try to get individuals, church leaders, pastors and prayer groups involved. D. Open your home for prayer groups who want to join the HSWLF. Give out the folder. Lead in united prayer at the set times or at random times. You will sense the power of God. E. Send us your suggestions, reports, and special prayer needs.

11. Time for your area. If you cannot figure out the time for your area, write us. What country are you in? Near what large city? We will try to figure it out for you.

12. Some live in areas where it is inconvenient to join with the worldwide group at the set times (2 A.M. Greenwich mean time—Thursday and Sunday). For these people we suggest the following: A. Join with other believers in your time zone each Wednesday and Saturday at 9 P.M. local time. Read the prayer resistance aloud at these times. B. Whenever you can do so, join in with the worldwide prayer group at the set times. This will involve sacrifice for some. God will bless you for it. Victory is ours in Jesus' name!

Finally: pray always. The HSWL prayer covenant does not take the place of your regular prayer life. It is an added emphasis. It is very powerful. It will bring new blessing to your life. *Do not read the resistance if you are not a born again Christian—that would greatly endanger you.*

CHAPTER 11

SKIRMISHES ON THE FRONT LINES
Battles and Victories

President Ronald Wilson Reagan characterized the Soviet Union as "an evil empire." He was not speaking of all the people of Russia, but of the Communist Regime that dominates the nation. He was not wrong to call that regime an evil empire. We have learned how to invade evil empires, not with ICBM rockets or atomic warheads, but with the power of intercessory prayer. Let me tell you a story that is a testimony to the power and the grace of God.

In 1958 I attended a youth leaders' conference in New England. On the way back to West Virginia, where I was active in serving as a pastor, I stopped over in New York City for a couple of nights. While there we visited the United Nations. The area was cordoned off by the police because Nikita Kruschev, supreme ruler of the Soviet Union, had made a surprise visit to the UN. While standing and watching the activity around the UN, Mr. Kruschev's limousine brought him to the UN buildings. A policeman pointed him out to us. As I looked at Mr. Kruschev a strange thing happened to me. Suddenly I wanted to weep for the man who had been called a "bloody butcher." Protesters with banners filled the area, and when they realized it was Kruschev in the limousine, they began to shout and curse him. God began to speak to me that we should pray for the man's salvation. I carried that burden away from New York with me that day. In the months that followed, Ramona and I interceded for Mr. Kruschev. We asked the church to pray for him. We had programs on several radio stations at the time, and we asked the audience to pray for his deliverance. We got a few critical letters for that, but most people really did pray for him. This continued for quite some time, and then we heard that Mr. Kruschev had been put out of office.

Some time later a number of Christian publications carried a strange story. A Russian sea captain had defected in Canada. He said that he was a born-again Christian. This man claimed that while on vacation at a Black Sea resort he and some of his friends were having a secret prayer meeting in a motel room. Into that room walked Nikita Kruschev. They all were terrified and thought, "We're dead."

Seeing the fear written on their countenances, Mr. Kruschev said, "Don't be afraid. I am one of you. I have just recently accepted Jesus as my Savior." The sea captain claimed that they talked for a long time and that Nikita Kruschev asked them to pray for him. Shortly after that Kruschev was put out of office supposedly because of crop failures in the Ukraine. Some believe it was because they found out he was a Christian believer. Perhaps we should not be dogmatic, but here is the rest of the story.

When Nikita was a little boy, the Orthodox priest in his town paid him money to memorize verses from the Bible. He wanted to win the boy to the church, but it seems that Kruschev, while he learned a lot of verses, never accepted Jesus as his Savior. In later years, Kruschev would sometimes quote a Bible verse in a speech and then cover his embarrassment by saying, "That is an old Russian proverb." Someone has written a book or booklet listing the Bible references in his speeches. I saw a copy of that booklet at a convention but do not know where to get a copy. If you know anything about it, please let me know.

I wanted to believe what I read in the Christian magazines, but did not know if it was authentic; therefore, I refrained from speaking publicly about Kruschev's alleged conversion.

One day Ramona and I were visiting my cousin Margarita Osborne in St. Petersburg, Florida. Margarita said, "David, there was a wealthy lady who spoke to our women's group at church recently. She travels all over the world and holds prayer meetings wherever she finds people who are interested. Usually the groups are small, and usually private. This lady told us how she went with a tour to Moscow, and while there, met some Russian Christians who invited her to a prayer meeting in a private home. She said that while she was there the wife of the deposed Russian dictator, Nikita Kruschev, came into the room. Mrs. Kruschev gave witness to the fact that she and her husband had accepted Christ as Savior and Lord of their lives.

She further explained that the reason they gave no public witness was because of threats they had received as Kruschev was being put out of office. They were warned to be quiet about their new found religious experience. The consequences would not only fall on their own heads if they spoke out, but also on the lives of their families and friends.

I was so amazed. I asked Margarita if she was sure of what the lady said. Cousin Margarita said, ''Well, David, I have a tape recording of the speech the lady made. Would you like to hear it?'' I listened to the tape with utter fascination. It was exactly as Margarita had described it to me.

Do you think God's grace could extend to a man guilty of the deaths of millions of people put to death under his evil regime? I do, and I rejoice to share this testimony of a successful invasion of the ''evil empire.'' There is no iron curtain that can stop the moving of the Holy Spirit. There are no barriers that can stop God.

STRANGE ENCOUNTER

I presented the message on *Holy Spirit World Liberation* to a congregation in Malvern, Arkansas. After the service, I went to the home of one of the pastors, Rev. Paul Dougherty. Mrs. Dougherty gave me a diet cola to drink. I drank it too fast and I could feel a gas bubble forming in my stomach. It felt a bit uncomfortable. Suddenly I felt like a spear was thrust into me and I immediately lost consciousness. Ramona and the Dougherty's saw me go into convulsions, as my eyes rolled back in my head, and my limbs became stiff. Later Paul said he thought I was dead. Ramona thinks he may have meant that literally. I do not know for sure. At any rate, I am alive now. They began to pray for me immediately.

As soon as I lost consciousness I saw strange things. I felt like I was fully conscious but in another realm—the spiritual dimension. To my horror, hideous demonic figures began to advance toward me. I knew they were demons of death, and that unless God intervened, my life was over. The Bible reveals that Satan is the prince of death.

Suddenly I was aware of a comforting presence behind me. I glanced back and there were white-robed angels. They looked so serene and powerful. They raised their hands and a stream of spiritual power flowed from them and smote those demons of death, who began to retreat in confusion.

I came out of the unconscious state and was I sick! I began to experience ''projectile vomiting.'' Later the Doughertys and Ramona testified to the following, although I have no recollection of what I said—but I remember the vision. They told me that as I was regaining consciousness I said over and over, ''I have been in another place. I have seen the war. I have been in another place and I have seen the war.''

While I was still unconscious, the other pastor of the church, Paul Moore, was awakened by the Lord. He felt an immediate need to pray for me. A while later he called and asked if there was anything wrong with me. Another friend, who lived in Philadelphia, called my old phone number in West Virginia and found out where I was. He then called the number in Arkansas to ask if I was in need of prayer. It seems the Holy Spirit had awakened him with a heavy burden to pray for me.

We may wonder why God allowed something like this to happen. I will tell you what He impressed me with as I prayed about it later. I was preaching the concept of Holy Spirit World Liberation and end time warfare against the powers of darkness, but God decided that He would allow me to plunge into the conflict in a real way. I will assure you that I never took spiritual warfare more seriously than after that night in Malvern, Arkansas. I may not understand the experience fully, but I can say for sure that I know from personal observation that Ephesians 6:12 is no mere theory. The wartime is very real. In my case, prayer prevailed and the demons of death were defeated. That's the main point of all this, isn't it? We are in a warfare and Satan will attack us, but victory is provided by our Lord if we will avail ourselves of it. I hoped I wasn't taking the matter of spiritual warfare lightly when round two of the same kind of experience hit me. Actually, the circumstances were a little bit different.

WITCHCRAFT ATTACK AND SUBSEQUENT VICTORY

I was preaching on psychotronic warfare in the Evergreen Christian Center in Olympia, Washington. Before the service began, a local satanist and some of his followers came into the church, sat down briefly, went through some weird sort of motions and then left. Some of the church people knew who these people were, what they believed and practiced and later told me about it.

Some lesbian witches (it was reported to me by church members) sat in the service that night also. The believers who talked to me about these people say that they have a particular hatred of the Evergreen Christian Center fellowship.

The youth pastor and I had spent some hours on the local college campus that afternoon, sort of stirring things up spiritually. Some light encounters took place. We bought some New Age books that were available in the college book store.

The stage was set. Satanists, witches, what more could you ask for to promote a spiritual battle in a church?

While I was preaching I was almost overcome with unbelievably intense pain in my body. I began to sweat profusely as I gripped the pulpit and tried to continue. I rushed through my material as fast as I could, but I could not finish. Finally I told the pastor that I was in such pain I had to quit speaking. I staggered off the platform into the prayer room. Two registered nurses in the congregation came to my aid. A medical doctor who attends the church was there and came to help me. They assumed I was having a heart attack. One of the nurses called an ambulance. The pastor was out there leading the congregation in prayer for me. Some of the believers told me later that the witches thought they had accomplished their purposes and got up to leave the meeting. In the foyer they said to someone standing there (it was reported to me), "He's dead." They left smiling.

I looked up at the doctor and the nurses and said, "There is nothing physically wrong with me. This is a spiritual attack."

The doctor immediately said, "I confirm that what you are saying is true." The Christian nurses agreed, but the ambulance was on the way and shortly arrived. I was still in intense pain. The three medical people accompanied me to the hospital. I was administered oxygen while on the way to the emergency intensive care unit at St. Joseph's Hospital. EKG monitoring of my heart activity was watched continuously.

Another doctor was assigned to me at the hospital. As the doctor and nurses from the church prayed for me, and as the church people prayed, the pain began to leave. After spending several hours at the hospital the resident doctor said, "I am going to release you. I know you had some intense pain, but there is nothing wrong with you. Your heart is all right. Since the pain is gone, there is no reason for you to stay here." Praise the Lord!

I called Ramona. It was Wednesday night and I was supposed to return home to Missouri on Thursday. I told my wife that I would stay an extra day to rest and would come home on Friday. I had mentioned in the pulpit, before preaching that evening (Wednesday), that I would be returning home on Thursday. Late Thursday evening someone called Ramona and asked "Is D. Lewis there?" "D" Lewis? That seemed a little strange. People ask for Dr. Lewis or Reverend Lewis or just for David, but "D" Lewis? Ramona said, "No, he is not here." The lady's sing-song-like voice then asked, "Is this Mrs. D. Lewis?" Ramona replied, "Yes, it is." The strange caller said "Thank you." That was all. She hung up. We think that one of the witches was checking to see if she had succeeded. She probably thought she had killed me with a witch curse. But *glory to God, I am alive, by the grace of God whose mercy endureth forever.*

I have seen the face of the enemy and he is hideously grotesque. He has certain powers, but he cannot defeat us. "Greater is He that is within you than he that is in the world." There is victory in Jesus.

A STRANGE THING HAPPENED ON THE WAY TO PATMOS—TRIUMPH IN TURKEY

Revelation, chapters two and three, contain the Lord's message to the seven churches of Asia Minor. These sites are all located in the country today known as Turkey. A short while ago I was privileged to visit the sites of all the seven churches, and make a trip out to the Isle of Patmos in the Aegean Sea where John was in exile as he received the book of Revelation.

The ancient site of Laodicea lies in a plain below the mountain on which the Roman city of Heiropolis was located. Hot springs that are almost boiling create a setting where a healthy tourist trade flourishes today. The hot baths are popular for health and recreational reasons. By the time the waters have fallen down the mountainside and meandered through the valley to the ancient city site of Laodicea, the stream has become lukewarm. No good for drinking, nor are they hot enough for hot baths. John was no doubt using this local illustration when he said to the church at Laodicea, "I know thy works that thou art neither cold nor hot: I would thou wert cold or hot. So then because thou art lukewarm, and neither cold nor hot: I will spue thee out of my mouth" (Revelation 3:15, 16).

LUCIFERIAN ATTACK

Early in the morning Ramona and I were burdened to pray for special protection. We had a small tour group with us and, while touring in the Heiropolis above Laodicea, one of the ladies began walking along a low wall. I saw her fall off the wall, and leaving the normal walkway, I began to run toward her with the aim of helping her. Fortunately, she was not injured. While running toward her, I fell into a pit that was several feet deep. It could have been disastrous, but as I scrambled out of the hole, I found that I was completely uninjured. Now I was on guard, wary, with an uneasy feeling that this was more than a physical accident. The place seemed eerie, and I was glad to leave Laodicea.

PERGAMOS—WHERE SATAN'S SEAT IS

Before touring each site either I, or the Presbyterian minister who shared leadership of the group with me, would read the passage from Revelation that related to the ancient church that had existed there in New Testament times. We read of "Pergamos...even where Satan's seat is." Photography of each of the locations was very important to me, and this place was filled with photographic opportunities. For that reason, I left the tour group and local guide and went off on my own. Ancient Pergamos is perched on a very high cliff. There are marvelous ruins both on the cliff top and in the area below. Ramona was with me, carrying a camera tripod for me. At one point I began to walk down the slight incline toward the cliffside, the better to get photos of the dramatic view below.

I did not trip over anything. There was no reason for what happened. I was in no hurry, but as I walked toward the precipice of the cliff I had the impression that something pushed me—hard. I began to stagger forward in an awkward run, on the edge of falling, my arms flailing madly.

When Ramona spoke to the ministers' wives at a recent district clergymen's conference, she was not speaking from the standpoint of book learning and theory in her dissertation on the power of prayer. What we say to you has been tested in the crucible of experience.

Ramona saw me heading toward certain death should I plunge over that cliff and onto the rocks hundreds of feet below. She immediately cried out to Jesus. I heard her cry, but more importantly, Jesus heard her.

When my feet stopped at about three or four inches from the edge of the cliff, my arms still swinging, I knew that someone had heard that cry, for I felt the physical restraint of two mighty hands on my shoulders pulling me back.

In moments, my Presbyterian minister friend came running, looking for me with an urgent warning: "David," he cried, "Be careful, the Lord just revealed to me that Satan is trying to kill you here. As soon as I got this from the Lord I prayed for you. It was just a couple of minutes ago."

Deeply shaken, I looked at him and said, "I know it. It has already happened, but God heard your prayer and I am all right." We only told a few of the tour members what was going on. Most of them could not handle it. I told Rev. Ethel Calloway, who was with us, and she also confirmed that warnings had been given her by the Lord.

God does not always prevent the encounter with the enemy, but I am confident the victory is ours.

JOHN, THE PIMP

At night Athens Constitution Square is the haunt of pimps and every other type of unsavory character. This is not to speak ill of the great Grecian city, for it is no different than New York or any other great metropolis.

God spoke to one of the brethren as we were having a discussion in the lobby of the hotel. He told us that we were to go out into the streets and witness for Him. That seemed like an almost impossible task because missionary activity and open witnessing is illegal in Greece. Also very few people speak English there. Nevertheless, we obeyed and went out.

A pimp approached us and inquired if we would like to savor the favors of his stable of ladies of the night. We declined and offered to tell him about salvation through the Lord Jesus Christ. He listened politely for some time, and then angrily walked away. About half a block away he turned and came back saying, "Please tell me that again." We told him of the plan of salvation again, and the Holy Spirit moved on his heart. He knelt down right in the street as we prayed for him. Then and there he invited Jesus to come into his heart. He gave us his name, address and phone number. I wanted to tell him the name of the Full Gospel Church we had attended previously, but I forgot the name of the pastor, the name of the church, and its address.

A WORD OF KNOWLEDGE

We knew that man had to get into a church and find spiritual leadership if he was to make a change in his lifestyle.

The next morning one of the pastors was sitting in the hotel lobby with me and the Lord impressed us to leave the hotel. We wandered down the streets until we decided to go into a small coffee shop for a light breakfast. As we sat there drinking our coffee and eating a bun, a man stopped and began staring at us through the window of the little coffee shop.

Finally, he walked in and approached us. He looked at us in a peculiar fashion and then said, "Good morning, I am a Spirit-filled believer in Jesus Christ."

I replied, "So are we, please sit down and talk to us."

He said, "I never walk to work this way, but this morning the Lord impressed me to come by on this street. He said there was someone I was to meet. When I got to this coffee shop I felt this was the place. When I saw you, I knew I should speak to you. Do you know what I am here for?"

"Yes, I replied, "We led a man to Jesus last night and we know that he must get into a local church if he is to survive. The Lord sent you here so we could give you his name and address." Our Greek friend took it in stride, not seeing anything unusual about the way this had all been "arranged." After all, why should he?

CALIFORNIA DRUG BUST

I presented the Holy Spirit World Liberation concept at a church in Chula Vista, California. My oldest daughter, Becky, was about to get married, and she had told me that there was a certain large piece of pottery that she wanted from Mexico. The youth pastor from the Chula Vista Church took me down to Tijuana, Mexico, the next day where we made our purchase and then headed back for Chula Vista, which is just south of San Diego. As we approached the United States border, I said, "Pull the van over to the curb, God is impressing me that we are to pray about something right now." I told my friend that somehow we were to strike a blow, by the power of the Holy Spirit, against the drug traffic. We spent some time in prayer, and then bound Satan and pronounced a victory over the drug pushers.

We went on back to Chula Vista and I began to prepare for the evening service at the Son-Shine Inn, which is a youth outreach operated by Faith Chapel in La Mesa, California. I got to the meeting a bit early, and already there were about two or three hundred young people there. As I was standing talking to some of the people, the youth minister from Chula Vista came up to me with news that had him all excited. "Brother David," he enthused, "Guess what I just heard on the news!"

Before I could even ask what he had heard, he continued, "The prayer! It worked! It worked! I just heard that the San Diego police, working with the Mexican authorities, made one of the biggest drug busts of all time! And they said that it had looked like they had lost their lead when suddenly things broke for them and they were able to pull it off! That happened while we were praying at the border."

I was very pleased to hear that good report, but after all, it was what I expected. Why shouldn't we have victories over the dark powers?

A CHALLENGE FOR YOU

We invite you to get involved in Prayer Power Liberation. There is a death curse on President Reagan, known as the "zero curse." Maybe it is only superstition, but the devil loves and uses superstition. Satan is the prince of death and loves to create chaos in our nation. This has nothing to do with politics.

In 1840 an Indian witchdoctor, Tenskwatawa, brother of the Shawnee chief Tecumseh, confessed a death curse on newly elected president William Henry Harrison. The whole unusual story is told in my book *Can Reagan Beat the Zero Curse*. The "curse" was that Harrison would die in office, and in perpetuity, this curse would rest on our nation to the end that every president elected in a year ending in zero would die in office. He would not necessarily die in that term of office, but before he left the presidency. The computer readout indicated that it would be an average of 78.5 billion to one that that death cycle would continue from Harrison in 1840 to Kennedy in 1960. The so-called "zero curse" has struck down seven of our presidents. Only one president not elected in a zero year has died in office.

Maybe it's only circumstantial. At any rate, the secret service knows of thirty thousand Americans who have expressed a desire to kill President

Reagan. Files are kept on these people. A smaller "hot" list of about four hundred are known to have active plans to carry out their threats. These are watched very carefully.

VOODOO DOLLS

Christ for the Nations reports that an American company is manufacturing and distributing voodoo dolls in the image of President Ronald Reagan. Printed in *World Prayer & Share Letter*: Christ for the Nations by Mrs. Gordon Lindsey.

Americans are outraged by a new Ronald Reagan Voodoo Doll, which is being sold with stick pins and a vicious incantation to put a hex on the president. Experts warn that the crude, tasteless doll could pose a real physical danger to the President. "There are a lot of crazies out there," explains Dr. David Rosen, a psychologist in Chicago. Things like the Reagan voodoo doll support their paranoia and encourage them to act our their sick fantasies. Barbara Graham, a sociologist in Dallas, Texas, claims that evil consequences of the doll could reach right into our homes. Tasteless gimmicks like the Reagan voodoo doll mock the President and hold him up to ridicule in the public eye by demeaning the highest authority in the nation, all authority, right down to the parents, is challenged, she told Globe. Buyers are encouraged to stick pins into the three-color, eleven inch styrofoam doll as they chant a curse. Joseph De Louise, a parapsychologist in Chicago, fears the curse in sticking a pin in the President's effigy may actually have a harmful effect on Reagan. "What's really bad about all this is the use of God's name to complete the curse" explains De Louise, noting that the last two lines are part of an authentic voodoo hex. The doll is sold by a marketing firm that suggests that it might someday become a collector's item. God forbids the use of enchantment (Lev. 19:26, 31 and Lev. 20:6, 27).

Surely this is an enterprise born in the very heart of Satan. Ephesians 6:12 says, "For we wrestle not against flesh and blood, but against principalities, against powers, against rulers of the darkness of this world, against spiritual wickedness in high places." We must do spiritual battle against these powers of darkness. God is greater than voodoo!

AN EVIL WORD

Some time after my book *Can Reagan Beat the Zero Curse* was published, I received a letter from a man who identified himself as an American Indian. He wrote:

When a delegation of the Great Plains Indians came to the

White House, they were ushered in to the oval office and the spokesman of the group announced that they had come to see The Great White Father in The White House. Ronald Reagan looked up with his mouth open and blinked:

"Who?"

The power that has struck down every president since 1840 at twenty-year intervals was invoked on 10 November, 1839.

On that date, a medicine man stood stark naked in the exact center of the state of Kansas, which was still a territory then. Fed up, and disgusted with the treatment of his brothers and a long string of broken treaties personified by The Great White Father, he called for justice to the primal force that has existed before Zeus, Chrisna [sic], and Jehova [sic]. He called upon the God Eternal, which your god calls God. He named these various gods that are subject to the great unspeakable name and summoned that malevolent spirit to hear him cry for his people.

Then it was that the curse of the unspeakable dread name fell upon the White House and its residents, beginning in 1840 and extending until...restitution is made to the red man and their kin. Til the land is restored and the buffalo returned, the whites leave this continent. This is not ever to be. The land is unfit for anything, the buffalo is slaughtered, and you whites will never leave. So the presidents pay the price.

Lip service and prayers will not save this man who says Christ and serves the devil.

Personally, I loathe the bastard. He exhibits total ignorance and total political cunning. I will rejoice at his destruction by cabal or disease or the accident which awaits him.

This country deserves things like Reagan. It has become the very embodiment of evil and will drag the whole world down into the pit with her. Being what she is, how can she not have things like Reagan for commanders? But, compared to what is about to cancel him, your "God" can't cure acne.

There is the challenge. If you are reading this book after 1988 you will know whether we prevailed in prayer or not. If not, it is no indictment against God or His ability to answer. I simply do not know if Christians are taking this seriously or treating it as a light matter, or even just a strange curiosity. We have done our part in getting the warning out.

If you are reading this before 1988, and President Reagan is still alive, then there is time and opportunity for you to get involved in this particular challenge. Here is the prayer that has been distributed to thousands of believers on a small card:

Daily Prayer For Our President!

Almighty God, in the name of the *Lord Jesus Christ* we submit to Your perfect will. Grant to our nation a time of peace and liberty. Bind the evil forces that would rob us of these blessings. Bind the occult powers that have boastfully struck down our leaders in the past.

Preserve the life of our president, Your servant, *Ronald Wilson Reagan.* Prevent the prince of death from touching him.

By Your authority, Oh God, we bind Satan, we resist him, and command him not to touch President Reagan.

Thank You Heavenly Father, for the promise that You answer us according to Your will. In the name of the Lord Jesus Christ. Amen.

1 Tim. 2:1-4; James 4:7; 2 Cor. 10:3-5; Prov. 25:5; Prov. 14:34; Isa. 54:14-17; Eph. 6:12; Matt. 16:19

Pray this prayer daily. It may be there is still time to break the zero factor and proclaim victory to the glory of God.

> I exhort therefore, that, first of all, supplications, prayers, intercessions, and giving of thanks, be made for all men; For kings, and for all that are in authority; that we may lead a quiet and peaceable life in all godliness and honesty.
>
> 1 Timothy 2:1-4

Submit yourselves therefore to God. Resist the devil, and he will flee from you.

James 4:7

For though we walk in the flesh, we do not war after the flesh: (For the weapons of our warfare are not carnal, but mighty through God to the pulling down of strongholds;) Casting down imaginations, and every high thing that exalteth itself against the knowledge of God, and bringing into captivity every thought to the obedience of Christ.

2 Corinthians 10:3-5

Take away the wicked from before the king, and his throne shall be established in righteousness.

Proverbs 25:5

Righteousness exalteth a nation: but sin is a reproach to any people.

Proverbs 14:34

In righteousness shalt thou be established: thou shalt be far from oppression; for thou shalt not fear: and from terror: for it shall not come near thee. Behold, they shall surely gather together, but not by me: whosoever shall gather together against thee shall fall for thy sake. Behold, I have created the smith that bloweth the coals in the fire, and that bringeth forth an instrument for his work; and I have created the waster to destroy. No weapon that is formed against thee shall prosper; and every tongue that shall rise against thee in judgment thou shalt condemn. This is the heritage of the servants of the Lord, and their righteousness is of me, saith the Lord.

Isaiah 54:14-17

For we wrestle not against flesh and blood, but against principalities, against powers, against the rulers of the darkness of this world, against spiritual wickedness in high places.

Ephesians 6:12

And I will give unto thee the keys of the kingdom of heaven: and whatsoever thou shall bind on earth shall be bound in heaven: and whatsoever thou shall loose on earth shall be loosed in heaven.

Matthew 16:19

CHAPTER 12

UNITY OF THE CHURCH

In the vision (see chapter nine) the clear, simple message of the Holy Spirit came to me: "Let believers everywhere be united in prayer and faith."

The prayer and intercession concept had long been a part of our prophetic ministry emphasis. I never believed in a fatalistic doomsday message for the Church. The faith message has always been a part of our ministry to the body, but what about the concept of unity?

Some push for organizational ecumenicity—a super World Church. Others lament the "scandalous fragmentation of the Church." God began to teach me some great truths about the unity of the body of Christ.

UNITY ALREADY EXISTS

There is an essential unity in the body of Christ that no one but God created. No man can destroy it, not even the members of the body. The fundamentalist may refuse to fellowship with the pentecostalist. The traditional pentecostalist may refuse to sit with the charismatic from an old line denomination, but whether they *like it or not, they are united,* providing they are born again believers. I am not saying that all church members share this unity. I am saying that all born again believers share this unity. They may refuse to recognize it, but they cannot destroy it.

Jesus prayed to the Father that all believers might be one. He prayed for the unity of His Church. I cannot imagine that His prayer was unanswered. It is answered in a positional sense. The true Church is one. Unity exists. (See John 17:20-21).

The apostle Paul wrote of the essential unity of the Church in 1 Corinthians:

> For as the body is one, and hath many members and all the members of that one body, being many, are one body: so also is Christ. For by one Spirit are we all baptized into one body, whether we be Jews or Gentiles, whether we be bond or free; and have been all made to drink into one Spirit. For the body is not one member, but many. If the foot shall say, Because I am not the hand, I am not of the body; is it therefore not of the body? And if the ear shall say, Because I am not the eye, I am not of the body; is it therefore not of the body? If the whole body were an eye, where were the hearing? If the whole were hearing, where were the smelling? But now hath God set the members every one of them in the body, as it hath pleased him. And if they were all one member, where were the body? But now are they many members, yet but one body. And the eye cannot say unto the hand, I have no need of thee: nor again the head to the feet, I have no need of you.
>
> 1 Corinthians 12:12-21

Even if a believer denies being united with another believer, his denial is of no effect. All believers are part of the body of Christ, the Church.

WHAT IS NEEDED

What we need is not continual harping about the need to "create" unity. What is needed is not ecumenical or organizational unity. The so-called "ecumenical movement" is a failure. What we need is *recognition* of the organic unity that already exists in the body of Christ. There is no need for a super denomination. There is a need for all Christians of all churches to recognize that they are one in the Spirit. I do not insist that you join my church or agree with all my doctrine, but we are one in the body of Christ.

Let our unity be on a spiritual level. Let us recognize our common enemy and join ranks to battle Satan and bind the evil efforts of his servants.

The unity I speak of is positional. We enjoy it because of being in the body of Christ. What we need now is to recognize that unity and act as one in areas of essential agreement. We can be united in prayer and faith. Recognize the fact of positional unity. Strive for fulfillment of the ideals of unity. As Paul says:

> That there should be no schism in the body; but that the members should have the same care one for another. And whether one member suffer, all the members suffer with it; or one member be honored, all the members rejoice with it.
>
> 1 Corinthians 12:25-26

One way to unite with brothers and everywhere is to join in the prayer of the Holy Spirit World Liberation Movement. Our desire is to see believers all over the world joining in this powerful prayer concept. We can change the course of history. There are many roads we can travel from here to the Kingdom. The Kingdom of God in its eternal aspect is predestined. The road we travel from here to there is not. I am not referring to the individual's salvation. There is only one way to come to the Father, and that is through Jesus. What we are concerned with here is the quality of our future from now until the Second Coming of Christ.

CHAPTER 13

WITH JESUS AT
THE GATE OF HELL

In the spring of the year, rushing, icy waters fed by melting snow on Mount Hermon come pouring out of the foot of the mountain near the desolate village of Banias. Usually a brooding silence hangs over the place. A sense of gloom pervades the atmosphere. On the cliffside perches a small Druze house of worship, a shrine. It reminds one who has a sense of ancient history of the pervasiveness with which non-Biblical religions have dominated this foreboding region. It is like standing at the entrance of some evil domain.

We are in the very north of modern Israel. The waters from the mountains are a principal source of the Jordan River. Nearby are the Syrian and Lebanese borders. The Israeli Kibbutzim Hagoshrim and Kfar Blum are nearby, to the southwest.

It was here that Jesus made His most important prophecy. As far as the Church is concerned, it must be the most important prophecy of all time. Yet, though the passage in the Gospels is oft quoted, seldom is it regarded for its eschatological (end-time prophetic) value. I have called it the hidden prophecy of the Bible.

TWO CAESAREAS IN THE HOLY LAND

I first visited the Holy Land in 1968. One day we toured one of the most picturesque sites outside of Jerusalem—Caesarea Mare (Caesarea by the sea). This is where Peter preached to the household of the Roman centurion Cornelius. It was here that the Apostle Paul appeared before Felix, Festus, and Agrippa. A few days later we arrived at Caesarea Philippi, at the foot of Mount Hermon. The Israeli guide said that it was here that Peter made his great confession, and Jesus responded with one of the most significant utterances He ever made during His earthly ministry:

> When Jesus came into the coasts of Caesarea Philippi, he asked his disciples, saying, Whom do men say that I the Son of man am? And they said, Some *say that thou art* John the Baptist: some Elias; and others, Jeremias, or one of the prophets. He saith unto them, But whom say ye that I am? And Simon Peter answered and said, Thou art the Christ, the Son of the living God. And Jesus answered and said unto him, Blessed art thou, Simon Barjona: for flesh and blood hath not revealed it unto thee, but my Father which is in heaven. And I say also unto thee, That thou art Peter, and upon this rock I will build my church; and the gates of hell shall not prevail against it.
>
> Matthew 16:13-18

CAESAREA PHILIPPI

Caesarea Philippi was a mighty Roman city in the time of Jesus. It was located at the foot of Mount Hermon—the present location of Banias. The book of Judges records that the region was known as Baal-Hermon in early Biblical times. Baal was a particularly despised pagan god. The priests of Baal promoted wild sexual orgies as a part of Baal worship and the "god" demanded appeasement through human sacrifices. Frequently the children of Israel fell into the trap of Baal worship and suffered dire consequences as a result.

Centuries before the time of Christ the inhabitants of the region called their city Panias. This was in honor of the fertility god Pan who also demanded human sacrifices. In the spring of each year the Pan-priests cast a young virgin girl into the swirling waters of the stream issuing from the base of Mt. Hermon. The present name Banias is simply a corruption of the older Panias.

THE GREATEST PROPHECY

It was here in this strange atmosphere that Jesus chose to give the ultimate prophecy concerning the final destiny of His Church. "I will build my church; and the gates of hell shall not prevail against it." Here is the prophetic pronouncement that overshadows all others in importance to the Church. This is God's absolute, iron-clad guarantee that His Church will not fail. It will never be defeated.

UNEXPLAINED JOURNEY

Jesus had been ministering in the Galilee region. He left with his desciples and journeyed to Caesarea Philippi. It was one of the longest trips ever made by our Lord, the distance being about thirty-five miles from the Sea of Galilee to Mount Hermon. I suppose this would be a journey of over two days, since they had to walk through fairly rugged terrain and up through the Huleh Valley. As far as the Gospel record is concerned, no other ministry took place here. No crowds were assembled to be taught, fed, or healed. All that we have record of is the short conversation mentioned in Matthew's Gospel. Peter makes the great confession, "Thou art the Christ, the Son of the living God," and Jesus responds with the greatest single prophetic utterance, "I will build my church and the gates of hell shall not prevail against it."

Some have conjectured that the Transfiguration could have taken place on Mount Hermon, instead of the traditional Mount Tabor which is near Nazareth. The Bible simply does not tell us. After the great prophetic utterance, we see Jesus and the disciples a few days later in the Galilee area once again. It is possible, indeed more likely, that all Jesus did at Caesarea Philippi was engage in the conversation recorded in Matthew sixteen. The question has to be asked: Why did Jesus take His disciples on this rigorous journey to a place haunted by evil for centuries? Why choose such an unlikely spot for the most sublime of all utterances in the prophetic sphere?

WHY CAESAREA PHILIPPI?

Jesus did not make meaningless moves. How I pondered this strange question. Jesus, why did you go to Caesarea Philippi? It would seem fitting to make the ultimate prophecy in the more favorable clime, around the Sea of Galilee. There the multitudes followed you and heard your profound message. There you healed the sick, counselled the brokenhearted, and delivered the demoniac. If not Galilee, then the Holy City would be a suitable place for a prophecy of this magnitude. Go, Jesus, to the city of the great king for this supreme moment of revelation. In the very shadow of the temple raise your voice and make the announcement: "The gates of hell shall not prevail..."

But Jesus chose to go to a place overshadowed with the presence of the demonic, a place with a history of pagan worship and human sacrifice.

My question was not answered on that first trip to the Holy Land. It was months later, as I was researching various matters in the Library of Congress, that I began to look up references on Caesarea Philippi. Imagine my surprise when I found authors who suggested that the inhabitants of the Israel of Jesus' time had a special nickname for the Roman city of Caesarea Philippi. Just as New York is called the Big Apple; Chicago, the Windy City; and my hometown, Springfield, Missouri, is called the Queen City of the Ozarks— so Caesarea Philippi had a nickname. It is not so complimentary. They called it The Gate of Hell! Suddenly a lot of things fell into place. I knew why Jesus had undertaken the mysterious journey to Caesarea Philippi!

THE GATE OF HELL

Jesus wanted the disciples to hear Him make the great prophecy at the very citadel of hell rather than in the courtyard of the temple. He wanted them to have no doubt concerning the ultimate success of His mission. This was a show of strength and confidence. The disciples must have sensed that Jesus was shaking His fist in the devil's face. He marched right up to the gate of hell and announced that the Church, made up of ordinary men like the disciples, would not fail. He proclaimed that He would build the Church. Our Lord takes the *responsibility for the success and preservation of the Church upon His own shoulders*. The victory of the Church in the final sense does not depend on what you and I do, but upon what He has determined shall be; however, the translation of this victory factor into everyday reality in this time frame is largely up to us. We have the privilege of cooperating with God, of exercising the authority of the believer, and creating a climate of victory in these dramatic end times. This concept will be examined later in greater detail. This is one of the most important concepts to be linked to the teaching of eschatology (end time prophecy). It is, indeed, the neglected element in prophecy teaching. We must wake up to the fact that God has an end time victory program available to the Church. *Available does not mean inevitable*. "Faith without works is dead."

At this point we wish to emphasize that Jesus has taken the responsiblity of the ultimate victory of the Church upon His own shoulders. This is important. It prevents frustration when our own efforts fall short of success. It encourages us to start again and press on to victory.

The believer's response to the plan and purpose of God will determine our destiny in the eternal Kingdom. We will be judged (evaluated) according to our works (see 1 Corinthians 3). We never work to thwart the will of God but to understand and implement the will of God. We have no desire to change the will of God but to find, pursue, and fulfill the will of God.

WARNINGS ABOUND

Scores of dedicated men and women of God are warning us of coming calamities, persecution of the Church, and a host of other dire happenings that are "soon" to come upon us. Books are written on the subject. Television programs sound the message of coming doom.

It must be understood that judgmental warnings are given so the people of God can *do something about it, and avert the judgment* (2 Chronicles 7:14). The warning dreams, visions, and revelations that the Lord's servants are receiving are authentic (in many cases), but that does not mean that they will be fulfilled. An example of this is found in the story of the prophet Jonah and the city of Nineveh. Jonah declared that in forty days the city would be destroyed. The Bible states that this was the message God gave Jonah to declare to Nineveh. The King of Nineveh called his people to repentance. They responded and the judgment was averted. Nineveh was not destroyed in forty days as God had commanded the prophet to declare.

> Who can tell if God will turn and repent, and turn away from his fierce anger, that we perish not? And God saw their works, that they turned from their evil way; and God repented of the evil, that he had said that he would do unto them; and he did not.
>
> Jonah 3:9, 10

TURNING THE TIDE OF HISTORY

The warnings we are hearing should not be ignored. They are not empty ravings of fanatics. They are directly from the Almighty. Satan has mobilized his forces for the destruction of the Church. The devil is the author of anarchy, chaos and destruction. He wants to destroy our liberty and hinder the preaching of the Gospel. The enemy wants to fill you with a sense of fatalism and defeatism. He wants you to maintain a do-nothing attitude. Every believer is involved in this war as a soldier whether he is effective or not. We must realize our authority and exercise it to bind the powers of darkness, so we will be effective for the Kingdom.

Powerful people in high places would like nothing better than to repress the Church. How the secular man hates the fact that evangelicals have captured so much of the television and radio media for the preaching of the Gospel!

This must be stopped, they declare. God's people dare not give in to fatalistic defeatism. We can bind the spirit of Antichrist and keep the Church free to reach the world with the gospel. We can maintain this liberty until the trumpet sounds and we exit this world.

What can we actually do in this end time warfare? Shall we all become political activists and fight the powers of darkness on that level? Certainly Christian activism is important, for we are commanded to be "doers of the word and not hearers only" (James 1:22). However, this is not the role for every believer to fulfill. The foundation of victory is laid in the realm of spiritual warfare. Our weapon is intercessory prayer. We battle the powers of hell and bind the power of Antichrist. God will move as He finds dedicated people who will direct His Divine power against the kingdom of hell.

"For though we walk in the flesh, we do not war after the flesh; for the weapons of our warfare are not carnal, but mighty through God to the pulling down of strongholds" (2 Corinthians 10:4). The battle is won in the arena of faith and prayer. It is translated into reality by the good works of those who are called to move into the world system as activists. There will be no successes without winning the war in the spiritual realm.

The Holy Spirit working through the Church is revealed in 2 Thessalonians, chapter two, as the force that hinders the final Antichrist from being revealed before "his own season." The man of sin cannot be manifested as long as the Church is in the world. If we are a vehicle of the Spirit's restraint today, binding the powers of darkness to this extent by our very presence in the world, think of what we can do if we consciously exert the authority of the believer.

BROADER HORIZONS

We must totally submit to God and then actively resist the devil (James 4:7), not only in our personal lives but on a *national and international scale*. I suggest that we consciously bind those forces in all realms where activity is directed toward hindrance of the Church. They will be bound by the power of God as we exercise our throne rights and authority.

The enemy must not stop our end-time witness to the world. We must not give in to pessimism and doom-saying. Fatalism must be cast out as if it were a demon. Our Lord Jesus Christ guaranteed us victory when He shook His fist in the devil's face and said, "I will build my church; and the gates of hell shall not prevail against it." Will we respond to the challenge for our age?

CHAPTER 14

WHY DO WE PRAY?

Prayer seems to be illogical, but it is not. We hold certain premises that make prayer seem mystical and unreasonable. We say that God is all powerful. He is. We say that God loves us. He does. We claim that God is concerned about our needs. He is. We say that God is compassionate. He most certainly is. This raises some tough questions. A troubled person asked me, "David, if God is a God of love and compassion, why does He allow so much suffering and tragedy in the world? *Why doesn't He do something.*"

The scripture encourages me to believe that God is far more compassionate than any human being could ever be. "If ye then, being evil, know how to give good gifts unto your children, how much more shall your Father which is in heaven give good things to them that ask him?" (Matthew 7:13).

As an earthly father, this puzzles me. I have two lovely daughters. Never, in a time of need, would I require that one of my daughters come slavishly bowing before me, begging me to help her in her distress. In fact, if I knew of a need, I would try to minister to it even before she mentioned it to me. God is certainly more compassionate that I—and further, *He knows everything.* Why, then, must I beg him for answers to prayer? In fact, other than praise and worship, why is prayer necessary at all? It doesn't seem to make sense— but believe me, the most sensible and meaningful exercise in human life is prayer and intercession (in addition to praise and worship). Why is this so? We must consider the laws that govern the spiritual realm, the realm of prayer.

WHAT WILL BE WILL BE

Fatalism is a curse upon the Church and the world. It is so common in the Church as to be frightening. It is one of Satan's most effective weapons against the Church. It will do more to hinder the appropriation of end-time victory than almost any other thing.

I once heard a humorous story about a lady who believed in "What will be will be." One day she fell down the stairs in her house. At the bottom she picked herself up, brushed herself off and muttered, "Thank heavens that's over with."

A lady wrote me shortly before the Carter/Ford election. She said, "I am really confused. I heard that Tom Zimmerman said that Gerald Ford is a Christian and Jimmy Carter claims that he is a born again Christian. I just don't know who to vote for. I guess I just won't vote. After all God's will is going to be done anyway." What a compounding of errors! First of all, in a nation such as ours, one is surely obligated to register and vote if one is to be obedient to the teachings and commands of Jesus. He told his followers to render unto Caeser the things that are Caeser's and unto God the things that are God's. In His day, rendering to Caesar basically meant, "Pay your taxes and be quiet." Today the situation is different, but the principle is the same. We have a responsibility to the civil government. It is more than just paying taxes! In our government "of the people, by the people, and for the people" fulfilling citizenship responsibility (rendering unto Caesar) involves some participation in the process of government. How can you be pleasing to God if you do not even register and vote? That is surely the very minimal involvement.

CHRISTIAN FATALISM

The letter writer's final observation is the worst of her several errors. "I guess I just won't vote. After all God's will is going to be done anyway." Friend, look at the miserable condition of the world about you. Reflect on the crime, mayhem, abuse of other human beings, pornography, abortion, abridgment of citizens' freedoms, the wars and acts of terror that are endemic to our age. If you think for a moment that these things are the will of God, please don't ever bother to introduce me to the demon monster you worship. What pit of hell did you find your pagan god in? The God I serve is revealed in the Bible as a God of love and compassion. His will toward man is good. Jesus says that the devil is come to kill and destroy, but that He came to give us abundant life (John 10:10). Only with great reluctance does He punish the wicked (Ezekiel 33:11).

GOD'S WILL NOT ALWAYS DONE IN THIS WORLD

The fact is that God's will is not always manifested in this sinful world that presently is under the influence of the devil. God's will is done, in most cases, when believers who have abandoned the kingdom of darkness and joined in allegiance with our Lord intercede and work to bring His will to pass. This fact is proclaimed in the Bible and demonstrated in this world over and over again. What we see in terrible crimes of humanity and in the brutal spirit of barbarism that prevails today is a manifestation of the rebellion of mankind against the will of God. It is not a manifestation of the will of the Almighty.

TO KNOW AND ACCOMPLISH GOD'S WILL

We never seek to change or thwart the will of God. Our goal is to find out what the will of God is, and then to implement that will of God through intercession and good works. If we misunderstand His will in a given instance, we recall that the Bible says that when we pray He answers us according to His will. God has built in safeguards to protect the interests of His Kingdom and His subjects.

CHAPTER 15

FIFTEEN-YEAR-OLD GIRL DISCOVERS POWERFUL SECRET WEAPON

We have long been aware of the prophecies of the Old Testament that speak of the dramatic future release of the Russian Jews and their exodus out of Russia into Israel.

Jeremiah speaks of a time when the children of Israel will no longer speak of the greatness of God in terms of the Exodus out of Egypt under the leadership of Moses, but will say, "Great is the Lord that brought us out of the north country." See Jeremiah 16:14-16.

This is the account of a modern-day miracle. It is the saga of a fifteen-year-old girl who had a burden to intercede for a Russian Jewess whom she had never met.

SYLVA'S STORY

Nine Russian Jews and two Gentiles collaborated to "highjack" a twelve-passenger airplane in order to escape the oppressive Soviet regime in 1970. They were apprehended, jailed, tried, and put in prison. The plan was not to harm anyone, but to force out the crew and use the plane for escape. Mark Dymshitz, a pilot, was one of the "Leningrad Eleven," as they were later to be called. It was he who would operate the plane.

The only woman in the group was Sylva Zalmunson. This is her story. Sylva was born in Russia in 1944. She said, "I always felt the anti-Semitism...I always felt abused. And I was abused." She spoke of "massive propaganda that was directed (in Russia) against the Jews and Israel. All Jews will have to leave to be free human beings. Of three million in Russia, only one hundred thousand have gotten out...I had the feeling that there was no future for the Jewish nation in Russia, that there was a policy of discrimination and a future of spiritual assimilation." (Quotations from the book *Israeli Women Speak Out*, by Geraldine Stern.)

THE TRIAL

The trial of Sylva Zalmunson and the others of the "eleven" began on Dec. 15, 1970. She had been arrested six months earlier. At her trial she cried out, "Israel is a country to which we Jews are tied spiritually and historically...The dream of uniting with our ancient fatherland will never leave us...I don't doubt for a minute that someday I shall go and live in Israel. This dream, sanctified by two thousand years of hope will never leave me. *Next year in Jerusalem! If I forget thee, O Jerusalem, may my right hand lose its cunning.*" (Quoted from Edward Kuznetsov's book, *Prison Diaries*.)

PRISON

Sylva was sentenced to ten years' imprisonment under strict regime. She was placed into a forced labor situation. The child she was carrying miscarried. Her description of life in the Russian prison is too horrible to tell. Her husband and one of the other men were given a death sentence (which was later commuted to fifteen years in prison).

PROTEST IN THE WESTERN WORLD

Many people in the USA, Canada, and other Western nations mounted protest in behalf of these "eleven." It is true as St. James says that "faith without works is dead." By the same token, works without faith, without the backing of intercessory prayers, are often ineffectual.

A STRANGE EXPERIENCE

In December of 1973, I attended a B'nai B'rith meeting in San Diego, California. While sitting in the meeting at which a prominent senator and others spoke out on behalf of the Soviet Jews, I noticed that a matronly lady was staring at me almost continously. It began to make me nervous. Did I have egg on my tie? Had I cut myself shaving? Do I look so peculiar?

At the close of the meeting she came up to me at once, saying, "I feel compelled to give you something." I held out my hand and received a bronze star of David on a chain. On it were the words, "Prisoner of Conscience-USSR." On the reverse side was the name Sylva Zalmunson. The front said *"Let My People Go."* She explained to me about the "Leningrad Eleven" and that we should do all we could to protest their imprisonment. I replied that I was not Jewish, but a Christian, and that I would accept this as a prayer reminder and that I would pray for the release of Sylva. She looked at me rather dubiously, saying, "Well, I am not so sure I can believe in a God who would allow such suffering. Where was God during the Holocaust?" I answered her, "I will pray daily for the release of Sylva Zalmunson until the day she is released from prison, allowed to leave Russia and go to Israel. When you hear of her early release you will know that day that the God of Israel lives!"

I ordered some more medallions, and at Christmas gave one to each member of my family. We all began to pray for the release of Sylva Zalmunson. My daughter Sandy was 15 years old at the time. She Seemed to be particularly affected by this challenge. Often she would come to me through the months that followed and say, "Daddy, let's not forget to pray for Sylva."

SANDY'S STORY—BY SANDY LEWIS HOWELL

Let My people go...this is the cry from the heart of our Father! Yet how many of us ever do anything to see the fulfillment of these words?

There are 3½ million Jewish people in the Soviet Union today. The greatest desire of their hearts is to simply be allowed to immigrate to Eretz, Israel— their homeland. This is a statement of the fact that it seems I've known all my life, but for what purpose? I'm only one girl. What can I do to help 3½ million people? Can I go to Russia and with my voice alone bring about their release? When I was about 15 years old, God showed me one thing I could do. I could pray and intercede for their freedom. That was great, and yet I felt it wasn't enough. I wanted to pray for *specific* people, not just pray in general.

The Christmas I was 15, my father gave me a gift that I will always treasure. To many it might appear to be just a piece of costume jewelry, but it was so much more! It was the tool God used to cause me to be *very* specific in my prayers for the release of Soviet Jewry.

Along with the necklace was an explanation of who Sylva Zalmunson was. With 10 other Jewish people, she attempted to leave Russia by force, after having been refused visas. They were all caught, arrested, and sentenced to spend many years of their lives in prison. Sylva's only crime was the desire to live in the land of her fathers, the land God promised her people.

I started to diligently pray for two things: Sylva's release from prison and her immigration to Israel. I had no personal contact with Sylva (until 1973), but I prayed daily! God doesn't want us to pray only for those we know, but for the ones He tells us to pray for. I don't have words to describe my joy the day—nine months later—when I read the following in the *Jerusalem Post*: "Sylvia Zalmunson—the *only* one of the Leningrad 11 to be released before the sentence was up is seen here praying at the Western Wall in Jerusalem." The article went on to say that it was very unusual and that there was no reason for her release. I knew the reason though. It was because of the prayer of faith. Because I knew it was the will of God for Russia to let His people go, I could pray in complete confidence, knowing it would be done. "Now faith is being sure of what we hope for and certain of what we do not see!" (Hebrews 11:1). Since then, I have received several more of these prisoner of conscience necklaces. The uncanny thing is that every one I got was one of the Leningrad 11. I took one at a time and prayed until nine were released. I heard about the last one when I was 19 years old. I met the sister of the last one before his release. My father had met this lady, told her of my intercession, then introduced her to me at a senatorial reception in Washington, D.C. She cried and asked me if I'd pray for her brother. I have to admit that I too cried when I saw him on the news, in 1982, being treated with a reception by the Israeli government upon his immigration to Israel!

Most of us will never go to Russia or be in a position of *political* power to demand their release; but we are all in a position of *spiritual* power, and when we pray we can literally *demand* their release. Praying in faith will move the hand of God to deliver them. We all have this wonderful opportunity to bring pleasure and joy to our Father God when we release Him to move His people out of Russia and into Israel, through our prayers!

Beyond prayer, we can act on behalf of Soviet Jewry by writing letters to our Senators and Congressmen, by getting up petitions for their release and sending them to the Russian Embassy, by holding public prayer demonstrations—locally and nationally, and by having church-wide intercessory prayer meetings and fasts.

God *will* answer our prayers, but it's up to us to pray! God has spoken His will about the exiled in Jeremiah 30 and 31.

We must pray until we have the assurance that all who want to go to Israel *can*—then we can say with joy and power, "*Next year in Jerusalem!*" (Note: The nine Jews of the "Eleven" have been released. The two Gentile Russians are still in prison.)

This story is just one illustration of the power of prayer. God intervenes in human affairs when He is invited to do so. Let there be millions of believers who will enter into the warfare of intercessory prayer and call for our Father's intervention. We command the enemies of God to release the Jews of the USSR! Will you answer the call to renewed intercessory prayer? Faith, prayer and good works together will bring the answer—and the release of the Jewish people of Russia.

AFTERMATH

In November of 1983, we found Sylva Zalmunson, living in Rishon LeZion, a suburb of Tel Aviv, Israel. We were privileged to visit her and her family. When Sandy told her the story and presented a copy of our newspaper, *The Jerusalem Courier*, Sylva wept. She said, "I could hardly believe it when they let me out of prison. There was no reason for it. Now I begin to understand." She knows now that God truly answers prayer in a miraculous fashion.

Sandy still is burdened for those languishing in prison in Russia, and for those whose very freedom is threatened. She now does work for CHRISTIANS UNITED FOR ISRAEL and heads up the Department of Concern for the Russian Jews. We need people to back up this undertaking with intercessory prayer. There is a need for people to write letters to Jewish "refusnik" families (people who have applied for permission to leave Russia and have been refused). Letters from the outside world can literally save the lives and liberty of these people. Sandy (Lewis) Howell will send you a package of explanation and instructions if you wish to help with the letter writing project. There is no charge for this service.

Send your request to: **P.O. BOX 11115, SPRINGFIELD, MO 65808**

Sylva Zalmunson, her child
and Sandy (Lewis) Howell

CHAPTER 16

WAR IN HEAVEN

War in Africa, war in South East Asia, war in the Middle East—this is conceivable. But *war in heaven?* War in the very domain of God? This staggers the human mind (Revelation 12:7-9).

From Genesis to the closing paragraphs of Revelation the theme of conflict is woven into the fabric of God's Word. The apostle John summed it up: "For this purpose was the Son of God manifested: that he might destroy the works of the devil" (1 John 3:8).

The pages of history flow crimson with the spilled blood of youth. Human history is a sorry saga of continued conflict and clash of arms.

How sad are the by-products of man's brutality to his fellowman. The Vietnam conflict consumed 26 billion U.S. dollars each year—this in a world in which 10,000 people die of starvation every 24 hours. If man could stop all the world's war machines, perhaps he could really work on the problem of poverty.

And, alas, not only the warrior bleeds from the bomb blasts, but also the stunned innocent. When Jesus said, "Ye shall hear of wars and rumors of wars" (Matthew 24:6), He was not putting a curse on mankind. He was sadly recognizing the inability of sinful man to solve his deepest problems.

One often hears the question, "Why do wars and suffering continue? How can a loving God allow such evil?''

God does not want anyone to perish, but the Bible reveals there is a war against God and His purposes. The evils of earthly wars are by-products of the war now raging in the realm of the spiritual, the supernatural.

Why is there conflict in that realm? The Bible informs us that it is a continuation of Lucifer's early rebellion against God. Why did Lucifer rebel? Why did he try, with partial success, to win the allegiance of the angel hosts of heaven? Jesus said of Satan that "he...abode not in truth" (John 8:44). This great angel departed from reality when he disbelieved the claims of God.

How could Lucifer hope to supplant the position of God Himself? The devil began to question both the claims and the nature of the Almighty. He doubted God's claim to omnipotence. He thought it possible to topple the rulership of God. He declared, "I will be like the Most High" (Isaiah 14:14). Of all of God's titles, Lucifer chose to say, "I will be like the Most High; I will be the sovereign of the universe."

Why did God create an angel that had the power of becoming a devil? Why did He create an earthly paradise that could become a kingdom of evil? In creating angels and men God didn't create robots. Creatures without freedom are not capable of love or true fellowship. God's determination is finally to "bring many sons unto (His) glory" (Hebrews 2:10). Sons—not puppets!

True love is based on the power of choice, on freedom of will. When the glowing bride stands beside her beloved at the marriage altar, she is saying to the world, "Of all my acquaintances, I choose him."

No one can force another human being to love him. If it were possible to force another to conform to a course of actions that seemingly denoted affection, then slavery—not love—would be the final product.

God has given every intelligent being the power of choice. Those who serve and love God eternally will do so because they chose to do so. Angels passed through a probationary testing, and their choice was final and irrevocable— just as the choice you make in this life will be final when your personal probation and testing on this earth are finished.

But why did God allow Lucifer a continued existence after Lucifer failed the test? Of course, God could have dealt immediately with Satan, but that would have tended to give credibility to the devil's lying charges against God. It seems he charged that God is not all He claims to be, but instead is a tyrant, ruling merely by priority of existence and not really motivated by benevolence.

In a slave nation the resister is dealt with severely and immediately. Try shouting, "Down with the Premier!" in a dictatorship. You will land in jail or a slave labor camp.

In a free nation the dissenter is allowed to picket; he has a voice; a chance to prove himself, and even if he commits treason he is given a trial and further right of defense.

God manifested His superior power by dealing with Satan in a limited sense, and by putting certain restrictions on him. His final doom was pronounced, but this sentence will not be carried out until Satan, by his own actions, has proved the claims of God; that no good can be produced independent of God and His benevolent rulership.

It is independence from God that has produced the chaos we see on this planet. Satan has dominion over this world. Jesus recognized him as the "prince of this world" (John 12:13). Paul called him the "god of this world" (2 Corinthians 4:4). How clear it is then that I cannot borrow my standards of life and conduct, my ethics, from a bankrupt world system. I cannot accept the new morality or situation ethics proposed by worldly clergymen.

The whole world lies in darkness; so even when the system produces apparent good, I must be wary and always turn back to the Book of God for my guidelines of conduct and character. I cannot accept the evolutionary concepts of its scientism as opposed to the claims of Genesis with its clear account of God's Creator relationship to the earth.

Cosmologists emphasize the insignificance of the earth in comparison with the rest of the universe. We are told that halfway out to the observable limits of the universe lie the recently discovered quasi stars. Quasars are millions of times as large as our own sun and give off billions of times as much heat and light. So one could ask, how can this tiny earth be of any significance in the plan of God? How can it be the eye of the storm in the conflict of the ages?

Before you read any further, see if you can answer this question: In what country is Waterloo, where Napoleon was defeated, located?

Almost everyone knows that at Waterloo one of the most decisive battles in the history of the western world was fought. Had Wellington not defeated Napoleon there, the USA might well be a French-speaking nation! Yet in spite of its importance, few I have questioned could quite remember where Waterloo is located. I have heard people guess that Waterloo is in England, France, Italy, Spain, and Germany. The fact is that Waterloo is in Belgium.

Waterloo may be an insignificant spot in itself, but where it is located is not the important thing—*what happened there* is what gives it historical importance.

It seems that this earth is the Waterloo of the universe for the devil. It is here that the sovereign God, as decreed, will defeat the power of evil and make an open show of Satan's lies before all created beings. The Bible even speaks of God proving Himself; of justifying His actions; not because He is forced to do so, but because a God of love would choose to do so for the well-being of His creatures. "We have become a spectacle to the world—a show in the world's amphitheater—with both men and angels as spectators" (1 Corinthians 4:9, Amplified).

Earth is under observation!

> But ye are come unto mount Sion, and unto the city of the living God, the heavenly Jerusalem, and to an innumerable company of angels.
>
> Hebrews 12:22

> Likewise, I say unto you, there is joy in the presence of the angels of God over one sinner that repenteth.
>
> Luke 15:10

> I charge thee before God, and the Lord Jesus Christ, and the elect angels, that thou observe these things without preferring one before another, doing nothing by partiality.
>
> Timothy 5:21

Wars rage in our own sphere of perception and also in the supernatural dimension about us. Led by Michael, heaven's storm troopers do battle with the forces of hell (Revelation 12:7; Daniel 12:1).

So when you face struggles, remember it isn't because God doesn't like you or wants to give you a bad time. It is because we are in a war. You are a vital part of this action. You are called to be a soldier in the army of God.

Sometimes the Church is not so much a mighty army with banners as it is a guerrilla band, determined to infiltrate every level of the enemy's world structure and win away from him those who will become loyal followers of our King. At other times we rally the troops and march forth "terrible as an army with banners." May God grant it!

By sending Jesus to die on the cross and then to come forth victoriously from the grave, God put the lying devil to open shame. God has proved the greatness of His love and the rightness of His reign. "It was determined to demonstrate and prove at the present time (in the now season) that he himself is righteous" (Romans 3:26, Amplified).

Even in the midst of hostile and adverse conditions, God is preparing a people who love Him and who will serve Him eternally. What victory belongs to those who win the overcomer's crown in the agnostic climate of these times when Satan is making his last desperate stand! "Woe to the inhabitants of the earth...for the devil is come down unto you, having great wrath, because he knoweth that he hath but a short time" (Revelation 12:12).

All history approaches its climax. All Divine prophecy finds its fulfillment in the person and return of our Lord Jesus Christ. All profane history finds its end-product in that man of sin, the human Satan who will have a short reign before the righteous Kingdom of our God begins on earth, in its millennial aspect.

There are but two camps today: that of Christ and that of Antichrist. Where do you stand? Which side are you on in this all-important war? You cannot be neutral, for Jesus said, "He that is not with me is against me" (Matthew 12:30).

For those on God's side the message of Christ's return is a blessed hope (Titus 2:13). It is not doomsday—it is "hopesday." God's intervention is the one hope for the survival of our world now under the rampaging attack and raging dominion of Satan.

Where do you stand in the conflict of the ages? Will you join the Holy Spirit World Liberation Movement?

> Have your eyes caught the vision?
> Has your heart felt the thrill
> To the call of the Master
> Do you answer, I will
> For the conflict of the ages
> Told by prophets and by sages
> In its fury is upon us
> Is upon us today!

CHAPTER 17

BATTLE FOR THE MIND

Satan is making his last-ditch stand prior to the return of Christ for His Church and the onset of the "great sorrows." The arena of battle is crowded with satanic gladiators in the garb of political and religious false prophets. Earth prepares for the two beasts of Revelation 13 to make their grand entrance and seduce the nations politically and spiritually.

> We wrestle not against flesh and blood, but against principalities, against powers, against the rulers of the darkness of this world, against spiritual wickedness in high places.
>
> Ephesians 6:12

The National Association of Evangelicals reports more Christian martyrs under communism than in all the previous history of the Church. Another source says that over 25 million Christians have died for their faith in Europe and Asia in this century alone!

Early in the Russian revolution of 1917, and later in China, crude methods of torture and extermination were used extensively. Today, however, much of the conflict is on the psychological level. The forces of good and evil are engaged in an all-out battle for the minds of men.

Riots, rebellion and revolution flourish on every continent, led not by the ignorant but by a new intelligensia, skilled in the techniques of mental control and psycho-politics. Shirer says in *The Rise and Fall of the Third Reich* that Hitler learned early of two things absolutely essential for domination of the populace: spiritual-mental terror and physical terror. Today the mind-battle intensifies as the end-time struggle for the soul of man looms large before us, indeed is upon us today.

REVOLUTION AND COUNTERREVOLUTION

In the religious world there is renewed interest in the supernatural works of God. We thank God for the great charismatic renewal of the churches. We give praise to Him for the resurgence of evangelical Christianity with emphasis on a supernatural "born again" experience in the life of the God-seeker.

Quentin Edwards, pastor of a classical pentecostal church, said of the Neo-Charismatic movement:

> I believe that the movement has created a greater openness toward the things of God than ever before. Without the moving of the Holy Spirit in the charismatic awakening, this so-called born-again-experience movement would not have made the impact that it has. Most of the leading outspoken witnesses in the evangelistic movement have also come into this charismatic experience. I think it is significant that 85% of the people being reached on foreign mission fields are reached through people involved in the charismatic experience and renewal.
>
> (*Restoration,* Spring 1978 edition; Article: "Open Forum on the Charismatic Renewal," p. 13.)

TWO-FOLD REVIVAL

Daniel the prophet indicated that there would be a sort of two-fold revival in the end times:

> ...the words are closed up and sealed till the time of the end. Many shall be purified, and made white, and tried; but the wicked shall do wickedly; and none of the wicked shall understand; but the wise shall understand.
>
> Daniel 12:9,10

As the tide of true God-sent revival mounts, there is a satanic counterrevolution. Satan attempts to copy the supernatural works of God for diabolical purposes. He is the master counterfeiter. Rather than deny the supernatural, he promotes a glib, very appealing, pseudo-supernaturalism that damns the souls of men to hell. As the Holy Spirit revival prepares the Bride for the Bridegroom, the occult revival prepares the harlot and her children for the Man of Sin. The metaphysical movement from astrology to Satanism paves the way for the human Satan who is sure to boast great psychic powers. Paul speaks of the coming of this wicked deceiver:

> Even him whose coming is after the working of Satan with all power and signs and lying wonders, and with all deceivableness of unrighteousness in them that perish; because they received not the love of the truth that they might be saved.
>
> 2 Thessalonians 2:9,10

ANTICHRIST PROCLAIMS DIVINITY OF MAN

In the modern psychic revival there is little tendency to recognize the devil as he is described in the Bible. Most of the works of darkness are attributed falsely to the power latent in the human spirit. That there is an ESP factor could be argued, but if it exists at all, it is of limited power, and finds its effective amplification in the occult realm by demonic interference and control. Ego tripping humanity does not recognize the sinister power behind the scenes. Man seeks to be his own God. That is the basis of secular humanism. Man is the supreme reality. There is no God but man. That is the core-teaching of the New Age Movement.

As man finds self-exaltation in humanistic paranormal experience, hearts are unwittingly prepared for the man of sin who will proclaim himself to be "god" as representative of the divinity of humanity. "When you bow to worship me you will be worshipping the deity of all humanity—you will be worshipping yourself through me." That will be the line of the Antichrist. "Men today represent the final product of human evolution. Homo Sapiens has become Homo Superior. Only man is worthy of the worship of man. There is no god 'out there.' The only god there is is the 'god' that is right here—in the human mind and spirit. Man is god and god is man. In the humanist New Age religion, all cooperating citizens of the new world federation will bow to the world leader as a focal point of the worship of man."

HELL'S THEOLOGIANS

It is interesting to note that the coming world-beast will be able to quote

---

modernist theologians to bolster his philosophical position: "I worship God through man. To know God is first to know man, and to know man is to worship the divinity in him...Man is my best expression of deity, and so I bow reverently at this shrine." The "theologian" Feuerbach said, "Religion...in its essence believes in the divinity of man. Man has his God in himself."

Jehovah is crowded out of the picture for modern man. Man becomes his own deity. "There is no room for Him," wrote Bishop John A. T. Robinson in *Honest to God*: "not merely in the inn, but in the entire universe, for there are no vacant places left. We are reaching the point at which the whole conception of a God 'out there' which has served us so well since the collapse of the three decker universe, is itself becoming more of a hindrance than a help." Robinson advocated the acceptance of "Christian" atheism, although later he reversed some of his extreme views.

CHARIOTS OF THE FRAUDS

From the mystic world of another "New Age" cult we hear that cosmic beings from outer space have come to earth in "flying saucers" to prevent man from destroying himself with atomic weapons. Soon they will raise up a human leader. Endowed with great powers, this leader will effect a confederation of nations, and wars will be stopped, bringing peace to a tortured earth. This is another group being psychologically prepared for "the king of fierce countenance" who shall "by peace destroy many" (Daniel 8:23,25). (See *Aquarian Revelation,* Brad Steiger.)

Erich Von Daniken's theories have swept the world like wildfire. After a weak resistance much of the academic world has capitulated to his fantasies. Von Daniken claims that God is simply a mythological being invented by early primitives who could not understand the alien visitors (extraterrestrials) who have been visiting earth for centuries in their space craft. Early man's misinterpretation of these visitations gave rise to myths about gods, devils, angels and other supernatural beings. The Bible is a compilation of these myths. On a recent TV talk show it was claimed that the books by Von Daniken have now reached 40,000,000 in circulation. This would include *Chariots of the Gods, Gods from Outer Space,* and *Gold of the Gods.*

In the foreword to Von Daniken's *Gods from Outer Space,* Wilhelm Roggersdorf writes that Von Daniken is "Completely free from all prejudices." (*Gods from Outer Space,* Von Daniken; Bantam, 1972, p. 7.)

Incredible! "Free from all prejudices." In the foreword to *Chariots of the Gods* Von Daniken speaks of "...traditional archaeology, constructed so laboriously and firmly cemented down"...and "There is something inconsistent about our religion." (*Chariots of the Gods,* Von Daniken; Bantam, 42nd printing, 1973, p. 7.)

How free is Von Daniken from "all prejudices"? I talked to Von Daniken some time ago. I found him anything but free from prejudices. When asked why he formulated his theory, he said, "Religion—I am against religion." Free from all prejudice? Note that the anti-God and anti-Christ attitude predated the formulation of the theory!

When the world dictator does emerge, he will be equipped to wage his war of deception on an almost unimaginable scale. His "coming is after the working of Satan with all power and signs and lying wonders" (2 Thessalonians 2:9). He will sway the masses with mob psychology, and perhaps with other techniques yet unknown or now in the experimental stages.

Experiments are already being conducted in ESB, electronic stimulation of the brain. An electronic conductor is inserted into the brain, and behavior is controlled through artificial stimulation. Subjects can be made to hate or love, to be happy or depressed, to be distrubed or tranquil. Dr. Curtis R. Schafer, speaking at a national electronics conference, said, "A child could be socketed a few months after birth, and the once-human being, thus controlled, would be the cheapest of machines to create and operate."

Dick Russell writes, "The making of a Frankenstein-like 'terminal man' is scarcely a scalpel's length away." Russell tells of a 651-page report printed by the Senate Subcommittee on Constitutional Rights: *Individual Rights and the Federal Role in Behaviour Modification.* The report was work done under a United States Senator and is "a chilling revelation of government financed experiments to control behaviour with drugs, computers, brain surgery, radio transmitters implanted in the skull and other means." Russell writes: "The experts credit their success to a mind science behaviorism which denies man's consciousness and views him merely as a series of responses conditioned by his environment. Man is a machine with sometimes faulty cogs, a composite of bits of behaviour. He is the highest of the animals." ("Unsavory Business of Mind Control," by Dick Russell; *Argosy Magazine,* November 1975, p. 29.)

Howard Estep, a respected prophecy teacher and publisher of the monthly *Prophetic News Letter,* reported in February 1975:

> Please note carefully something which recently came to light through the United Nations organization. A *dispatch by the UPI from the U.N. headquarters tells us,* "Satellites orbiting the earth can beam messages directly to television sets in viewers' homes *to brainwash people without them even knowing it.*

"By sending out subliminal messages that are recorded only in viewers' subconscious, the technique *can be used to mass-hypnotize* and influence politics of other countries.

"The use of subliminal messages is banned in some Western European nations but not in the United States. The system could be abused *to spread false news or indoctrinate unsuspecting audiences*," the report said. The report was prepared for Secretary General Kurt Waldheim by a U.N. task force."

"...All the world wondered after the beast...and as many as would not worship the image of the beast should be killed" (Revelation 13:3,15). No one scoffs at the possibility of worldwide communications and control, now that communication satellites twinkle among the stars and intercontinental television systems are in operation.

Author Margie Casady wrote for *Psychology Today Magazine* that Harvard lawyer and psychology lecturer Ralph Schwitzgebel describes electronic monitoring systems that could be used to keep track of "dangerous" people. Casady commented:

Unless society becomes more humane in its use of technology, it is no surprise that researchers like Schwitzgebel hang up their crude tools rather than refine new ones that might put us all under the watchful eye of Big Brother.

(*Psychology Today*; January, 1975, p. 84)

The coming Antichrist can demand that people all over the world watch certain programs on their television sets. Even the means to check on those not complying is available for use (and being used for television viewer surveys for ratings purposes). A mobile antenna can now be pointed at a home to determine whether the television is in use, how many are turned on, and what channel or channels are being watched. (See *Newsweek*; March 16, 1964, p. 90.)

No wonder Antichrist is pictured in Revelation as having power to detect and slay a multitude of resisters in the tribulation period.

It is possible to bombard the subconscious mind with visual signals flashed on a television screen for such a short time that the conscious mind is not aware of them, but which have a hypnotic effect on the subconscious.

For more information on this subject see the article "How to Keep From Being Manipulated," by a Nashville attorney, Eleanor Tyler Mead (*Christian Life Magazine*; May 1976. Begins on p. 16). Mead warned:

In these last days, Satan's battle for the soul is really the struggle for the mind. The contest is fought for the memory, the nerve cells, the subconscious, and ultimately, for the will.

The first study of subliminal perception came to public attention in the late 1950s. At that time, legislators and the public were shocked at the implications involved in subliminal or subaudial perception. Legislation was introduced in several states and in the United States Senate to prohibit the use of subliminal techniques in public advertising. Though these many laws were introduced during this period and their introduction received wide publicity, none was ever enacted. So despite the fact that most people believe they have been protected from these subliminal tactics, there is no legal prohibition against their use.

This was written in 1976. At this date we are unsure of whether prohibitions against subliminal techniques have been enacted or not, or in what areas any restrictions might exist. Mead continues:

The first experiments in subliminal perception were based upon a tachistoscope (a film projector with a high speed shutter which flashes messages every five seconds at 1/300th of a second). This machine originally was used to flash messages super-imposed over motion pictures in theaters. During a six-week test of the machine in theaters, messages were flashed stating, "Eat Popcorn—Drink Coca Cola." Popcorn sales increased more than 50 percent; Coca Cola sales, more than 18 percent.

This crude beginning with the tachistoscope has developed into a fine art. Today, commercial research firms offer mechanically induced subliminal messages to anyone who can pay their fee. They are being commercially used every day in North America. And there are non-mechanically induced subliminal techniques just as effective.

An Assemblies of God minister who visited behind the Iron Curtain reports that most full-gospel pastors there have been imprisoned and many subjected to mental assault through the diabolical scheme of brainwashing. Beria, the master psycho-politician of Russia, developed this technique by building on the findings of Pavlov. The theory is that the brain may be "washed" and new patterns of thinking implanted. Methods used in brainwashing would sound fantastic if we did not have proof of their use.

When an injection of lysergic acid diethylamide (LSD) is administered, it induces a state of total loss of reality for several hours. After several such injections the subject can hardly discern reality and becomes suspectible to brainwashing.

Beria is quoted as saying, "Among Pentecostal groups healing campaigns are conducted which, because of their results, win many to the cult of Christianity...You must recruit...a smashing of all religious healing."

It is significant to note that according to authentic reports, they have never been able to brainwash one truly Spirit-filled child of God. As Jesus said, "Greater is he that is in you, than he that is in the world."

Edward Hunter, author and foreign correspondent, stated that the factors he found in common in all who successfully resisted mental assault were "faith, prayer, and strong convictions."

A Lutheran pastor from behind the Iron Curtain stated at the 1958 World Conference of Pentecostal Churches that the only way the brethren could hold out in faith under these conditions was to be baptized in the Holy Spirit!

Satan attacks with new and unusual weapons in his battle for the minds of men today, but thank God, our armor and our sword are as effective as ever against the principalities and powers and the rulers of the darkness of this world.

"Wherefore take unto you the whole armor of God, that ye may be able to withstand in the evil day...And take the helmet of salvation, and the sword of the Spirit, which is the word of God: praying always..." (Ephesians 6:13-18).

CHAPTER 18

LET'S STOP PLAYING GAMES WITH BIBLE PROPHECY

"Can You Top This" was the name of a popular television show a number of years ago. A panel of comedians would be given a subject. Each in turn would recall or manufacture a joke on that subject. A laugh-o-meter measured and displayed the response of the audience. When prophecy is treated only as a "mind trip," or mere intellectual exercise, frustration sets into the minds of the teachers of the message as well as the hearers. To keep the attention of prophecy "buffs" the teacher has to come up with material more sensational than the last fellow. A sort of "one-up-man-ship" game is the result.

WHAT DOES IT HURT?

Should we overlook these abuses of the prophetic message? We cannot do this. Bible prophecy is a message of great dignity and purpose. Fantasies should not be mixed with truth. Yet fanciful stories are constantly promoted to "prove" that Bible prophecy is being fulfilled. Antichrists are discovered and exposed, dates are set for the Rapture of the Church. The prophetic "can you top this" game goes on and on.

You cannot destroy God with lies. You cannot destroy His prophetic plan with distortions. Yet, great harm is done by using prophecy for the promotion of vain nonsense. While you cannot destroy prophecy, you can certainly *destroy credibility.* You can render it almost impossible for people to take the message seriously. Repeated date setting merely causes an endless cycle of disappointments. Name candidates for the office of the antichrists and you create the impression that prophecy is not a subject to be taken seriously.

VULTURES IN THE ARMAGEDDON VALLEY: When I read the account of how vultures are gathering in the Armageddon valley of Israel (obviously in preparation for the great final battle) my interest was aroused. Fantastic! Such a wealth of detail in the account! A new kind of vulture had been observed. The females were laying two and three eggs instead of the usual one. The vultures were multiplying at a *prodigious* rate. This was heralded by the authors (one in a book, one in a tract) as a distinct fulfillment of the prophetic word. One can still hear preachers talking about it on television. Even though the story has been discredited, it has its promoters. These are not dishonest men. They simply believed what they read. The flaw is that they did not take the time to check out the data before using it.

When I heard the story, my initial reaction was positive. This is exciting. Upon reflection I thought, "I have been through the Armageddon valley many times. I cannot recall seeing even one vulture." Just in case I had missed something previously, the next time through the valley I looked everywhere with a pair of binoculars. I could detect no vultures. Next, I asked many people who lived in the valley about it. I asked farmers, kibbutzniks, merchants, etc. No one could recall seeing any unusual vulture activity.

One day a Jewish guide told my group the story of the vultures. This guide is a good man and normally very reliable. Not wishing to embarrass him I took him aside at lunchtime and questioned him about the vulture story. He assured me that it was absolutely true. There is indeed a new breed of vultures. The females are laying two and three eggs instead of the usual one. I then asked him, "Have you ever seen any of the vultures?" After a long, thoughtful pause he replied, "Rev. Lewis, I think I remember seeing one, once, a long time ago." I asked the guide, "Where in the world did you get this story? There is no truth in it." The Israeli looked at me woefuly and said, "I was given a book by an American pastor. It was in the book. He called it to my attention." After a moment of reflection he asked, "Rev. Lewis, surely they wouldn't print it if it wasn't true, would they?"

I mentioned to him that I was a member of the Society for the Protection of Nature in Israel, and that in one of our recent publications we were informed that, lamentably, the vulture population had steadily decreased in Israel for the past continuous eight years. They are an endangered species. I had also written to a major university in Israel and gotten a reply on the question.

The answer was the same as in the *SPNII* bulletin.

There is no doubt in our minds that somehow there will be swarms of carrion-eating birds to consume the fallen bodies after Armageddon, but I do not think we need fantasies to assist God in bringing this to pass. he can bring swarms of migrating vultures into the land when it is time for them to be there.

BEAST COMPUTER IN BRUSSELS

Another popular fantasy is interesting to us because we can analyze its origin and the rise of its popularity. The story is commonly told that there is a huge, three-story computer in Brussels, Belgium. It is named "The Beast." It was programmed by Heinrich Eldeman and has the capability of giving an identity number to every living person on earth for the purpose of buying and selling through electronic funds transfer. This, of course, leads up to the administration of the mark of the beast (Revelation 13:16-18). Unfortunately, some skeptical Christian authors have "thrown out the baby with the bathwater." Detecting the several flaws in the story, they make fun of the whole thing; but we know that the scripture will be fulfilled. There will be an Antichrist who will administer a mark-number. It will be for the purpose of participating in a new world economic system.

In the early 1960's C. M. Ward described a powerful computer system located in Brussels. It had all the capabilities mentioned. This is neither fantastic nor impossible. Ward seemed to have solid sources of information. There was no mention of its being three stories in height, nor was it called "the beast." Ward put this in print in a small booklet in 1962.

Early in the 1970's an author, Joe Musser, wrote a novel titled *Ride a Pale Horse*. It was published by Zondervan and sets the scenario for the computer/beast story. Later Musser wrote the copy for a tabloid tract for the David Wilkerson ministry. It was a newspaper style tract designed as if published after the Rapture of the Church. In the tabloid was an account of a three-story computer—The Beast—in Brussels. Someone typed out the contents of that story and sent it to *Moody Monthly* as a news item. *Moody Monthly* is normally a very careful and reliable publication. This time, however, someone failed to check up on the source of information. The account was printed as fact in the spring of 1974. The story took off like wildfire. It is still cited as evidence that the reign of the Antichrist is at hand. The reign of the Antichrist may be near at hand as evidenced by the humanist movement, the New Age Movement, and a host of other Antichrist forces that are at work; but the promotion of fantasies only destroys the credibility of the message. I think the devil must like that very much. Since he is the great deceiver, if he can weave deception into one of our most powerful messages, then he has certainly dealt us a blow.

There is evidence that a vast computer network for electronic funds transfer has been developed.

A highly placed informant in the Canadian National Government in Ottawa, Ontario, gave us the following information a few years ago: "Burroughs Corporation of Paoli, Pennsylvania, has just completed delivery of a multicomputer system to the European Economic Headquarters in Brussels, Belgium." He further informed us that the system is designated *SWIFT*, an acronym standing for *System for Worldwide International Funds Transfer.*

We should not ignore the phenomena of our times that illustrate the fulfillment of prophecy. The key to correct understanding is to interpret the world from the viewpoint of the Word, not to try and fit world events between the lines of the Bible. This is not a moot point, it is a major consideration in the interpretation of Biblical prophecy and the times in which we live.

THE SOLUTION

The solution to this problem is not to ignore the message of Bible prophecy. I appeal to pastors, evangelists, and teachers—don't cast aside the powerful teaching of eschatology. Don't abandon the field to fanatics. Over a third of the Bible is prophecy. Declare the whole Word of God.

Declare the truth of the Word. Indeed one should use current illustrative material, but check out your sources when new and exciting things seem to be fulfilling prophecy. Believe me there is no lack of material. If you are unsure of information you wish to share with your congregation or class, simply be honest with them. Tell them, "I have some interesting information but it is not verified. I offer it for its 'curiosity value' and for our further research." Develop reliable sources of information.

Emphasize that prophecy is not merely for speculation. It is more than intellectual exercise. It is a call to action. We can, and should, implement the plan and purpose of God for our age through intercession and good works. Challenge your class to zero in on specific world and national conditions in the warfare of intercessory prayer. Become a part of the fulfillment of end-time prophecy rather than just an observer of events. Join the *Holy Spirit World Liberation Movement!* (See chapters nine and ten.)

> For we have not followed cunningly devised fables, when we made known unto you the power and coming of our Lord Jesus Christ, but were eyewitnesses of his majesty. We have also a more sure word of prophecy; whereunto ye do well that ye take heed, as unto a light that shineth

in a dark place, until the day dawn, and the day star arise in your hearts:

Knowing this first, that no prophecy of the scripture is of any private interpretation.

For the prophecy came not in old time by the will of man: but holy men of God spake as they were moved by the Holy Ghost.

2 Peter 1:16,19-21

CHAPTER 19

THE DEBATING GAME

Some of the harshest judgments are passed against brethren by proponents of either the pre-tribulation, the mid-tribulation, or the post-tribulation positions. Cruel insults are hurled in the name of Christ and the truth. Books are written about "The Rapture Cover-up" and "The Rapture Hoax." Let's see if we can get this subject in a proper sense of proportion and see if there is any possible reconciliation. One book recently published and widely circulated declares an intention to attempt such a reconciliation of the three positions. The reconciliation turns out to be a demand that you agree with the author or you are a deceiver and a liar. I think we can do a little better than that without anyone feeling compromised.

First of all let's think of this: All Bible-believing Christians agree on eternity. Christ is king and shall reign forever. That, after all, covers most of the territory. Most of us agree on a literal Millennium, a thousand-year theocratic Kingdom here on earth, with Jesus reigning from the throne of David in Jerusalem. It almost seems ridiculous that brethren fall out over a disagreement concerning a three-and-a-half or seven-year period of time.

DOES IT MAKE A DIFFERENCE?

I have no desire to persuade you to change your doctrine relating to the Tribulation. I am perfectly happy to discuss it with any person who can enter into a controversial discussion without becoming upset or angry. I will not discuss doctrine with anyone who cannot control his own spirit. I am frequently approached by people who are determined to persuade me that my position on the Rapture is wrong. I have been studying prophecy since I was 11 years old. I have been preaching the prophetic Word since 1954. Frankly, I have not heard a new argument on this particular subject in the last two decades. Why is it so important to people to persuade others of their position on this minor point of doctrine? Of course I would like for everyone to agree with my position, but I have laid that aside because there are much larger issues at stake in this end-time warfare. It is time to join ranks and confront our common enemy with the strength of unity. My brethren are not my enemies, regardless if they agree with all my doctrines or not. There are foundational doctrines that are a basis for fellowship, such as the nature of God, the deity of Jesus Christ, etc., but the doctrine of the pre-, mid-, or post-tribulation Rapture is not one of them.

HOW DOES IT AFFECT YOU?

What effect does your position on the Rapture have on your spiritual life? I have met pre-tribbers who are survivalists. I have met post-tribbers who were escapists. I have met people in both camps who were spiritual giants, and others who were carnal—as babes in Christ. I am convinced that even if your doctrinal argument is right, if your spirit is wrong, then you are going to be ineffectual in the end-time struggle.

UNITED WE STAND

Here is a tentative statement I think we can all agree on. If you have an insight to share with me for the improvement of this statement please write and let me know of your ideas.

"I believe that Jesus Christ is the Son of God. He is Lord of Lords. I believe that He is coming back to earth again. I believe His Kingdom is eternal. It is my determination to live for Him regardless of circumstances. Whether it is good times or bad I determine to live for Him. I want to be ready when He comes, whenever it is. As long as I am in this world I determine to resist evil. I will rebuke and bind the spirit of Antichrist. I will never give up."

Yes, I will tell you what my personal position on the Rapture happens to be, but this is not an effort to persuade you. That is not the purpose of this book. We are dealing with larger issues here. I believe in a pre-tribulation Rapture. But I have problems with my pre-trib brethren. I find that pre-tribulationism is used to promote escapism of the wrong kind. I say of the wrong kind because there is a sense in which escapism is legitimate. Adam got us into a sin trap. Jesus came into the world to provide an escape for us. Salvation allows me to escape from eternal damnation. Healing gives me an escape from sickness, but there is an unhealthy escapism in the mind of the person who comes to me and says, "Brother Lewis, I am so glad the Lord is going to rapture us and take us out of the world before anything bad can happen to us."

PRE-RAPTURE TRIBULATION

While I believe in a pre-trib Rapture, I also believe that there can be pre-Rapture tribulation. Jesus said that His followers would have tribulation in this world. The Church has been in that general tribulation for the past 1900 years. In various times and places the Church has undergone horrible persecution and even martyrdom. There was no rapture for the martyred Christians in the Roman Empire. There was no rapture for those slain in the Inquisition. There was no rapture for the millions of martyrs killed for their faith by the communists in Russia and China. If you do not heed and practice the principles set forth in this book we may see persecution in our own nation even before the Rapture of the Church. The choice is up to you. This is both a wonderful, and yet, an awesome idea. God allows us to select the kind of future we will live in. Isn't it time for you to join the Holy Spirit World Liberation Movement?

CHAPTER 20

NUMBER, NUMBER, WHO'S GOT THE NUMBER?

Ridiculed by its enemies, abused by its friends, ignored by many, Bible prophecy is nonetheless a powerful factor of God's Word. Man cannot destroy the God of prophecy, nor the prophecies of God, but the credibility of the message has been badly damaged in the minds of men. Perhaps the eschatological message has been hurt more by its professed supporters than by all of its enemies put together. To the extent that a sensible treatment of the subject is neglected by sober pastors and theologians, a vacuum is formed in the Church. Into that vacuum flow the rantings of cultists, fringe area fanatics, and the ponderings of secular futurologists.

THE QUEST FOR TOMORROW

People want to know the future. It may be mere curiosity for some, but for others it is a sincere desire to know and cooperate with the purposes of God. There is a ready-made podium for the person who speaks out concerning the future. Opportunists fill the mail with circulars and newsletters of doubtful value. There is a strange competition to see who can come up with the next sensational (often falsely reported) prophetic phenomenon that proves "prophecy is being fulfilled right before your very eyes and indeed *the end is here,* so send me your tithes and offerings while we still have a few days left...."

This author is a traditional interpreter of Bible prophecy. I believe in a pre-millennial Rapture of the Church and coming of the Saviour as the most logical model for outlining the end-time pronouncements of the New Testament. I'm not looking for any argument with mid- or post-tribbers. We determine to live for Christ regardless of circumstances, whether it be affluence and liberty or a fulfillment of mankind's darkest dreams. My whole life has been dedicated to the study of prophecy; its declaration my calling. And, yes, I do believe that prophecy is being fulfilled before our very eyes at an ever accelerating pace, but I am concerned with the erosion of confidence in the message caused by today's parlor prophets and their tricky games.

CRYING WOLF

One of Aesop's fables tells of a shepherd boy who got bored with his tedious job. He decided to play games with the emotions of the nearby villagers and cried, "Wolf! Wolf!" in mock distress. When the villagers rushed to his aid, the boy laughed at their gullibility. The trick actually worked a second time, but credibility in the boy's cry was lost. Of course, when a wolf really attacked the flock no one answered his cry of real distress.

The Church is constantly beset with false alarms. Who should be blamed if people no longer listen, if prophecy is ignored? There is a renewed interest in the message right now, but what if Jesus does not come by the year 2001—will anyone be listening then? We should declare the message in such a manner that it will still be valid at that time, and yet prepare the people of God for the return of Christ at any time. It will take more than prophecy mind trips and game playing.

The ever popular Dating Game has been recycled over and over with slight variations, but always with the same tragic results. Then there is the Waiting Game, Monopoly (not by Parker) and the Debating Game. One of the most popular of the prophecy games is Number, Number, Who's Got the Number?

> And he [the beast-antichrist] causeth all, both small and great, rich and poor, free and bond, to receive a mark in their right hand, or in their foreheads: And that no man might buy or sell, save he that had the mark, or the name of the beast, or the number of his name. Here is wisdom, Let him that hath understanding count the number of the beast: for it is the number of a man: and his number is Six hundred threescore and six.
>
> Revelation 13:16-18

It is my viewpoint that since the Antichrist will not be identified until after the removal of the restraining force (2 Thessalonians 2:1-8) it is impossible now to identify the man of sin. The power restraining the son of perdition is the Holy Spirit as operative through the Church. The omnipresent Spirit of God cannot be removed from the earth at any time. It is the Church that God uses to bind evil in this world (James 4:7, Matthew 18:18, etc.) that will be removed at the time of the Rapture. It is an exercise in futility to try and identify the Antichrist in this season. Those converted during the Tribulation will be able to make the identification, and the words of Revelation 13:17 are addressed to them.

Many will recall widespread preaching during the World War II era that Mussolini or Hitler was the Antichrist. Since the slogan VV IL DUCE was widely used by Mussolini and the Fascist regime, and because the Roman numeral value of the slogan/title is 666, many were sure of a positive identification. Mussolini was identified as the beast. In the past, various popes, Judas Iscariot, Nero, Napoleon, Stalin, Mao T'se Tung, and a host of others have been identified as the final Antichrist. One prophecy preacher's mailer announces, "*I SAW THE ANTICHRIST,* an extremely informative, realistic, dynamic, futuristic presentation of prophecy written as though you are going through it right now. This book is a fascinating first of its kind, utilizing his fabulous knowledge of Bible prophecy and his unlimited imagination of how things will be." I don't know who he saw, as I failed to order the book. This prophet of woe is not alone in his attempt to see the Antichrist.

The pastor of a Fundamental Bible church in Indiana assured us that the late Nelson Rockefeller was the "coming world dictator." When your favorite candidate dies it sure ruins the *NNWGTN* game. A Chicago pastor's literature informs us that the Antichrist is "Syrian President Hafez Assad—the man whose number is 666." His essay claims, "This fact has been revealed to me by God the Almighty through His Holy Spirit."

Death of a nominee seems to be no problem to "The man whose name counts Solomon—The Last Prophet." His literature showing that "The name Giovoni Batesta Montini equals in both Greek and Hebrew, the name of Satan," is still being circulated. He says, "Giovoni Batesta Montini was known as Pope Paul the Sixth...he is the sixth incarnation since Jesus Christ died on the cross." Using the spelling Paulus and combining numerological computations based on both Greek and Hebrew this author "proves" that the late Pope Paul is the Antichrist. Of course Pope Paul the Sixth is dead.

A California-based prophecy preacher would no doubt take exception to the foregoing identifications of the beast. In a bestselling book he suggests that the Antichrist is Juan Carlos, King of Spain, but then we remember that in the same book (copyright 1974) he projected that September 6, 1975, was the probable date for the Rapture of the Church.

We have collected published "proof" that Richard Nixon, Jimmy Carter, Menechem Begin, Anwar Sadat, Pierre Elliot Trudeau, Henry Kissinger, Ronald Reagan, George Bush, Saddam Hussein, and a host of others can be positively identified as the Antichrist, all with the number 666. Some are sure that John Kennedy is not really dead. Soon the "beast" will be healed of his deadly head wound and will be worshipped as a god, thus becoming the world dictator.

As long as Satan can divert people's attention from the true purpose of prophecy, he has rendered them ineffective in fulfilling the real purposes of God. We are called not only to analyze the prophetic revelation, but to live our lives in a manner supportive of the ongoing works of the Almighty. Prophecy is for participants, not spectators and game players. Our task is to combat and bind the spirit of Antichrist in all its manifestations.

MARK, NAME OR NUMBER

The Revelation 13 passage reveals some very important data for these end times. First of all, there is going to be an economic change that can only be described as an upheaval. Secular futurologist Alvin Toffler calls it the coming Eco-Spasm. Next, a repressive regime will force people to cooperate with the new system or they will not be able to buy or sell. Finally, there will be an antichrist who will be the ultimate human villain.

While the Antichrist is prominent in prophecy, he is not the star of the end-time drama. He rules worldwide for only 42 months. The star of the drama is the King of Kings who reigns forever and forever. His name is Jesus. "For the testimony of Jesus is the Spirit of prophecy" (Revelation 19:10). Any system of prophetic teaching or analysis should ultimately and supremely glorify the Lord Jesus Christ, not the Antichrist.

CHAPTER 21

THE DATING GAME

When is Jesus coming back? When is the world coming to an end?

A lot of people think they have the answer and are setting dates. *Newsweek* magazine referred to the emphasis on the apocalypse as the "boom in doom."

I firmly believe Jesus is coming back. Over 300 Bible prophecies pointed to the first coming of Jesus. They were all fulfilled. The New Testament has 257 references to the future, literal return of Jesus to this planet. They too will be fulfilled.

No one can destroy the plan of God, but a lot is being done to erode people's confidence in Bible prophecy. In fact, more damage is done to the credibility of the message by the Bible's friends than by its enemies!

Our Saviour clearly warned: "But of that day and hour knoweth no man, no, not the angels of heaven, but my Father only" (Matthew 24:36). In spite of that plain statement, schemes for dating the Rapture, the beginning of the Millennium, or the end of the world are recycled over and over.

Let's take a brief look at the checkered history of the bewildering world of the date-setters.

Augustine suggested that the world would probably end in A.D. 1000. From about 950 to 1000 wealthy landowners all over Europe were encouraged to deed their holdings to the church in exchange for pardon for their sins.

Early in the last century, Dr. R. C. Shimeall wrote a book predicting that the Millennium would come in 1868. In that same century a converted Jew, Joseph Worlf, began prophesying that Jesus would come to the Mount of Olives in 1847. Lady Hester Stanhope converted to his doctrine, moved to Palestine, and established residence on the Mount of Olives. She kept two beautiful white Arabian horses in stables there. One was for Jesus to ride through the Golden Gate. Presumably the other was for her to accompany Him.

In 1918 H. C. Williams wrote a volume entitled *The Revelation of Jesus Christ*. In it he said: "A.D. 1914 is the time limit set in the Scriptures for the concurrence of the war: that the war broke out and continues in all details as described by the prophets is a complete fulfillment of the prophetic record."

In the same book Williams predicted that 1934 would mark the downfall of the Gentile nations, and in 1972 the Millennium would begin.

In 1975 a widely circulated book proclaimed that probably the Rapture would take place on September 5 or 6, 1975.

Following the interpretations of this man, others began to preach the September 1975 date. One pastor even borrowed large sums of money, which he had no way of paying back, to invest in missions. In a sermon he explained that he had nothing to worry about since Jesus was sure to come back on September 5, 1975.

This is the stuff that spiritual tragedies are made of, for on September 7 the bubble burst. Only eternity will reveal the tragedies created by those playing the dating game.

Date-setters claiming to be a part of the Church and citing Biblical authority can potentially play havoc with the credibility of the Second Coming concept in the minds of millions. When people are disappointed with date-setting failures, they are tempted to "throw out the baby with the bathwater." Their downfall is in not being able to distinguish between the valid and solemn message of Christ's coming and the perversion of it as perpetrated by false shepherds, opportunists, and the deluded.

Date-setting is not just an historic phenomenon. At present numerous books and periodicals are predicting that the Rapture must take place in 1988. This is based on an interpretation of Jesus' words in Matthew 24:34: "Verily I say unto you, This generation shall not pass, till all these things be fulfilled."

They say a generation is 40 years. Israel (the fig tree referred to in Matthew 24:32) became a nation in 1948. So 1948 + 40 = 1988.

There are several flaws in this superficial reasoning.

First, the generation concept is not that firmly fixed in Scripture. I am not sure that Exodus with the 40-year generation, nor the Book of Job with the 35-year generation, nor the statement that the days of man are "three score and ten''—indicating a 70-year generation—are to be taken as precisely describing a generation. The date-setters choose whichever one fits their scheme.

Secondly, why select 1948 for the year when the "fig tree' put forth its leaves? Why not the return of the Jews in the 1880's? Why not the founding of Zionism by Theodor Herzl in Basel, Switzerland, in 1897? Why not the founding of Tel Aviv, the first all-Jewish city in modern times, established in 1909?

1917 would be a likely year due to two major events: General Allenby's liberation of Jerusalem and Arthur James Balfour's famous declaration that "His Majesty's government view with favor the establishment in Palestine of a national home for the Jewish people, and will use their best endeavors to facilitate the achievement of the object...."

The capture of old Jerusalem by the Israelis in 1967 is considered as a possibility by many.

May we suggest that it was not our Lord's intention in this passage to provide a means of fixing the time of His return, since He immediately says this would be an impossibility (Matthew 24:36).

Thirdly, the word translated "generation" is *genea* and does not necessarily mean a literal generation. W. E. Vine's *Expository Dictionary of New Testament Words* gives one possible translation of *genea* as "a race of people."

Many outstanding scholars agree on that translation. If that is correct, then Jesus is simply declaring the indestructibility of the Jewish people. This would fit the context best.

I believe the coming of Jesus is imminent. He could come back today. But He may not.

I have believed that since I was 10 years old. If you had asked me then if I thought I would grow to be a man of fifty years of age, I would have said that it was highly unlikely. After all, Jesus is coming soon.

I am still anticipating His coming. I will continue to proclaim His coming as imminent. But soon? I am not sure how you define that word *soon,* and the closer one gets to defining the word, the closer one is to being a date-setter.

It is better to live as if Jesus were coming today and yet prepare for the future as if He were not coming for a long time. Then you are ready for time and eternity.

A friend once asked the great evangelist Dwight L. Moody, "Mr. Moody, if you knew Jesus was coming back at six o'clock this evening what would you do today?" I am sure the questioner was surprised at Moody's answer for he said, "If I knew Jesus was coming back this evening at six o'clock, this afternoon I would plant apple trees." That is a beautiful answer.

If you knew Jesus was coming back tonight, what would you do today? If there is something you would feel compelled to rush out and do, then you had better do it, for Jesus might come back tonight! On the other hand, if you are daily living your life in His will, then you would not have to change one thing you are planning to do!

God designed His revelation to us so that we are always living on the edge of eternity, and yet always planning for our future here. Suppose He had revealed the very date of the Rapture of the Church 1900 years ago? I doubt if the Church would even be in existence now. It is good to live in anticipation, but to realize that we do not know when the trumpet will sound. Go ahead and make your five-year and twenty-five-year plans. If the Lord comes before you complete your venture, so be it. We won't mind the interruption in the least!

The moment you set a date for the coming you upset this Divine balance, and you create havoc and distrust in the body of Christ. I tell you date-setting is a sin and should be denounced from every pulpit as such. Pastors, if you ignore the subject of prophecy or accept some of the modern re-interpretations of prophecy, you have solved nothing. Only by diligent study of and declaration of the Word of God in this realm will you bring real hope and good works with stability to your flock. Ignore prophecy, and the fanatics and distorters will have a field day. Nature abhors a vacuum. If you create a spiritual vacuum by ignoring the prophetic Word, false teachers will supply something to fill that void.

Jesus said: "Watch therefore; for ye know not what hour your Lord doth come...Therefore be ye also ready: for in such an hour as ye think not the Son of man cometh. Who then is that faithful and wise servant, whom his lord hath made ruler over his household, to give them meat in due season? Blessed (happy) is that servant, whom his lord when he cometh shall find so doing" (Matthew 24:42-46).

We are not undertaking a mere intellectual exercise here. This dating game is dangerous.

In 1832 William Miller first preached: "And so, brethren, it has been revealed to me that the world is coming to an end. Repent, repent, I say, for you have but 11 years to be washed clean in the blood of the Lamb. In mighty fire and terror the world will end in 1843."

As 1843 approached, anticipation turned into a kind of madness. People abandoned homes, farms, material possessions, and even children to gather in homes, praying as they waited for the last trump.

In Westford, Massachusetts, about 500 people gathered wearing white robes to wait for the Coming. When the midnight hour of December 31, 1842, arrived, an old town drunk, known as "Crazy Amos," blew a trumpet outside the fine old mansion where the people were gathered. Pandemonium broke loose, and several were seriously injured in the stampede. Outside they found not Jesus, but a bleary-eyed, laughing, old drunkard.

Historians record a darker side of the debacle. Following disappointment upon disappointment and a continual readjusting of the dates, many lost their minds. The asylum at Worcester, Massachusetts, became so overcrowded that a large hall had to be appropriated to house the deranged.

In New Hampshire, New York, Vermont, Maine, and parts of Pennsylvania the lunacy rate is said to have increased 300 percent in 1843-44 as a result of the date-setting.

Usually rational people went everywhere in flowing white robes, ready for ascension. Suicides became common in the face of disappointment.

When it was all over, the disillusioned faithful went back to try to pick up the pieces of the lives they had abandoned. Many became atheists.

Modern date-setters are getting ready to rerun a tragedy of that magnitude—or worse. As world crises mount, people will find the date-setters' schemes alluring as a psychological escapism.

A book publisher recently told me, "If you want to write a best-seller in the field of prophecy, name the Antichrist and set a date." There is something sinister behind that suggestion!

Newsweek for September 16, 1974, carried an article entitled, "The Doomsday Effect." It said that in 1982 all nine planets of our solar system will be in conjunction—that is, in a straight line in relation to the sun and all on one side of the sun. The combined gravitational pull may cause great storms on the sun. These storms could alter wind directions on earth, and this in turn could slow the speed of Earth's rotation and trigger the worst earthquakes the world has ever known. I wrote several articles refuting the idea. I commented on it over T.V. and on our monthly cassette service, the Audio Prophecy Digest.

A number of nationally known Bible teachers had used this as a basis for suggesting that the world would be in the Tribulation by 1982, but we could not accept it. Our conservative approach turned out to be right.

A periodical out of Florida calculated that the Rapture would take place soon, and that the Millennium would begin by 1979. Other dates being set are 1992, 1993, and 2000.

2000! It has an almost magical appeal! I recently heard a minister declare: "A day is as a thousand years and a thousand years as a day with the Lord. There were seven days of creation. It has now been six 'days' or 6,000 years from creation (or will be about A.D. 2000, according to Usher's chronology). That leaves one day of a thousand years—the Millennium. so the end has to come by the year 2000."

Let us consider a possibility. If Jesus tarries in His coming, the date-setters will have a heyday as the year 2000 approaches. It will be like a fever. It will sell pamphlets and books by the millions, but if Jesus does not come back by the year 2000, it is hard to imagine any credibility being left for the Bible prophecy message unless we begin a strong program right now to offset the heresy of date-setting.

Ignoring it will not make it go away. Only by preaching the true and dignified message of the Lord's return and by strongly denouncing date-setting can we hope to maintain confidence in the Bible message of Jesus' return.

Pastors, evangelists, teachers—please do not ignore the prophecy message because it is too complicated, or because it has been abused by fanatics. *Preach the Word.* Only truth, strongly declared, overcomes error.

I hope Jesus comes back before A.D. 2000. I am ready for Him to come right now, but if we are still here in A.D. 2001, the Bible prophecy message will be just as valid as it is today. The question is, will anyone be listening?

CHAPTER 22

SOUND DOCTRINE
An Important Key to
End-Time Victory Over Error

"They were astonished at his doctrine" (Matthew 22:33).

> Give ear, O ye heavens, and I will speak; and hear, O earth,
> the words of my mouth. My doctrine shall drop as the rain,
> my speech shall distil as the dew, as the small rain upon
> the tender herb, and as the showers upon the grass: Because
> I will publish the name of the Lord: ascribe ye greatness
> unto our God. He is the Rock, his work is perfect: for all
> his ways are judgment: a God of truth and without iniquity,
> just and right is he. They have corrupted themselves, their
> spot is not the spot of his children: they are a perverse and
> crooked generation.
>
> Deuteronomy 32:1-5

CORRUPT DOCTRINE

"They have corrupted themselves." "For there must be also heresies
among you, that they which are approved may be made manifest among you"
(1 Corinthians 11:19). Jesus warned, "false prophets...if it were possible...
shall deceive the very elect" (Matthew 24:24). The apostle Peter wrote,

"there shall be false teachers among you, who privily shall bring in damnable heresies" (2 Peter 2:1). These false teachers are likened to Balaam who had an anointing of the Lord and prophesied true prophesies, but misused his gift (verse 15). Not only are we told that false prophets come as "angels of light," but Jesus also tells us to "Beware of false prophets which come to you in sheep's clothing" (Matthew 7:15).

ANTI-DOCTRINE PREACHERS

"I don't preach doctrine, I just preach the Word of God." That is what the preacher said! How many times have you heard that from a pulpit or from the television evangelist? What a total contradiction that statement embodies! Doctrine is teaching. Any person who reads a Bible passage must stop with the mere reading if he does not want to preach or teach doctrine, for the minute you say one word to explain the passage, you are sharing doctrine. Doctrine can be good or bad. The word is used in the Bible (KJV) 56 times. About 45 of the passages speak of doctrine in a favorable light—pure doctrine, good, sound doctrine, the doctrine of Christ, etc. Only 11 of the passages speak of false doctrine, corrupt doctrine, etc.

YOU MUST CHOOSE

Since every teacher states doctrine, and since there are contradictions, you are forced to choose. The church I belong to, the Assemblies of God, has a clear doctrinal statement, and it is based on a high regard for the Word of God. We interpret the Bible very literally (except where symbolism is demanded by the context, and even then we allow the Bible to interpret its own symbols so that we can arrive at the literal meaning conveyed by the symbol).

The preachers who tell you that doctrine is not important for the most part are men who do not accept literal interpretation of the Bible. They hide behind the claim that they do not preach doctrine, yet they have rigid and highly defined doctrinal structures which they energetically promote and urge you to accept. Their inconsistency is further noted in the manner in which some of these allegorists accuse those of us who believe in literal interpretation—in the Rapture, the Millennium, and the fact that God still has a plan to be fulfilled in national Israel—of teaching error. Some say we are satanically deceived and in devilish heresy. If doctrine is so unimportant to them, why are they making such an issue over what we believe? I have always been able to co-exist with those who disagreed with me on certain points as long as both sides could agree to behave like true Christians.

I think every church that claims to be based on the Bible has some kind of statement of faith (doctrine). You should know what the church you attend believes. The church I belong to has a "Statement of Fundamental Truths." I do not claim that our statement is better than the one your church has, but it is the one we have, and as far as I can see it is simple, concise, and entirely based on Biblical truths. I have nothing to hide from the reader of this book. I am an ordained minister of the Assemblies of God. I believe this book will be read and appreciated by members of every Christian church. We do not claim to be exclusive in any sense of the word. We are just a part of the body of Christ and the end-time Holy Spirit Movement. I minister in churches of almost every denomination and fellowship. My membership in the Assemblies of God has not cut me off from the rest of the body of Christ.

In case you want to know what I believe as a minister of the Assemblies of God, here is our Statement of Fundamental Truths. I would never demand that you agree with this entire statement as a basis of fellowship. It is simply what we believe the Bible teaches in certain areas.

General Council of the Assemblies of God
Statement of Fundamental Truths
ARTICLE V—CONSTITUTION

The Bible is our all-sufficient rule for faith and practice. This Statement of Fundamental Truths is intended simply as a basis of fellowship among us (i.e., that we all speak the same thing, 1 Cor. 1:10; Acts 2:42). The phraseology employed in this Statement is not inspired nor contended for, but the truth set forth is held to be essential to a full-gospel ministry. No claim is made that it covers all Biblical truth, only that it covers our need as to these fundamental doctrines.

1. The Scriptures Inspired

The Scriptures, both the Old and New Testaments, are verbally inspired of God and are the revelation of God to man, the infallible, authoritative rule of faith and conduct (2 Tim. 3:15-17; 1 Thess. 2:13; 2 Peter 1:21).

2. The One True God

The one true God has revealed Himself as the eternally self-existent "I AM," the Creator of heaven and earth and the Redeemer of mankind. He has further revealed Himself as embodying the principles of relationship and association as Father, Son, and Holy Ghost (Deut. 6:4; Isa. 43:10,11; Matt. 28:19; Luke 3:22).

THE ADORABLE GODHEAD

(a) Terms Defined

The terms "Trinity" and "persons" as related to the Godhead, while not found in the Scriptures, are words in harmony with Scripture, whereby we may convey to others our immediate understanding of the doctrine of Christ respecting the Being of God, as distinguished from "gods many and lords many." We therefore may speak with propriety of the Lord our God, who is One Lord, as a trinity or as one Being of three persons, and still be absolutely scriptural (examples, Matt. 28:19; 2 Cor. 13;14; John 14:16,17).

(b) Distinction and Relationship in the Godhead

Christ taught a distinction of Persons in the Godhead which He expressed in specific terms of relationship, as Father, Son, and Holy Ghost, but that this distinction and relationship, as to its mode is *inscrutable* and *incomprehensible,* because *unexplained.* Luke 1:35; 1 Cor. 1:24; Matt. 11:25-27; 28:19; 2 Cor. 13:14; 1 John 1:3,4.

(c) Unity of the One Being of Father, Son and Holy Ghost

Accordingly, therefore, there is *that* in the Son which constitutes Him *the Son* and not the Father; and there is *that* in the Holy Ghost which constitutes Him *the Holy Ghost* and not either the Father or the Son. Wherefore the Father is the Begetter, the Son is the Begotten, and the Holy Ghost is the proceeding from the Father and the Son. Therefore, because these three persons in the Godhead are in a state of unity, there is but one Lord God Almighty and His name one. John 1:18; 15:26; 17:11,21; Zech. 14:9.

(d) Identity and Cooperation in the Godhead

The Father, the Son and the Holy Ghost are never *identical* as to *Person;* nor *confused* as to *relation;* nor *divided* in respect to the Godhead; nor *opposed* as to *cooperation.* The Son is *in* the Father and the Father is *in* the Son as to relationship. The Son is *with* the Father and the Father is *with* the Son, as to fellowship. The Father

---

178

is not *from* the Son, but the Son is *from* the Father, as to authority. The Holy Ghost is *from* the Father and the Son proceeding, as to nature, relationship, cooperation and authority. Hence, neither Person in the Godhead either exists or works separately or independently of the others. John 5:17-30,32,37; John 8:17,18.

(e) The Title, Lord Jesus Christ

The appellation, "Lord Jesus Christ," is a proper name. It is never applied, in the New Testament, either to the Father or to the Holy Ghost. It therefore belongs exclusively to the *Son of God.* Rom. 1:11-3,7; 2 John 3.

(f) The Lord Jesus Christ, God with Us

The Lord Jesus Christ, as to His divine and eternal nature, is the proper and only Begotten of the Father, but as to His human nature, He is the proper Son of Man. He is, therefore, acknowledged to be both God and man; who because He is God and man, is "Immanuel," God with us. Matt. 1:23; 1 John 4:2,10,14; Rev. 1;13,17.

(g) The Title, Son of God

Since the name "Immanuel" embraces both God and man in the one Person, our Lord Jesus Christ, it follows that the title, Son of God, describes His proper deity, and the title Son of Man, His proper humanity. Therefore, the title, Son of God, belongs to the *order of eternity,* and the title, Son of Man, to the *order of time.* Matt. 1:21-23; 2 John 3; 1 John 3:8; Heb. 7:3; 1:1-13.

(h) Transgression of the Doctrine of Christ

Wherefore, it is a transgression of the Doctrine of Christ to say that Jesus Christ derived the title, Son of God, solely from the fact of the incarnation, or because of His relation to the economy of redemption. Therefore, to deny that the Father is a real and eternal Father, and that the Son is a real and eternal Son, is a denial of the distinction and relationship in the Being of God; a denial of the Father and the Son; and a displacement of the truth that Jesus Christ is come in the flesh. 2 John 9; John 1:1,2,14,18,29,49; 1 John 2:22,23; 4:1-5; Heb. 12:2.

(i) Exaltation of Jesus Christ as Lord

The Son of God, our Lord Jesus Christ, having by Himself purged our sins, sat down on the right hand of the

Majesty on high; angels and principalities and powers having been made subject unto Him. And having been made both Lord and Christ, He sent the Holy Ghost that we, in the name of Jesus, might bow our knees and confess that Jesus Christ is Lord to the glory of God the Father until the end, when the Son shall become subject to the Father that God may be all in all. Heb. 1:3; 1 Peter 3:22; Acts 2:32-36; Rom. 14:11; 1 Cor. 15:24-28.

(j) Equal Honor to the Father and to the Son

Wherefore, since the Father has delivered all judgment unto the Son, it is not only the *express duty* of all in heaven and on earth to bow the knee, but it is an *unspeakable* joy in the Holy Ghost to ascribe unto the Son all the attributes of Deity, and to give Him all the honor and the glory contained in all the names and titles of the Godhead except those which express relationship (see paragraphs b, c, and d), and thus honor the Son even as we honor the Father. John 5:22,23; 1 Peter 1:8; Rev. 5:6-14; Phil. 2:8,9; Rev. 7:9,10; 4:8-11.

3. The Deity of the Lord Jesus Christ

The Lord Jesus Christ is the eternal Son of God. The Scriptures declare:

(a) His virgin birth (Matt. 1:23; Luke 1:31,35).
(b) His sinless life (Heb. 7:26; 1 Peter 2:22).
(c) His miracles (Acts 2:22; 10:38).
(d) His substitutionary work on the cross (1 Cor. 15:3; 2 Cor. 5:21)
(e) His bodily resurrection from the dead (Matt. 28:6; Luke 24:39; 1 Cor. 15:4).
(f) His exaltation to the right hand of God (Acts 1:9,11; 2:33; Phil. 2:9-11; Heb. 1-3).

4. The Fall of Man

Man was created good and upright; for God said, "Let us make man in our image, after our likeness." However, man by voluntary transgression fell and thereby incurred not only physical death but also spiritual death, which is separation from God (Gen. 1:26,27; 2:17; 3:6; Rom. 5:12-19).

5. The Salvation of Man

Man's only hope of redemption is through the shed blood of Jesus Christ the Son of God.

(a) Conditions to Salvation

Salvation is received through repentance toward God and faith toward the Lord Jesus Christ. By the washing of regeneration and renewing of the Holy Ghost, being justified by grace through faith, man becomes an heir of God, according to the hope of eternal life (Luke 24:47; John 3:3; Rom. 10:13-15; Eph. 2:8; Titus 2:11; 3:5-7).

(b) The Evidences of Salvation

The inward evidence of salvation is the direct witness of the Spirit (Rom. 8:16). The outward evidence to all men is a life of righteousness and true holiness (Eph. 4:24; Titus 2:12).

6. Ordinances of the Church

(a) Baptism in Water

The ordinance of baptism by immersion is commanded in the Scriptures. All who repent and believe on Christ as Saviour and Lord are to be baptized. Thus they declare to the world that they have died with Christ and that they also have been raised with Him to walk in newness of life (Matt. 28:19; Mark 16:16; Acts 10:47,48; Rom. 6:4).

(b) Holy Communion

The Lord's Supper, consisting of the elements—bread and the fruit of the vine—is the symbol expressing our sharing the divine nature of our Lord Jesus Christ (2 Peter 1:4); a memorial of His suffering and death (1 Cor. 11:26); and a prophecy of His second coming (1 Cor. 11:26); and is enjoined on all believers "till He come!"

7. The Baptism in the Holy Ghost

All believers are entitled to and should ardently expect and earnestly seek the promise of the Father, the baptism in the Holy Ghost and fire, according to the command of our Lord Jesus Christ. This was the normal experience of all in the early Christian Church. With it comes the enduement of power for life and service, the bestowment of the gifts and their uses in the work of the ministry (Luke 24:49; Acts 1:4,8; 1 Cor. 12:1-31). This experience is distinct from and subsequent to the experience of the new birth (Acts 8:12-17; 10:44-46; 11:14-16; 15:7-9). With the baptism in the Holy Ghost come such experiences as an overflowing fullness of the Spirit (John 7:37-39; Acts 4:8), a deepened reverence for God (Acts 2:43; Heb. 12:28), an intensified consecration to God and dedication to His work (Acts 2:42), and a more active love for Christ, for His Word and for the lost (Mark 16:20).

8. The Evidence of the Baptism in the Holy Ghost

The baptism of believers in the Holy Ghost is witnessed by the initial physical sign of speaking with other tongues as the Spirit of God gives them utterance (Acts 2:4). The speaking in tongues in this instance is the same in essence as the gift of tongues (1 Cor. 12:4-10,28), but different in purpose and use.

9. Sanctification

Sanctification is an act of separation from that which is evil, and of dedication unto God (Rom. 12:1,2; 1 Thess. 5:23; Heb. 13:12). The Scriptures teach a life of "holiness without which no man shall see the Lord" (Heb. 12:14). By the power of the Holy Ghost we are able to obey the command: "Be ye holy, for I am holy" (1 Pet. 1:15,16).

Sanctification is realized in the believer by recognizing his identification with Christ in His death and resurrection, and by faith reckoning daily upon the fact of that union, and by offering every faculty continually to the dominion of the Holy Spirit (Rom. 6:1-11,13; 8:1,2,13; Gal. 2:20; Phil. 2:12,13; 1 Peter 1:5).

10. The Church and Its Mission

The Church is the Body of Christ, the habitation of God through the Spirit, with divine appointments for the fulfillment of her great commission. Each believer, born of the Spirit, is an integral part of the General Assembly and Church of the Firstborn, which are written in heaven (Eph. 1:22,23; 2:22; Heb. 12:23).

Since God's purpose concerning man is to seek and to save that which is lost, to be worshiped by man, and to build a body of believers in the image of His Son, the priority reason-for-being of the Assemblies of God as part of the Church is:

a. To be an agency of God for evangelizing the world (Acts 1:8; Matt. 28:19,20; Mark 16:15,16).
b. To be a corporate body in which man may worship God (1 Cor. 12:13).
c. To be a channel of God's purpose to build a body of saints being perfected in the image of His Son (Eph. 4:11-16; 1 Cor. 12:28; 1 Cor. 14:12).

The Assemblies of God exists expressly to give continuing emphasis to this reason-for-being in the New Testament apostolic pattern by teaching and encouraging believers to be baptized in the Holy Spirit. This experience:

a. Enables them to evangelize in the power of the Spirit with accompanying supernatural signs (Mark 16:15-20; Acts 4:29-31; Hebrews 2:3,4).
b. Adds a necessary dimension to worshipful relationship with God (1 Cor. 2:10-16; 1 Cor. 12, 13, and 14).
c. Enables them to respond to the full working of the Holy Spirit in expression of fruit and gifts and ministries as in New Testament times for the edifying of the body of Christ (Gal. 5:22-26; 1 Cor. 14:12; Eph. 4:11,12; 1 Cor. 12:28; Col. 1:29).

11. The Ministry

A divinely called and scripturally ordained ministry has been provided by our Lord for the threefold purpose of leading the Church in: (1) Evangelization of the world (Mark 16:15-20), (2) Worship of God (John 4:23,24), (3) Building a body of saints being perfected in the image of His Son (Eph. 4:11-16).

12. Divine Healing

Divine healing is an integral part of the gospel. Deliverance from sickness is provided for in the atonement, and is the privilege of all believers (Isa. 53:4,5; Matt. 8:16,17; James 5:14-16).

13. The Blessed Hope

The resurrection of those who have fallen asleep in Christ and their translation together with those who are alive and remain unto the coming of the Lord is the imminent and blessed hope of the church (1 Thess. 4:16,17; Rom. 8:23; Titus 2:13; 1 Cor. 15:51,52).

14. The Millennial Reign of Christ

The second coming of Chist includes the rapture of the saints, which is our blessed hope, followed by the visible return of Christ with His saints to reign on the earth for one thousand years (Zech. 14:5; Matt. 24:27,30; Rev. 1:7; 19:11-14; 20:1-6). This millennial reign will bring the salvation of national Israel (Ezek. 37:21,22; Zeph. 3:19,20; Rom. 11:26,27) and the establishment of universal peace (Isa. 11:6-9; Ps. 72:3-8; Micah 4:3,4).

15. The Final Judgment

There will be a final judgment in which the wicked dead will be raised and judged according to their works. Whosoever is not found written in the Book of Life, together with the devil and his angels, the beast and the false prophet, will be consigned to everlasting punishment in the lake which burneth with fire and brimstone, which is the second death (Matt. 25:46; Mark 9:43-48; Rev. 19:20; 20:11-15; 21:8).

16. The New Heavens and the New Earth

"We, according to his promise, look for new heavens and a new earth wherein dwelleth righteousness" (2 Peter 3:13; Rev. 21, 22).

Why would anyone say that those who believe in this, or a similar statement of doctrine, are divisive? I can fellowship with any brother or sister in the Church who would agree on some statement similar to seven of the sixteen points of this statement, to wit: 1. Inspiration of the Scriptures, 2. One True God, 3. Deity of the Lord Jesus Christ (including His bodily resurrection from the dead), 4. The Fall of Man, 5. The Salvation of Man, 6. Resurrection of the Body, 7. Literal Return of Jesus Christ.

Even if we should disagree on the other nine points, there is still a basis to consider each other brethren and sisters in the body of Christ. We have *true* unity through our organic connection in the body, not through total doctrinal agreement. We cannot seek unity for the sake of unity at the cost of unacceptable compromise. We cannot be silent when a vast majority of believers in the Evangelical, Fundamentalist, Pentecostal, and Charismatic churches are slandered because they believe in the Rapture, the Millennium, and that Israel has a place in the future plan of God. These accusations demand a responsible answer.

Before you listen to some of the people who are encouraging you not to believe in the "doctrines" of your church, take a look at what the Bible says about doctrine. Here is a listing of every mention of the word doctrine in the Scripture:

> My doctrine shall drop as the rain, my speech shall distil as the dew, as the small rain upon the tender herb, and as the showers upon the grass:
>
> Deuteronomy 32:2

> For thou hast said, My doctrine is pure, and I am clean in thine eyes.
>
> Job 11:4

> For I give you good doctrine, forsake ye not my law.
>
> Proverbs 4:2

> Whom shall he teach knowledge? and whom shall he make to understand doctrine? them that are weaned from the milk, and drawn from the breasts.
>
> Isaiah 28:9

> They also that erred in spirit shall come to understanding, and they that murmured shall learn doctrine.
>
> Isaiah 29:24

> But they are altogether brutish and foolish: the stock is a doctrine of vanities.
>
> Jeremiah 10:8

> And it came to pass, when Jesus had ended these sayings, the people were astonished at his doctrine:
>
> Matthew 7:28

> Then understood they how that he bade them not beware of the leaven of bread, but of the doctrine of the Pharisees and of the Sadducees.
>
> Matthew 16:12

> And when the multitude heard this, they were astonished at his doctrine.
>
> Matthew 22:33

> And they were astonished at his doctrine: for he taught them as one that had authority, and not as the scribes.
>
> Mark 1:22

And they were all amazed, insomuch that they questioned among themselves, saying, What thing is this? What new doctrine is this? for with authority commandeth he even the unclean spirits, and they do obey him.

Mark 1:27

And he taught them many things by parables, and said unto them in his doctrine.

Mark 4:2

And the scribes and chief priests heard it, and sought how they might destroy him: for they feared him, because all the people was astonished at his doctrine.

Mark 11:18

And he said unto them in his doctrine, Beware of the scribes, which love to go in long clothing, and love salutations in the marketplaces,...

Mark 12:38

And they were astonished at his doctrine: for his word was with power.

Luke 4:32

Jesus answered them, and said, My doctrine is not mine, but his that sent me.

John 7:16

If any man will do his will, he shall know of the doctrine, whether it be of God, or whether I speak of myself.

John 7:17

The high priest then asked Jesus of his disciples, and of his doctrine.

John 18:19

And they continued steadfastly in the apostles' doctrine and fellowship, and in breaking of bread, and in prayers.

Acts 2:42

Saying, Did not we straitly command you that ye should not teach in this name? and, behold, ye have filled Jerusalem with your doctrine, and intend to bring this man's blood upon us.

Acts 5:28

Then the deputy, when he saw what was done, believed, being astonished at the doctrine of the Lord.

Acts 13:12

And they took him, and brought him unto Areopagus, saying, May we know what this new doctrine, whereof thou speakest, is?

Acts 17:19

But God be thanked, that ye were the servants of sin, but ye had obeyed from the heart that form of doctrine which was delivered you.

Romans 6:17

Now I beseech you, brethren, mark them which cause divisions and offences contrary to the doctrine which ye have learned; and avoid them.

Romans 16:17

Now, brethren, if I come unto you speaking with tongues, what shall I profit you, except I shall speak to you either by revelation, or by knowledge, or by prophesying, or by doctrine?

1 Cor. 14:6

How is it then, brethren? when ye come together, every one of you hath a psalm, hath a doctrine, hath a tongue, hath a revelation, hath an interpretation. Let all things be done unto edifying.

1 Cor. 14:26

That we henceforth be no more children, tossed to and fro, and carried about with every wind of doctrine, by the sleight of men, and cunning craftiness, whereby they lie in wait to deceive;

Ephesians 4:14

As I besought thee to abide still at Ephesus, when I went into Macedonia, that thou mightest charge some that they teach no other doctrine.

1 Timothy 1:3

For whoremongers, for them that defile themselves with mankind, for menstealers, for liars, for perjured persons, and if there be any other thing that is contrary to sound doctrine;

1 Timothy 1:3

If thou put the brethren in remembrance of these things, thou shalt be a good minister of Jesus Christ, nourished up in the words of faith and of good doctrine, whereunto thou hast attained.

1 Timothy 4:6

Till I come, give attendance to reading, to exhortation, to doctrine.

1 Timothy 4:13

Take heed unto thyself, and unto the doctrine; continue in them: for in doing this thou shalt both save thyself, and them that hear thee.

1 Timothy 4:16

Let the elders that rule well be counted worthy of double honour, especially they who labour in the word and doctrine.

1 Timothy 5:17

Let as many servants as are under the yoke count their own masters worthy of all honour, that the name of God and his doctrine be not blasphemed.

1 Timothy 6:1

If any man teach otherwise, and consent not to wholesome words, even the words of our Lord Jesus Christ, and to the doctrine which is according to godliness;

1 Timothy 6:3

But thou hast fully known my doctrine, manner of life, purpose, faith, longsuffering, charity, patience,

2 Timothy 3:10

All scripture is given by inspiration of God, and is profitable for doctrine, for reproof, for correction, for instruction in righteousness:

2 Timothy 3:16

Preach the word; be instant in season, out of season; reprove, rebuke, exhort with all longsuffering and doctrine.

2 Timothy 4:2

For the time will come when they will not endure sound doctrine; but after their own lusts shall they heap to themselves teachers, having itching ears;

2 Timothy 4:3

Holding fast the faithful word as he hath been taught, that he may be able by sound doctrine both to exhort and to convince the gainsayers.

Titus 1:9

But speak thou the things which become sound doctrine:

Titus 2:1

In all things shewing thyself a pattern of good works: in doctrine shewing uncorruptness, gravity, sincerity,

Titus 2:7

Not purloining, but shewing all good fidelity; that they may adorn the doctrine of God our Saviour in all things.

Titus 2:10

Therefore leaving the principles of the doctrine of Christ, let us go on unto perfection; not laying again the foundation of repentance from dead works, and of faith toward God.

Hebrews 6:1

Of the doctrine of baptisms, and of laying on of hands, and of resurrection of the dead, and of eternal judgment.

Hebrews 6:2

Whosoever transgresseth, and abideth not in the doctrine of Christ, hath not God. He that abideth in the doctrine of Christ, he hath both the Father and the Son.

2 John 9

If there come any unto you, and bring not this doctrine, receive him not into your house, neither bid him God speed;

2 John 10

But I have a few things against thee, because thou hast there them that hold the doctrine of Balaam, who taught Balac to cast a stumblingblock before the children of Israel, to eat things sacrificed unto idols, and to commit fornication.

Revelation 2:14

So that thou also them that hold the doctrine of the Nicolaitans, which thing I hate.

Revelation 2:15

But unto you I say, and unto the rest in Thyatira, as many as have not this doctrine, and which have not known the depths of Satan, as they speak; I will put upon you none other burden.

Revelation 2:24

DOCTRINES:

But in vain they do worship me, teaching for doctrines the commandments of men.

Matthew 15:9

Howbeit in vain do they worship me, teaching for doctrines the commandments of men.

Mark 7:7

Which all are to perish with the using; after the commandments and doctrines of men?

Colossians 2:22

Now the Spirit speaketh expressly, that in the latter times some shall depart from the faith, giving heed to seducing spirits, and doctrines of devils;

1 Timothy 4:1

Be not carried about with divers and strange doctrines. For it is a good thing that the heart be established with grace; not with meats, which have not profited them that have been occupied therein.

Hebrews 13:9

(*Strong's Concordance*)

I would like to further suggest that the antidote to multiplied error and confusion is to be firmly grounded in the Word of God and to know what you believe. Then you will not be swept away by "every wind of doctrine" that blows your way.

Paul was desirous that "the name of God and his doctrine be not blasphemed...If any man teach otherwise, and consent not to wholesome words, even the words of our Lord Jesus Christ, and to the doctrine which is according to godliness; He is proud, knowing nothing, but doting about questions and strifes of words, whereof cometh envy, strife, railings, evil surmisings...from such withdraw thyself'' (1 Timothy 6:1,3-5).

DOCTRINE OF THE RESURRECTION

Some of the anti-doctrine teachers are telling us that the first resurrection takes place when we are saved. This is a direct contradiction of the entire fifteenth chapter of 1 Corinthians. Paul condemned Hymenaeus and Philetus for exactly this same false teaching:

> Study to shew thyself approved unto God, a workman that needeth not to be ashamed, rightly dividing the word of truth. But shun profane and vane babblings: for they will increase unto more ungodliness. And their word will eat as doth a canker: of whom is Hymenaeus and Philetus; *Who concerning the truth have erred, saying that the resurrection is past already; and overthrow the faith of some.*
>
> 2 Timothy 2:15-18

The denial of a resurrection at the time of the Rapture is just one example of the multiplied false doctrines that are blowing like a gale-force wind through the charismatic and pentecostal movements.

NEW TESTAMENT MEANING OF DOCTRINE

In conclusion, we present a treatment of the word "doctrine" as it appears in *Vine's Expository Dictionary of New Testament Words*. We use *Vine's* because of its easy availability, and because it is simple for the non-Greek-reading student to use and understand.

DOCTRINE

1. DIDACHE denotes teaching, either (a) that which is taught, e.g., Matthew 7:28, A.V., "doctrine," R.V., "teaching;" Titus 1:9, R.V.; Revelation 2:14,15,24, or (b) the act of teaching, instruction, e.g., Mark 4:2, A.V., "doctrine," R.V., "teaching;" the R.V. has "the doctrine" in Romans 16:17. See Note (1) below.

2. DIDASKALIA denotes, as No. 1 (from which, however, it is to be distinguished), (a) that which is taught, doctrine, Matthew 15:9; Mark 7:7; Ephesians 4:14; Colossians 2:22; 1 Timothy 1:10; 4:1,6; 6:1,3; 2 Timothy 4:3; Titus 1:9 ("doctrine," in the last part of verse: see also No. 1); 2:1,10; (b) teaching, instruction, Romans 12:7,

"teaching;" verse 16, A.V., "the doctrine," R.V., (correctly) "thy teaching;" 5:17, A.V., "doctrine," R.V. "teaching;" 2 Timothy 3:10,16 (ditto); Titus 2:7, "thy doctrine."

Notes: (1) Whereas *didache* is used only twice in the Pastoral Epistles, 2 Timothy 4:2, and Titus 1:9, *didaskalia* occurs fifteen times. Both are used in the active and passive senses (i.e., the act of teaching and what is taught), the passive is predominant in *didache,* the active in *didaskalia*; the former stresses the authority, the latter the act (Cremer). Apart from the Apostle Paul, other writers make use of *didache* only, save in Matthew 15:9 and Mark 7:7 (*didaskalia*).

(2) In Hebrews 6:1, logos, a word, is translated "doctrine," A.V.; the R.V. margin gives the literal rendering, "the word (of the beginning of Christ), and, in the text, "the (first) principles (of Christ)."

DEFENDING THE GOSPEL

We did not declare war on the new wave of non-literal preachers. We were content to cooperate with them on any level we could, and promote true unity in the body of Christ. That has always been our goal.

What I would prefer to do would be to simply continue preaching the good news of salvation, end-time victory for the Church, and the blessed hope of our Lord's return; but "Beloved, when I gave all diligence to write unto you of the common salvation, it was needful for me to write unto you, and exhort you that ye should *earnestly contend for the fatih which was once delivered unto the saints.* For there are certain men crept in unawares..." (Jude 3,4a). Following Paul's example, we would be "bold to speak the Word without fear...Some indeed preach Christ even of envy and strife; and some of good will...I am set for the defense of the gospel" (see Philippians 1:14-17).

CHAPTER 23

LITERAL INTERPRETATION OF THE BIBLE

You can read the Bible through in one year by reading three chapters daily and five chapters on each Sunday.

As you read the Bible you discover that it has a lot to say about the future. Some of the predictions were fulfilled after the prophet's time, so from our perspective these prophecies fall in the category of predictions that have already been fulfilled. Hundreds of prophecies have never been fulfilled. They will see a fulfillment in our future. Why are we interested in the future? Well, we had better be interested in the future because that is where we will be spending all the rest of our lives, for both time and eternity. Prophecy has many values in addition to informing us about events of the future. There are many applications of God's prophetic plan for the present season.

Over one-third of the Bible is prophetic in nature. Jesus talked more about the future Kingdom than any subject with the exception of redemption (salvation). Prophecy was the second emphasis in the Master's earthly teaching ministry. Dr. Paul Lee Tan points out that one out of every twenty-five verses in the New Testament has to do with the Second Coming of Christ. That is to say nothing of the hundreds of passages that teach on various other prophetic subjects and future events.

IT'S REAL

I believe Jesus, the Son of God, is real. I believe salvation, healing, and the infilling of the Holy Spirit are real. I believe Jesus and the Christian experience are real because of two things. First of all, these concepts are declared in the infallible Word of God, the Bible. Secondly, we have experienced salvation, healing and the ministry of the Holy Spirit in our lives. In addition to this, we have observed the power of Jesus Christ at work transforming the lives of others. We have plenty of empirical evidence to satisfactorily prove that God is real and His Word is all we claim it (and that it claims) to be.

WHAT ABOUT PROPHECY?

How strange it is to observe those who say prophecy is not literal. There are brethren who want everything in the Bible relating to our Christian experience and walk to be literal. But when it comes to prophecy there is some kind of problem. This is the exception to the rule. Prophecy is to be non-specific, or "spiritualized." This is a good place to mention that literal is not the opposite of spiritual. We hold that there are literal realities in the physical and in the spiritual realms.

PROPHECY IS BEING LITERALLY FULFILLED

When we see the exponential increase of knowledge (Daniel 12:4), the population explosion (Matthew 24:7; famine), the unprecedented rise of false Christs and false prophets, the worldwide Holy Ghost revival (Joel 2:28,29), and a host of other prophecies in the process of fulfillment, how could we say that prophecy is not to be taken literally?

ISRAEL IS REAL

What an embarrassment the nation of Israel is to the non-literal interpreter of the Bible. As long as there was no Israel, the allegorists (non-literal interpreters) could feel fairly comfortable. They have long claimed that Israel is finished in the plan of God. The Church has displaced Israel. All the prophecies in the Old Testament relating to the Jews are now transferred to the Church. That system of interpretation did much better before May 14, 1948. Many of the allegorists have become so bitter in their spirits over Israel becoming a nation in spite of their erroneous teaching that they have become theological anti-Semites. This is alarming when one ponders the fact that Hitler could never have succeeded in his persecution of the Jews had the German people not been conditioned by theological anti-Semitism in both the Roman and Protestant churches of Germany. Hitler and his henchmen often quoted prominent church theologians to provide a basis for their treatment of the Jewish people.

LITERAL SECOND COMING OF CHRIST

We are "Looking for that blessed hope, and the glorious appearing of the great God and our Saviour Jesus Christ" (Titus 2:13).

A great preacher in London, of liberal persuasion, said to his congregation that the blessed hope Paul wrote of was not to be taken as a literal future coming of Jesus back to this world. "The blessed hope," he declared, "was fulfilled on the Day of Pentecost when the Holy Spirit was outpoured on the early church." How strange! Too bad the good reverend didn't check his Bible references a little more closely. Paul wrote to Titus of the "blessed hope" many long years after the Day of Pentecost. Also note that after the Day of Pentecost there are one hundred and fifty-seven references to a future, literal return of Jesus to this world.

As the disciples watched Jesus ascend into heaven, God sent messengers to them to say, "Ye men of Galilee, why stand ye gazing up into heaven? This same Jesus, which is taken up from you into heaven, shall so come in like manner as ye have seen him go into heaven" (Acts 1:11). *This same Jesus*!!! Not a new kind of Christ, not a social influence of the Church, not a "spirit" Jesus, but *this same Jesus* will come back again. Fanny Crosby had the inspiration of the Holy Spirit when she wrote the famous hymn, "I shall know Him, I shall know Him, as redeemed by His side I shall stand. I shall know Him, I shall know Him, by the print of the nails in His hand." *This same Jesus*!

DANGERS OF THE NON-LITERAL APPROACH

One of the worst manifestations of the allegorical system of interpretation of the Bible is that it leans toward a rejection of Israel, and whether it is admitted or not, this is theological anti-Semitism! I use the word anti-Semitism in its popular, not its technical sense. To most people the word means hatred of or persecution of the Jewish people. Theological anti-Semitism is the natural bed-fellow of the active anti-Semite. The philosophical anti-Semite provides the approval, and in a sense, the inspiration for the active anti-Semite who lights the fire in the gas ovens at Auschwitz and Dachau. Hatred of the Jews is continuous because it is a satanic phenomenon. The Holocaust is not mere history, it has a potential future. That is why *we must be concerned about wrong interpretation of the scriptures!*

It is my conviction that a rational end of allegorism (non-literal interpretation

---

195

of the Bible) will lead one to agnosticism. Thank God some of our evangelical brethren who accept the non-literal sense of the Word evidently are not too logical.

BIBLICAL ANARCHY

Allegorism introduces anarchy into the whole matter of Biblical interpretation.

Anarchy is a situation where every man becomes a law unto himself. There is no clear law of guidance in any universal sense. In the realm of doctrine, you can make the Bible say anything you want it to say. Consider: If you say such and such a verse does not mean what it says, and then you proceed to ascribe a meaning to the verse that is not clearly implied in the context, what is to stop me from using your system of interpretation on any verse in the Bible? Thus every man becomes his own law maker and we have utter chaos. No one can make any real sense out of the Bible. If it can mean anything you want it to mean then it may mean nothing.

A logical man must finally ask the question, "If it doesn't mean what it says in this passage or in such and such a passage, how can I be sure any of it means anything?" Follow the allegorical system far enough and you will likely become an agnostic. An agnostic is not like the atheist who says, "There is no God." The agnostic says, "No one can know anything for sure."

AN EXAMPLE

A number of years ago a teacher in a fundamentalist (pentecostal) Bible college began to reject literal interpretation of the Bible. He taught allegorism in his classes. He began to teach amillennialism (there will be no literal 1000-year Millennium). This created a certain friction with the denominational heads of the school. It was mutually agreed that it would be best for him to leave the school. He also left the denomination and found ordination in one of the older, more "liberal" churches. He is now the pastor of a large church of that denomination in Seattle, Washington. Recently the *Seattle Times* featured this pastor in a lengthy article titled, "Jesus the Man." The article was subtitled, "Pastor's sermon sparks debate among peers." The *Times* quoted the controversial minister, "Jesus is Jesus, God is God, and Jesus," he says flatly, "is not God. I stress the full humanity of Jesus and that's what gets controversial because there's always a bunch of people around who say Jesus is God...the problem is that many religious persons, especially those who take the Bible literally, don't probe beyond the surface."

ANOTHER LIKE JESUS?

The Seattle newspaper further states: "In addition to running head on into those who interpret the Bible literally, (he) sparks debate through his belief *that another human, like Jesus may be part of God's plan for the future.*" This is an awesome concept and strangely disturbing. Ponder the words of Jesus, "I am come in my Father's name, and ye receive me not. If another shall come in his own name, him ye will receive" (John 5:43). Many understand this to be a prophecy of the coming humanist Antichrist, the very son of perdition!

The Seattle pastor is further quoted as saying, "I'm willing to say Jesus is unique, but not God."

IT'S LOGICAL

You can prove anything with logic. Given a false premise to begin with one can "prove" a lie with the system of logic. Just because a thing is logical does not mean it is true. If you accept the concept of non-literal interpretation of the Bible then it is logical to come to conclusions like those of the liberal pastor described in the *Seattle Times.* Only a literal approach to the Word of God steers us clear of such a course. If your beginning premise is that the Bible is the Word of God and that it means what it says, then you will come to correct conclusions. You will still have questions, for we "see through a glass darkly," but you will have a basic and solid understanding of the Word and of God's plan for the future. Prophecy is not intended to mystify you. Peter writes that we have a "more sure word of prophecy," and that it is "a light in a dark place." Prophecy clears things up for you. It will not confuse you. Don't accept the "cop outs" of the lazy Christian who would rather watch T.V. for hours on end rather than pursue the truth of God's Word. Reject the literal interpretation of the Scripture, however, and you will end up with wild concepts totally out of harmony with what the Bible is actually trying to teach. Origen allegorized the parable of the good Samaritan (Luke 10:30-37) and came up with the following: The man who fell among thieves is Adam. The robbers are the Devil and his demonic hordes. The priest represents the law. The Levite stands for the prophets. The good Samaritan is Jesus Himself (imagine that). The beast is the Lord's body. The inn is the church. The two pence represent the Father and the Son, and the Samaritan's statement, "When I come again," refers to the Second Coming of Christ. Countless examples of such fanciful interpretation could be offered. Is it any wonder that allegorization creates such confusion? Suffice to say, the allegorist disagree among themselves on almost everything. Chaos and anarchy characterize any system that rejects literalism. Literalism recognizes symbols in the Scripture, but allows Scripture to interpret its own symbols, and seeks the literal truth conveyed by the symbol. Even the allegorist will admit that the symbol means "something." That something is the literal truth we strive to discover. Never do we make a symbol out of anything that makes plain sense by itself. 1000 years is 1000 years. 144,000 Israelites means exactly that.

Further note that just because a passage has a symbol in it does not warrant making everything in the passage symbolical. For a thorough study of this entire subject see *The Interpretation of Prophecy* by Dr. Paul Lee Tan.

CHAPTER 24

PSYCHOTRONIC WARFARE
SOVIET ULTIMATE WEAPON—
THE ONLY WAY TO DEFEAT IT

Scientists such as Doctors Targ, Hararey, and Putoff have written about a new mind war technique being developed by the U.S.S.R. Columnists such as William Broad and Jack Anderson have written about it. "Nova," a program on National Public Television, has given documentation concerning this research. If these men are correct, the Soviets are trying to link the human mind with computers, tap into the ESP factor of the human mind, and, with the use of powerful "psychotronic generators," use this sheer mental energy as a weapon of war.

FROM THE BIBLE

In 1955 I was studying the book of Daniel intently. Certain passages seemed obscure and hard to understand. I was reading of the coming world ruler (Antichrist, as identified by John) in several passages. He is the covenant maker/breaker who defiles a future temple. This abomination of desolation is mentioned in the seventy weeks vision:

> Seventy weeks are determined upon thy people and upon
> thy holy city, to finish the transgression, and to make an
> end of sins, and to make reconciliation for iniquity, and

> to bring in everlasting righteousness, and to seal up the vision and prophecy, and to anoint the most Holy. Know therefore and understand, that from the going forth of the commandment to restore and to build Jerusalem unto the Messiah the Prince shall be seven weeks, and threescore and two weeks: the street shall be built again, and the wall, even in troublous times. And after threescore and two weeks shall Messiah be cut off, but not for himself: and the people of the prince that shall come shall destroy the city and the sanctuary; and the end thereof shall be with a flood, and unto the end of the war desolations are determined. And he shall confirm the covenant with many for one week: and in the midst of the week he shall cause the sacrifice and the oblation to cease, and for the overspreading of abominations he shall make it desolate, even until the consummation, and that determined shall be poured upon the desolate.
>
> Daniel 9:24-27

This event, the abomination of the Temple (holy place), is clearly yet in the future as it is referred to by Jesus as taking place just before the ''great tribulation'' (Matthew 24:15-21).

The apostle Paul refers to the same profane action of the coming man of sin (Antichrist) in the Second Thessalonian letter:

> Let no man deceive you by any means: for that day shall not come, except there come a falling away first, and that man of sin be revealed, the son of perdition; Who opposeth and exalteth himself above all that is called God, or that is worshipped; so that he as God sitteth in the temple of God, shewing himself that he is God.
>
> 2 Thessalonians 2:3,4

Again Daniel refers to the abominator (defiler) of the temple. Here Antichrist is referred to as the willful king.

> And the king shall do according to his will; and he shall exalt himself, and magnify himself above every god, and shall speak marvellous things against the God of gods, and shall prosper till the indignation be accomplished: for that that is determined shall be done. Neither shall he regard the God of his fathers, nor the desire of women, nor regard any god: for he shall magnify himself above all. But in his

estate shall he honour the God of forces: and a god whom
his fathers knew not shall he honour with gold, and silver,
and with precious stones, and pleasant things.

Daniel 11:36-38

Who or what is the "God of forces" the willful king, Antichrist, honors?
(Daniel 11:38). The next puzzle was a strange phrase in the King James
translation of Daniel 11:24,25, referring to the "forecasting of devices...."

> He shall enter peaceably even upon the fattest places of the
> province; and he shall do that which his fathers have not
> done, nor his fathers' fathers; he shall scatter among them
> the prey, and spoil, and riches: yea, and he shall forecast
> his devices against the strong holds, even for a time. And
> he shall stir up his power and his courage against the king
> of the south with a great army; and the king of the south
> shall be stirred up to battle with a very great and mighty
> army; but he shall not stand: for they shall forecast devices
> against him.

Daniel 11:24,25

Some modern translations render "forecast his devices" as "he shall devise
plots." However, the marginal rendering in many King James Bibles gives
the alternate translation from the Hebrew as "He shall *think his thoughts*
against the strong holds," or "he will project his strong mental energy against
the fortresses." Is this possible? At any rate, coupled with the fact that 2
Thessalonians, chapter two, describes the man of sin, the Antichrist, as a
miracle worker who "comes with lying signs and wonders"; and the book
of Revelation describes his cohort, the false prophet, as having the power
to work miracles in the sight of men (Revelation 13), I projected the idea
in my preaching as early as 1955 that the Antichrist, and possibly other
military leaders, would try to harness mental energy and use it for military
purposes.

I believe it is happening now and that we should be concerned, not for
sensationalism or to produce despair, *but because we, the believers, can do
something about it.* We alone can do something to stop it.

SOURCE OF POWER

There are two sources of supernatural power available to man. You can
find the power of God operative in your life if you are a born-again Christian.
There are supernatural "gifts of the Spirit" that are to be in operation in
the Church (1 Corinthians 12). One can also, in league with Satan, tap the

201

dark powers of the demons, the power of the devil himself.

What about the "third source"—the human mind? Is there not an ESP factor at work in the human psyche? Frankly, if it exists at all it is at such a low level as to be insignificant for all practical purposes. Search for it, try to develop it and you fall prey to demon power that will amplify your mind energy and dominate you; but the power will not be yours—it is from another source. Pursue it far enough, and you will become demon possessed.

Where does the Antichrist (the beast in Revelation 13) get his power? John clearly tells us: "...and the dragon gave him his power, and his seat, and great authority" (Revelation 13:2b). The dragon is Satan, not Red China as some have fancied. This is confirmed in Revelation 12:9: "And the great dragon was cast out, that old serpent, called the Devil, and Satan, which deceiveth the whole world." One of the important principles of Bible interpretation is that the Bible must be allowed to interpret its own symbols. Never do we bring outside information to the Word to understand its symbols. They must be interpreted internally, within the Bible itself.

The beast, Antichrist, gets his power from the devil. The Antichrist is a normal human being who receives supernatural abilities, even miracle-working powers, directly from the devil. *Now Daniel's "god of forces" is identified.* It is Satan himself who is the "god of forces."

My early 1955 conclusion, based on scripture alone, was that the Antichrist and other end-time military leaders would try to harness psychic mental energy and somehow use it as a weapon of war.

Following a lead from columnist Carl Alpert, who wrote an article reprinted in *The Jewish Digest*, titled "The Prophet of Zichron Yaakov," we journeyed to Zichron Yaakov, near Haifa, in Israel. There we met Avraham and Elenora Shifrin. With our camera crew we produced three half-hour programs on the subject of the fate of Christians and Jews in the U.S.S.R. Shifrin had been imprisoned in a slave labor camp in the Soviet Union for fourteen years. We did a fourth T.V. program on psychotronics.

The Soviets had imprisoned him because of his activities after Israel was declared a nation in 1948. He encouraged Jews to go back to the land of their fathers. For this he was imprisoned in Russia. He is now free from that bondage and lives in the land of Israel. Elenora, his wife, also suffered persecution at the hands of the Soviets while living there, before she met Avraham.

Shifrin has first-hand knowledge of the strange work going on in Russia. He is sympathetic to the idea of human parapsychological research, so he is coming from a totally different base than that from which we are approaching the subject.

Here is a transcript of what the Shifrins had to say in the T.V. interview we produced. The copy reads roughly because English is not Shifrin's native tongue. We have slightly edited the copy where absolutely necessary to make his meaning plain. Nothing of the actual meaning of his words has been changed. Square brackets indicate our added clarification.

SHIFRIN INTERVIEW

AVRAHAM SHIFRIN:

And why I know about this in my days when I was a political prisoner in Siberia, we establish contact with parapsychological secret institution in Moscow. And when I was released [from Russia to go to Israel] at this time I began [continued] my connections. I was very close, privately, with Solomon Gerlestein who was the director of this institution. I had contact with many other people.

ELENORA SHIFRIN:

Excuse me, when you said "we in the camps established contacts" you didn't mention that in the camps you had a group of people who started [studied] the problems of parapsychology. And therefore they had a special interest in establishing these contacts.

AVRAHAM SHIFRIN:

We had a special Yoga group in the Soviet concentration camps and that's why they were so interested to contact us. And when I began my contacts with Gerlestein, Mazar and others in Moscow, I understood that they work for the KGB and the army from the very beginning. And till 1970 I was in contact with them in the Soviet Union. Afterwards, when I came to Israel I didn't interrupt my contacts with some of these people in the Soviet Union. That's why till now I have information about their work in these institutions. What I can tell you in short? Because about this I can speak hours about their work. They work until 1971 in Moscow in a very big institution. It was secret work but then they decided to make it absolutely secret. They made many laboratories throughout all the Soviet Union. In Leningrad and in Moscow and also in many other places. And they work absolutely independent. One laboratory doesn't know what work is being done in another laboratory.

ELENORA SHIFRIN:
They work independently of one another but all of them
are controlled by the government.

AVRAHAM SHIFRIN:
Independently—they work for the KGB and for the army.
For the army they prepare clairvoyance, which can give
suggestions how to move troops because they know how
[the] enemy moves their troops. And they have it now on
a very high level. In Baku they have special laboratoriums,
working on how to kill people from a distance. In Almatar
[spelling of names may be wrong] they have a special
laboratory on how to cause heart attacks artificially for
people. They have many different directions of their work.
They have special institutions on how to change the
weather. And you know, in the United States and Europe
with your experience, that they really can make, during
very good weather, instantly three meters of snow on your
streets. They need it for the days of war, to stop your trucks
in the beginning of the war. Now they work in a very
serious way, how to influence brains of people, the thinking
of people. How to make from people dolls [puppets]. They
work in post hypnosis. How to send killers which will kill
people, and they will not know what they do. Post hypnosis
is when someone work like automaton in the hands of
another man which sits in Moscow and can send directions
to the killer in the United States. They have all this under
the governmental level. And it is very serious. They have
professors, and doctors, and hundreds and hundreds of
engineers which work on their equipment. I maybe will give
you one example which they made experiments which they
made not long ago in the Soviet Union. Dr. Ilyushin
invented a special generator which can make powers of
parapsychological individuals more powerful. In the city
Ivanervol they have knitting factories. They have thousands
of women, and they have no men there.

ELENORA SHIFRIN:
This is a city where the population is almost entirely women
and it is a very tragic situation.

AVRAHAM SHIFRIN:
Women without men. And women live in very bad mood
because of this separation. And they put these generators
in this plant. They change depression into happiness and
enthusiasm. They can make artificially either joy or
depression in the United States. They can impress your
soldiers or officers in their underground command staff
rooms, and when you must push on the button to send the
rockets, your officers will not push these buttons. In the
day or in the hours. Because you show on your TV
programs these command staff rooms and faces of these
officers which are responsible for this work with atomic
rockets. When they know these rooms and these faces they
can concentrate their generators on these people and these
men or these people they will be in depression or hesitation
in the hour or in the minute that they must make decisions.
That's why I must tell you that with parapsychology they
make now, the science of the future. And they make special
weapon of the future. And they will work with these
weapons in the days when they will meet. Because they
concentrate all this work in the special secret institutions
under the government and you don't oppose them in the
United States.

ELENORA SHIFRIN:
And what is important to mention that inside the Soviet
Union in order to keep it a complete secret they officially
announced that parapsychology is nonsense, it does not
exist, and they prohibited all open parapsychological
laboratories. They prohibited to work in parapsychology
all those scientists who refused to cooperate with the army
and the KGB in this matter. They arrest them. We now
know the names of dozens of parapsychologists who are
arrested for just studying these problems because they
wanted to study these problems independently, not for the
KGB. And it is very dangerous for them because they
understand that as well as they prepare parapsychological
weapons, people who understand the danger can prepare
parapsychological defense. Therefore they are trying to get
rid of all parapsychologists who are able to prepare defense.

AVRAHAM SHIFRIN:

We now have proofs that when there was no electricity, you remember those days in New York, the blackouts—in 1979. It was the work of the parapsychologists in Russia. The changing of the weather in the United States was their work. I myself have seen experiments of Dr. Romann in the Soviet Union, when he made on himself a heart attack. All the equipment registered it. Then he stopped it and became again healthy.

ELENORA SHIFRIN:

He did it in front of big audience. It was all fixed [observed] on machines (electrocardiogram). It was witnessed by dozens of people.

AVRAHAM SHIFRIN:

They can operate from a long distance, and make heart attacks on people and who knows, if this man was killed or if it was a normal heart attack? When they sent their officials to the White House and sometimes minor officials are sent to the State Departments, to know the rooms and then they participate with clairvoyants in secret meetings of your president in the oval room. They got this news without machinery because the clairvoyants bring them this news. That is why we must be very serious today about parapsychology in the Soviet Union. They make from this a weapon and they will participate in the next war with these weapons.

ELENORA SHIFRIN:

I think it is also very important to mention that even if we believe that a similar research is starting in the United States, if it is kept [a] complete secret the way they do it in the Soviet Union, it may become as dangerous as it is in the Soviet Union. Because also in the United States people who possess this power can use it against their own American population, the way they do it in the Soviet Union. And if it is not checked openly by the public it will become a dangerous weapon in the hands of a very small handful of people in your own country.

AVRAHAM SHIFRIN:

Because it is so dangerous for your democracy if someone

will change your brains, will influence your way of thinking, will make from you dolls [puppets], and it is in defense of [by means of] these generators, parapsychological generators. That's why we must be serious.

ELENORA SHIFRIN:
This knowledge is not new. The ways have always existed. There always [were] some who are witchcraft specialists, all kinds of voodoo doctors. The difference is that they could do it on the individual level and now in the Soviet Union they developed machines that can be handled by people who are personally unable to influence anybody but who can use those machines to influence masses of people.

AVRAHAM SHIFRIN:
For example, we know that they try to influence your senators and congressmen, when they go to vote. And they do it.

KREMLIN ASPIRATIONS FOR PSI WAR

The Soviet military and the Kremlin wish to use PSI-war techniques to spy on U.S. installations, planning meetings, individual's activities, etc. This is to be done either through bio-electronically amplified telepathy (distance viewing) or another technique known as astral projection, which is a very old psychic technique.

They wish to use psychotronic generators with mind-computer links to remotely hypnotize and control important leaders. Further, this "force" will be used to control the mood of masses of people, for example, to cause mental depression.

Using powers similar to voodoo and witchcraft they hope to be able to actually kill people from a remote distance.

Using amplified telekinetic power they seek the ability to disable our weapons systems. Telekinesis is the ability to move physical objects by the power of the mind, without touching the objects physically. If such a thing could be developed, then they could blow up our rocket launches on takeoff by controlling a critical part of the mechanism, or they could prevent ignition of our rockets before takeoff. The former seems most likely, for if they disabled the rocket or craft before takeoff, it could easily be corrected and the launch procedure would continue.

One could think this is all a fantasy, except for the fact that some of our own scientists and military people are taking the matter very seriously.

VOICES FROM THE U.S. MILITARY

Science Digest (May 1984) suggests that the Pentagon is searching for psychic weapons. It seems that some of our military people feel that the way to protect the U.S.A. is to get into the demonic mind war race with the Soviets. *Science Digest* states, "The Soviet Union is believed to spend tens of millions of dollars on the study of psychic abilities, or PSI, while the United States spends little more than $500,000 a year, most of it from private sources and foundations" (p. 38). Citing a 1963 report titled "Research into PSI Phenomena Current Status and Trends of Congressional Concern," it is concluded that PSI force could be useful to the military. The same article cites scientist, Dr. Russell Targ (co-author of the book *Mind Race*) as saying that a conference for which he spoke in Alexandria, Virginia, was attended by "plenty of the military." The article further tells of PSI experiments conducted at SRI (formerly Stanford Research Institute) in Menlo Park, California. SRI is one of our nation's major "think tanks."

Omni, an avant-garde monthly science magazine, has a slick, expensive, if rather bizarre appearance. *Omni* for April 1984, published "Psychic Warriors" by Ronald M. McRae. The author cites the December 1980 edition of *Military Review,* the professional journal of the United States Army, which contained an article titled "The New Mental Battlefield: Beam Me Up Spock" by Lieutenant Colonel John B. Alexander. Although the editor of *Military Review* attached a humorous title to the article, Alexander, the author, was taking the matter very seriously. He tells of "weapons systems (now in existence) that operate on the power of the mind and whose lethal capacity has already been demonstrated." Lethal capacity—the power to kill by mind force! Alexander also wrote of causing disease or death for no apparent cause (from remote distances) and of spying by PSI force. *Omni* author McRae states, "There are individuals in top defense posts who take psychic warfare very seiously which is why psychic research may get as much as $6 million annually. Reliable figures are unavailable, in part because much of the research is hidden in the secret intelligence budget and in part because even unclassified programs are disguised."

WITCH AND OCCULT POWER

McRae claims to possess documentation that a fortune-teller, known as Madame Zodiak, was employed along with at least 34 other psychics to track Soviet submarines. Should America be dabbling in these psychic pools of demonic powers? My answer is no. Our solution to the defense dilemma is unusual but entirely believable to the born-again Christian. At this point let me simply say that I do not think we should be fighting demon power with demon power.

A 1972 report of the U.S. Defense Intelligence Agency came to similar conclusions as have been mentioned, that the Soviets are developing mind weapons which "sooner or later might enable the Russians to do some of the following:" (Without quoting exactly I will summarize.) Mind power (PSI) could be used for spying, remote hypnosis, killing people and disabling U.S. military equipment—including spacecraft.

A later study published by the DIA in 1978 indicated that PSI weapons in the Soviet Union "would pose a severe threat to enemy military embassy, or security functions."

McRae's article in *Omni* states that "in 1981, the Air Force seriously considered buying 'psychic shields' for its missile crewmen. The shields, produced by a member of the USPA (United States Psychotronic Association) would be *activated by a drop of blood or a lock of hair from the bearer.*" (Emphasis added.) That last phrase is descriptive of what takes place in many witchcraft "spells" which involve the use of blood, hair or other organic matter from the subject. The long feature article in *Omni* further cites military people, CIA personnel, and White House staff members, etc.

On January 17, 1984, a weekly T.V. program, "Nova," was released on the National Public Broadcasting System (PBS) which explored "*The Case of ESP.*" The narrator and several of the participants suggested the possible military uses of psychic mind-force. The narrator said, "The U.S. is not the only nation where psychic powers are being explored as potentially useful tools. Russian scientists have studied several subjects who claimed to have extraordinary psychokinetic abilities. Nina Kulagina could reportedly move small objects without touching them...studies by the United States Defense Intelligence Agency conclude that the Soviets may be exploring the use of psychic powers to control people's behaviour." From this point the discussion launched into the field of military application of PSI-force. A complete transcript of the "Nova" telecast can be obtained for $3.00 by writing to: "Nova—WBGH Transcripts," 125 Western Avenue, Boston, Massachusetts 02134.

The United States Psychotronics Association, Inc., recently held its annual conference from June 27 to July 1. One of the topics discussed by speaker Tom Bearden was "Soviet Weather Engineering over the USA" and "Update on Soviet Psychotronic Weapons." Ron McRae and Sue Merrow further explore this subject in Jack Anderson's magazine, *The Investigator—Views Behind the News*. The article "Psychic Warfare" cites retired Lt. Col. Thomas E. Bearden claiming that "the Russians have already deployed third-generation psychotronic weapons. These include the 'photonic barrie modulator' which can induce death or illness from thousands of mi' away...."

What I am sharing with you is not hidden in a dark corner. You have read about psychotronic warfare in popular columns in the great daily newspapers of America, in articles written by well-known journalists.

Jack Anderson wrote a series of articles on the subject. In a column titled "The Race for Inner Space" Anderson says: "U.S. intelligence agencies won't talk about it, but they are rushing to catch up with the Soviet Union in what one scientist jocularly calls 'the race for inner space'—psychic research...The CIA and the Pentagon have an obvious interest in this phenomenon. If they could get psychics to throw their minds behind the Iron Curtain, there'd be no need to risk the lives of human agents. The CIA sent representatives to a parapsychology conference in Virginia...In fact, the CIA is now seriously pondering the possibility of raising 'psychic shields' to keep Soviet remote viewers away from our secrets. I asked my skeptical associates Dale Van Atta and Joseph Spear to find out how remote reviewing has become almost universally accepted in the intelligence community. They gained access to top-secret briefings on the subject." Anderson then proceeds to describe what they discovered about the CIA's code-named *Project Grill Flame*. According to Jack Anderson, the results of the project were impressive.

In another column, "Secret Psychic Research," Anderson states, "In past columns I have reported on secret projects to adapt psychic phenomena to military purposes. For example, in laboratory experiments, psychics have been used to spy on the Soviets by *projecting their minds out of their bodies*." (Emphasis added.) This last phrase describes an ages-old demonic practice known as "astral projection." Anyone who is at all familiar with the occult will recognize this terminology. Anderson claims that Congressman Charles Rose of North Carolina was an advocate supporting legislature which would (if passed) encourage "research into the more promising areas of this mysterious field."

William J. Broad, who writes for the *New York Times,* stated that "The Pentagon has spent millions of dollars, according to new reports on secret projects to investigate extra-sensory phenomena and to see if the sheer power of the human mind can be harnessed to perform acts of espionage and war." The William Broad column also claims that Charlie Rose, "a member of the Select Committee on Intelligence," has promoted research in the area of "mind-war" techniques.

In a letter to one of our correspondents, Congressman Don Sundquist (Tennessee) confirms Charles Rose's interest in PSI war studies:

> Dear Morton:
> Thank you for writing me regarding your concern over

our government's psychic research. It was good to hear from you.

I contacted the House Select Committee on Intelligence and learned that Congressman Rose is no longer a member of that Committee. Apparently during Congressman Rose's tenure on the Committee, he did sponsor legislation calling for studies in para-psychology, but I can assure you that no occult worship studies or aid to these groups is currently in operation.

Sundquist confirms past interest and activity that has existed in the field of para-psychology. Our research and that of a number of others indicates that this activity is on-going.

The documentation in our bulging files is so extensive that we can only give you a "tip of the iceberg" glimpse of it.

Combat Arms (May 1985), a paramilitary "Journal of Defense Technology" has Edith Kermit Roosevelt's article "Psychic Warfare" beginning on page 76. The subtitle of the article proclaims "Advanced parapsychology techniques may lead to brain wars and mind control!"

An extremely important article appeared in *Omni,* August 1985, titled "PSI Soldiers in the Kremlin" by Douglas Starr and E. Patrick McQuaid. The authors claim "They labor in the bowels of government labs, searching for waves to harness the mind." These authors are initially skeptical. When we note their final conclusions we are forced to take this material very seriously. This well-documented article was prompted by an interview with physicist August Stern, who was previously a researcher in a Soviet military laboratory. He is an eyewitness to some very weird experiments with the power of the mind. The authors tell of Kruschev's trip through India and how deeply he was impressed by the Hindu yogis. He said, "We will have our own yogi—tomorrow."

New American Magazine, October 1985, devotes its entire front cover to promoting the article "ESPionage—the K.G.B. and the CIA Are Thinking About Psychic Power." The author, Edith Kermit Roosevelt, is a former United Press International reporter, and currently specializes in Science Journalism. Roosevelt cites Dr. Robert G. Jahn, Dean of Princeton's School of Engineering/Applied Science, as speculating that ESP could have implications on high technology with the potential of "disturbance of the memory function of a single micro-electronic chip." The Central Intelligence Agency (CIA) sponsored a study which was executed by Airesearch Manufacturing of California. The finished report was titled *Novel Bio-Physic Information Transfer Mechanisms* (NABIT). This study suggests that

Soviets are involved in PSI research involving mental patients as well as adept parapsychologists. "The Russians may be implementing the next logical step—to reinforce psychic functioning in certain gifted individuals after having discovered the basic communication carriers." This report is cited extensively in the *New American* (December 1985).

The Soviets are, no doubt, developing the ultimate weapon, demonically empowered psychotronic generators, using the human mind as a channel. With the human brain linked to a computer and with PSI generators amplifying the powers being channeled, the potential results are truly awesome. No wonder Revelation chapter 9 speaks of demon armies being loosed from the pit to wreak their havoc upon all mankind.

POWER OF THE HUMAN MIND?

I do not believe that the human mind alone has the power to accomplish all the Soviets hope to do with the mind war machines. The final Antichrist gets his power from the dragon (Satan) as we read earlier in Revelation 13:2. The human mind is just a channel for this demonic power.

Is the situation hopeless? What can be done to stop this frightful menace? What about our own U.S. military being involved in the mind war? The next chapter offers the Christian answer to the mind wars.

CHAPTER 25

GOD'S ANSWER TO PSYCHOTRONIC WEAPONS
Victory in the Mind War

Our nation does need supernatural defense, but we do not need a psychic bag of tricks. It is tragic to think that some of our military leaders are trying to harness powers which are demonic to combat the demonic powers flowing through the Soviet Union's military establishment. Do not be tricked into thinking we can use white magic to combat black magic.

ROAD TO ENDOR

King Saul was a popular military and political leader in ancient Israel. Strong-willed, he often acted contrary to the will of God. Finally he got to the place where he was totally out of touch with the Lord. Having experienced supernatural guidance from God in the past, he desired supernatural leading on a continuing basis. Since God was angry and not answering him, he decided to go to the witch (para-psychological medium) of the town of Ein Dor (Endor). When the celebrated poet Rudyard Kipling read of Saul's tragic adventure in First Samuel chapter twenty-eight he wrote:

> The road to Endor is the oldest road
>   And the craziest road of all.
> Straight it leads to the witch's abode

As it did in the days of Saul.
And nothing has changed of the sorrow in store
For those who go down on the road to Endor.

Rudyard Kipling

Tragic will be the results if the USA depends on demon power to defend us. We will end up deluded and defeated.

OUR GLORIOUS HERITAGE

Our nation was founded by people seeking religious freedom. They frequently expressed their dependence on God. In times of crisis our early leaders often called upon the Lord in supplication for His deliverance. Let's not throw away our heritage. In the face of the mind war threat we believers must bind together to rebuke and cancel the evil energies beamed out of the USSR. We must also call on God to set our own leaders straight. They must not lead us down the road to Endor. Saul's excursion into the paranormal realm of demons brought tragic defeat to Israel and death to himself. Satan would like to seduce and then slaughter us.

SPIRITUAL WARFARE

Here is the place and now is the time to put our beliefs to the test. We have long talked about spiritual warfare, and with good cause. The cause now is more overwhelming than ever. Never mind that it seems overwhelming, for "greater is He that is within you than he that is in the world."

No doubt secular humanists in the military establishment look with horror on what the Soviets are trying to do. No star wars nor high frontier defense would be effective in a mind war. There seems to be no defense possible without a counter effort which would harness the same mind powers the Soviets are trying to control and amplify with neurophones, magneto encephalograms, and psychotronic generators. Admittedly, we need a defense against these diabolical assaults against our nation, but what should be the nature of our defense?

WARFARE BEYOND THE MILITARY

In the beginning of this book we outlined the Daniel Factor as a three-fold ncept involving knowledge, intercession, and action as the means to end- e victory. We are fulfilling a watchman role in declaring this knowledge e body of Christ. "Thus hath the Lord said unto me, go set a nan...Let him declare what he seeth" (Isaiah 21:6). Now is the time for intercession. Now is the time for action. Now is the time for you to get involved in Holy Spirit World Liberation. This is war and it is war in the pure spiritual sense. That is why the only possible defense will come from the Church and not from the Pentagon.

We can act within the framework of the known will of God to bind Satan and to cancel his diabolical plan as long as the Church is here as God's restraining force. We must get involved for "We wrestle not against flesh and blood but [we wrestle] against principalities, against powers, against the rulers of the darkness of this world, against spiritual wickedness in high places" (Ephesians 6:12). The phrase "spiritual wickedness" is better translated "against wicked spirits."

This is an arena of conflict with which the military is not familiar, but the Church does not have trouble marching to war in this realm. We have been educated by the Word and the Holy Spirit for battle in this theatre of war. Not only we can, but we must prevail here. There is no other hope.

Misled military leaders talk about erecting psychic shields for the protection of our soldiers and missile men. As noted in the previous chapter these psychic shields will be activated by a drop of blood or a lock of hair from the individual to be protected. This is sheer witchcraft, but there is a different kind of shield that God's word speaks of with approval. "Above all, taking the shield of faith, wherewith ye shall be able to quench all the fiery darts of the wicked" (Ephesians 6:16). How fiery are the darts of the devil, but by using the proper shield we shall quench them all. The shield of faith is our protection.

Almighty God, we call on You now. Help us in this hour of danger. We seek only to know and do Your will. Cancel Satan's assignments against us. Put a shield around each believer, around the Church, and around our nation. Protect us from the demonic weapons of demented minds and diabolical machines. Thank you Heavenly Father, in the name of our Lord Jesus Christ, that we know Your power is greater than that of the devil and his servants. Amen.

THE GREAT SHIELD

"When the enemy shall come in like a flood, the Spirit of the Lord shall lift up a standard [Hebrew *Magen,* meaning shield] against him" (Isaiah 59:19).

I have heard people argue over where the comma should be placed in Isaiah 59:19. Some say it should read "When the enemy comes in, like a floc the Spirit of the Lord shall lift up a standard against him." Others say, it should read, "When the enemy comes in like a flood, the Spirit of Lord shall lift up a standard against him." What difference does it m

We already know that the power of God is superior to that of Satan. Don't look at the comma! Look at the fact that when Satan attacks, God's Spirit raises up a shield to protect us from the merciless onslaught. The word translated "standard" in the passage is "magen" in the original Hebrew and means "a shield." It is the same word translated "shields" in Psalm 47:9:

> O Clap your hands, all ye people; shout unto God with the voice of triumph. For the Lord most high is terrible; he is a great King over all the earth. He shall subdue the people under us, and the nations under our feet. He shall choose our inheritance for us, the excellency of Jacob whom he loved. Selah.
>
> God is gone up with a shout, the Lord with the sound of a trumpet. Sing praises to God, sing praises: sing praises unto our King, sing praises. For God is the King of all the earth: sing ye praises with understanding. God reigneth over the heathen: God sitteth upon the throne of his holiness. The princes of the people are gathered together, even the people of the God of Abraham: for the shields of the earth belong unto God: he is greatly exalted.
>
> Psalm 47:1-9

Think of it! "The shields of the earth belong unto God." Shoddy witchcraft psychic shields need a drop of blood from the user for activation. Our shield was activated by the blood of our Saviour on Calvary where He paid the supreme price for our redemption and protection. Just as some action, some act of your will, is necessary to receive the cleansing of His blood for salvation, even so faith and prayer are necessary to obtain all of God's protective power for these strange times.

The apostle Paul shares a great New Testament truth with us that is very important for our participation in defeating demonic forces being harnessed for the enslavement of humanity today:

> For though we walk in the flesh, we do not war after the flesh: (For the weapons of our warfare are not carnal, but mighty through God to the pulling down of strongholds;) Casting down imaginations, and every high thing that exalteth itself against the knowledge of God, and bringing into captivity every thought to the obedience of Christ; And having in a readiness to revenge all disobedience, when your obedience is fulfilled.
>
> 2 Corinthians 10:3-6

WILL IT WORK?

What if not enough people get involved? What if it doesn't work? What about all the apathy in the Church?

Gideon led 32,000 men to battle, but sent 31,700 of them home because they could not pass the fear and apathy tests. "Go home, sit by the fireplace, and eat popcorn. We three hundred will protect you—with the help of God." Gideon's tiny band was the instrument in the hand of God that dealt defeat to the enemies of Israel. See Judges 6,7.

God sometimes used marchers-around-the-walls, tambourine players, trumpet blowers, dancers, shouters, and praisers to go ahead of the army. Look out devil, here comes the Church of God marching down the road of time. Devil, you are doomed! We know that in the end we win (we read the last page of the Book), and some of us are finding out that we can bind and defeat you right here and now. We know that the final binding will be when you encounter Jesus, but devil look out for the awakening Church! We have taken all of your harrassment we are going to put up with. For too long you have sold us a pack of lies about how weak we are.

How the devil would like to make fatalists out of all God's children. How he loves for us to only look at the negative side of prophecy. Satan would love to promote faith in reverse, or negative faith. He knows God will give us what we believe Him for. Satan wants us to lose hope for "faith is the substance of things *hoped for.*" He wants us to take a "what will be will be" attitude, but we are now serving notice on Satan. We declare war, in Jesus' name, on the dark powers. We intercede for and confess victory in the psychotronic war in the name of Jesus, and for the glory of God!

Christian intercession, not physical arms nor use of dark power, is God's answer in this battle. Prayer alone can prevail. This is purely spiritual warfare and only God-appointed spiritual weapons will bring us the victory.

CHAPTER 26

WILL THERE BE AN ATOMIC WAR? THE DAY AFTER

Mushroom clouds rising above Kansas City! People running madly through the streets trying to escape—but there is nowhere to go! Devastation unheard of and unimaginable! Mankind without hope....

The ABC TV movie *The Day After* shocked this nation. Scenes of the apocalypse are painted vividly on the canvas of our minds. Jesus' words, "Men's hearts failing them for fear and for looking after those things which are coming on the earth" are coming to pass. The Lord prefaced this observation with "upon the earth distress of nations with perplexity, the sea and the waves (gentile nations) roaring" (Luke 21:25,26). The Lord's council to believers is very clear in this same chapter, "But when ye shall hear of wars and commotions, be not terrified: for these things must first come to pass" (Verse 9).

POINT OF VIEW

It is clear that the producers of the movie have political ambitions and wish to back the philosophy of the nuclear freeze movement. This makes me ve uneasy as we have pointed out in other publications that the so-called "pe movement" has ties to, and in some cases, is manipulated by the Sov

The communists want us to accept a position of despair. They want this country to be gripped with a feeling of hopelessness. Then there are those Americans who truly feel that it is better to "be red than dead," and it would be better to disarm unilaterally and let the communists conclude their move toward world domination. A better slogan would be *"neither red nor dead."* We can believe and act to ensure end-time victory for the Church and a preservation of our nation with freedom for all.

One hundred million Americans saw the movie *The Day After*. The impact of this powerful film is bound to have long lasting effects on the American psyche. After the film, well planned talk shows were all geared up to mobilize public opinion. The well orchestrated discussion continues. Rallies were held all over the country following the film showing on ABC. At Riverside Church in New York a large crowd saw the picture. After the film a weeping, stunned audience was shown on a TV special. One emotional speaker cried out, "We've got to stop this." The movie was not seen in Russia. In Lawrence, Kansas, the scene of much of the movie, a group of 1,500 held a candlelight meeting. All over Europe many who had not even seen the film (as well as some who had) held "peace" rallies, notable for their anti-West, anti-USA bias.

A Cable News Network commentator, Daniel Shorr, pointed out that the movie blamed the USA for the global catastrophe. It was clearly stated that the first atomic weapons used were US Pershing missiles. This is the type of missile that has been deployed in Europe by the USA and our allies. The bias of the movie makers seems quite clear. I hope I am not misjudging them, but I cannot escape my conclusion. The world view seems pretty hopeless.

WHY ARMAGEDDON?

There is another point of view. It is that of the Christian who believes that God has a plan for this planet. God will not allow man to finally and totally destroy all human life on this earth. Man will be allowed to go only so far, then God will intervene. Armageddon is not an exercise of wanton slaughter as some have supposed, but is a rescue program to prevent total destruction of life on earth. The Lord is depicted as destroying the earth destroyers (Revelation 12:18b). Jesus said that "except those days should be shortened (literally: strictly limited) there should no flesh be saved" (Matthew 24:22). It must be recognized that the Biblical concept of the end of the age is a rebuke to the person who rejects God's Word.

ON'T BE PLEASING TO THE UNBELIEVER

is point of view is going to produce hostility in the heart of the non-

Christian. The Bible indicates that there will be a growing hostility between the secular humanists (which movement culminates in the enthronement of the beast of Revelation, the Antichrist) and the believers, the followers of our Lord Jesus Christ. How the secularist bristles when he hears a word concerning the judgment of God upon a rebellious human race! "For this cause," the Bible says, "your good shall be evil spoken of." However, Christians are not altogether faultless in the way our views have been presented. The day after the showing of the *Day After* I listened to a Christian radio station. A call-in talk show was in progress. A young man called with the comment that the movie did not frighten him—after all, he was ready to go to heaven, so what did it matter if he went in a puff of atomic vapor? It is no wonder that such a view is repugnant not only to worldly minded people but to thinking Christians as well. God has not called us to escapism, fatalism nor irresponsibility. We are not to live selfishly unto ourselves. We are responsible for the quality of life right here and now.

IT WILL HAPPEN

Here is the rub. This is the place we come to strong disagreement with the non-believer. *The great devastation of earth is coming.* I cannot be dogmatic, but I think the scenes depicted in the book of Revelation are a picture of atomic war. We read of over 50% of earth's population dying in a short period of time (less than seven years) from wars, plagues, famines, and personal violence. A third of the green grass and a third of the trees are burned up. Rivers and seas are polluted. Men flee to the dens and the caves, and so horrible is the day that they call for the rocks and the mountains to fall upon them. Death is preferable to the awful conditions on earth.

A prominent senator said some years ago in a speech that man now had it in his power to fulfil the plagues of the apocalypse without the intervention of the Almighty. I reread the book of Revelation with that thought in mind. With certain exceptions, it would seem that his comments are potentially accurate.

WHERE, THEN, IS HOPE?

The element of hope is two-fold. First, we believe God has a plan for us that will be realized. His Kingdom will not fail. Secondly, we can restrain evil in this present age by means of spiritual warfare (prayer). We believe that the Lord will remove the Church prior to the seven years of the fir devastation. Don't think that this is final proof that we will esc persecutions, famines, earthquakes or even atomic war *before the ra* *of the Church.* If the Church acts in an irresponsible way, if we fail t the forces of evil through intercessory prayer, terrible consequences could be rained upon the world even before the final Tribulation. In the chapter "Agenda for Victory" we point out that God has a victory program available for the Church, but it is not inevitable. While the final outcome is assured, there are many variant paths we can trod toward the climax of the age. We can hold the forces of destruction at bay *if we have the will to do so*. God ever seeks a person to intercede that destruction should not come upon the land (Ezekiel 22:30).

Destruction is the result of mankind's rebellion against or neglect of the will of God (Ezekiel 22:30). When God lamented in Ezekiel's day that there was no one found to intercede, we read of His fury outpoured because of man's rebellion (Ezekiel 20:33-38 and Ezekiel 22:31). While these words apply to ancient Israel the principle involved applies to any age, including our own.

PEACE OR ARMAGEDDON

Of course Armageddon is coming, but it has been coming for nineteen centuries. No one called you to be a promoter of Armageddon. We are followers of the Prince of Peace, the Lord Jesus Christ. By effectual and fervent prayer we will stay the demons of destruction. By our good works we will contribute whatever we can to the quality of life in this age.

THE NATIONS' RIGHT TO DEFENSE

No one should think that I am advocating the nuclear freeze movement or the secularist red-oriented "peace movement." Dispensationalists tell us that in the age of human government God gave society the right to police itself and governments the right to defend their national interests. I agree with that concept. The greatest tragedy of our times would be to disarm with the naive hope that the Soviets would do the same and not attack us. That would be the very best way to insure that there would be an atomic war, or that there would be a red takeover of the Western world. Our freedom would be lost either way. The only way to survive is through strength. The Soviets believe in their doctrine of the inevitability of conquest. They will do everything in their power to conquer us. They are driven by the demon "god of forces."

‍HEN RESTRAINT IS REMOVED

‍timate evil is loosed on the earth when the restraining force described ‍ apostle Paul in 2 Thessalonians, chapter two, is removed. Since that force is removed simultaneously with the removal of the Church (rapture), it is logical to conclude that what is removed is the Church empowered by the Holy Spirit. The Spirit is not removed from the earth since He is omnipresent, God. We have examined this subject at length earlier and merely mention it here.

None of this makes the slightest bit of sense to the unbeliever or the secular humanist, but to the believer who knows the Author of the Book, it is comprehensible. My word to the non-Christian is, your only ultimate escape is by accepting Jesus Christ as your personal Saviour. Then you are prepared for anything.

Furthermore, the Christian who disagrees with the pre-tribulation rapture concept should not have any great problem with the general theme we are presenting. You can still practice your survivalism (not a bad idea for pre-tribulationists as well) to be prepared for any calamity, pre-trib or whatever. You pre-tribulationists can see that I do not accept your extreme views and attitudes of escapism either, even though I accept the doctrinal position. The biggest problem I have with the post-tribulationist is the sense of defeatism you could accept. My biggest problem with pre-tribulationists is the tendency toward escapism.

THEY DON'T HAVE TO HATE US

Those secularists who reject our eschatological (end-time) views can still co-exist with us as long as we occupy the planet together. We respect your right to believe whatever you want. We are determined to improve the quality of life as long as we are here. We have no desire to die in an atomic funeral pyre. We are not lusting for Armageddon. We are grieved at the rebellion of man that will finally cause God to remove restraint and allow man's hate to wreak its havoc on the earth. The cup of iniquity is almost full. Our great desire is that there will be a mighty worldwide revival, that millions will enter the kingdom of God through the new birth and insure a degree of tranquility until the trumpet of God sounds the end of the age. Then the dark power will be unleashed for a short time. Even then, after the Rapture, in His mercy God will insure the salvation of millions of souls through the witness of the 144,000 believing Israelites who will be powerful to declare His word in earth's darkest hour. A multitude no man can number will be brought to God through the service rendered by the 144,000 (Revelation chapter 7). Yes, there will be believers (saints) on the earth during the Tribulation. This is a tragic yet triumphant picture in the last book of the Bible. The beast of Revelation (Antichrist) makes war against the saints and he "overcomes them." (See Revelation 13:7.) It seems that this could be the Church, for the Church is commanded to overcome evil. The gist of 1 John 5:5 is that all born-again people in the Church are overcomers, through faith in our Lord Jesus Christ. So the saints of the time of great global trauma (Tribulation) are people saved after the rapture of the Church.

If you disagree with all this, don't be hostile. We will work for a better world as long as we are here, but we offer you a hope beyond this age as well. Shouldn't you consider what we have to say?

Let me summarize: 1.) We live in dangerous times. "This know also that in the last days perilous times shall come...men shall...despise those that are good...resist the truth...reprobate concerning the faith...their folly shall be manifest" (2 Timothy 3:1-9).

2.) There *may* be atomic war before the Rapture. Intercessors can prevent it if they have the will and the vision to do so.

3.) In the Tribulation (as the Bible describes) there will be a time of planetary devastation of unbelievable proportions. It is my opinion that atomic warfare is what the book of Revelation describes.

4.) The only way to be ready for the end times is to find a personal relationship with Jesus Christ—that is to be saved, born again.

5.) Since No. 2 (above) is possible—Christians would be wise to learn how to survive in a time of great distress. Do not take an escapist view. We do not know whether the Church will take the matter of intercession seriously or not.

6.) My personal point of view is that the Church is waking up. It is my strong hope and belief that we will *not* face atomic war before the Rapture, but I cannot guarantee this. We have serious choices set before us.

7.) What will *you* do about it?

CHAPTER 27

RESTRAINING EVIL

This chapter is for pre-tribulationists only. If this is offensive to you, please do not read this chapter. If you can handle it (the fact that this author believes in a pre-tribulation rapture) you still might get some good out of it, but I do not want my post-tribulational brethren to think that I am fighting with them. We are allies, not enemies. We have a difference of opinion, but we will not fight over it. We have too much in common and too much is at stake.

I believe that the restrainer in 2 Thessalonians, chapter two, is the Church. It is the presence of God's salt and light people that prevents the final manifestation of ultimate human evil, the appearance of the very man of sin, the son of perdition (Antichrist).

Traditionally it has been taught that the Holy Spirit is the restrainer. That is not exactly correct, it is only partially right. The Church has no power apart from the Holy Spirit. However, we cannot accept statements like, "When the Holy Spirit is removed from the world...."

THE HOLY SPIRIT IS OMNIPRESENT

One of the immutable attributes of God is that He is omnipresent is present at all times, everywhere, in every state of relativity and

How could the third person of the Godhead not be omnipresent? How could the Holy Spirit be "removed" from the world? I suppose the Psalmist David would be thought to be an awful extremist for saying, "Whither shall I go from thy spirit? or whither shall I flee from thy presence? If I ascend up into heaven, thou art there; If I make my bed in hell, behold thou art there" (Psalm 139:7, 8). The Holy Spirit has always been here. He was present at creation. He anointed men of God, prophets and priests in Old Testament days.

A CHANGE AT PENTECOST AND THE RAPTURE

Beginning with the day of Pentecost the Holy Spirit began to do unique things on earth. Using the Church as a vehicle of restraint against the forces of Antichrist is one of those Church Age ministries of the Spirit of God.

This aspect of the Holy Spirit's work will end when the Church is removed (raptured) at the end of this age. Then all hell breaks loose on this earth. Still, the Holy Spirit is here working in the tribulation period. He anoints the 144,000. They are "sealed" (a work of the spirit—Ephesians 1:13). After their witness is given there is the conversion of a multitude of Gentiles (Revelation 7). There is no salvation apart from the administrative work of the Holy Spirit. The Holy Spirit anoints the two mighty witnesses during the Tribulation (Revelation 11).

WHAT IS REMOVED?

In 2 Thessalonians, chapter two, we read of a hindering force that prevents the man of sin from being revealed. The mystery of iniquity (conspiracy of anarchy) is already at work in the secular world, the New Age Movement, etc., but the Antichrist cannot be revealed until something is removed. My purpose is not to solve the pre-mid-post Tribulation question, but I admit that I am a pre-tribulationist. This is not stated in a pugilistic manner. I am not disturbed at all if you disagree with me on this point, but I must make my following statement from my viewpoint as a pre-tribulationist. However, the principles involved apply to anyone who accepts any of these rapture concepts. The principle is that we are to resist Satan, we are to be a part of God's restraining force as long as we are here in this world, prior to the Rapture. Post-tribulationists will not give up the spiritual warfare if they are right and we go through the Tribulation. We will all agree to battle Satan's forces as long as we are here—in whatever era we find ourselves.

Pre-tribulationists will be interested in the John Lineberry translation and Kenneth Wuest translation of 2 Thessalonians, chapter two. Here is the Lineberry translation:

Now we are begging you, brethren, concerning the coming of our Lord Jesus Christ and our gathering together to (meet) Him. To the end that you be not quickly shaken from your mind (sober sense), nor yet be constantly troubled, neither by spirit (pretended prophecy or revelation), nor by word (pretended statement from Paul), nor by letter (pretended epistle or forged letter) as by us, as that the Day of the Lord has come (and) is here (now). Do not begin to let any one beguile you in any way (according to any manner or fashion), because *the day will not come (Day of the Lord)*, except there come the departure (Rapture of the Church) first, and the man of the lawlessness be revealed (unveiled, uncovered), the son of the perdition (eternal misery, doom, and destruction). He who opposes and exalts himself above (and) against every one that is called a god or an object of worship; so that he himself sits down, (takes his seat and keeps on sitting), in the temple of God, perpetually proclaiming that he himself is God. Do you not call to mind that, being yet with you, these things I kept on telling to you? In fact, now what is restraining (Antichrist) you know absolutely, to the end that he himself might be revealed in his (appointed, set, or suitable) time. For the mystery of the lawlessness already is working, only until he who is even now restraining be taken (removed) out of the way (midst). And then shall be revealed the Lawless One, whom the Lord (Jesus) shall slay (put out of the way) by means of the breath of His mouth and shall destroy (render inoperative, do away with) by means of the appearance of His coming (Second Advent). *Even him* whose coming is according to the working of Satan, in the sphere of every king of power and signs and wonders of falsehood (which is of such a nature as to be conscious and intentional). And in the sphere of every deceit of unrighteousness for those who are perishing, because the love of Truth they did not welcome, in order that they might be saved. And on this account, God is sending to them a working of error (an active power of misleading) to the end that they should believe the lie (the conscious, intentional falsehood of Satan). In order that they, all (of them), might be judged, who did not believe the Truth, but took pleasure in the unrighteousness.

Lineberry translates apostasia in its original sense as "departure" (2 Thessalonians 2:3). This refers to the rapture of the Church. In his commentary on 2 Thessalonians, Lineberry capably defends this position. With this Wuest agrees. In *The New Testament, an Expanded Translation* by Kenneth S. Wuest, 2 Thessalonians 2:3-4 is translated as follows:

> Do not begin to allow anyone to lead you astray in any way, because the day shall not come except the aforementioned departure (of the Church to heaven) comes first and the man of lawlessness is disclosed (in his true identity), the son of perdition, he who sets himself in opposition to and exalts himself above everyone and everything that is called a god or that is an object of worship, so that he seats himself in the inner sanctuary of God, proclaiming himself to be deity.

Dr. Roy Hicks, General Supervisor of the Foursquare Gospel Churches comments further on the translation of apostasia as a departure: "I have had the privilege of consulting several Bibles from the fifteenth century. Some of them present 2 Thessalonians 2:3 as follows:"

> Let no man deceive you by any meanes for (that day shall not come), except there come a departing first, and that that man of sinne be disclosed, (even the sonne of perdition... (Geneva Bible)

> Let no man deceave you by eny meanes, for the Lorde shall not come excepte there come a departynge fyrst, and that synful man be opened, the sonne of perdicyon...(Great Bible).

> Let no man deceave you by eny meanes, for the Lorde commeth not, excepte ther come a departinge fyrst, and that that synfull man be opened, the sonne of perdicion... (Tyndale).

Hicks continues: In The New Testament—an Expanded Translation, Mr. Wuest translates 2 Thessalonians 2:3 as follows:

> Do not begin to allow anyone to lead you astray in any way, because that day shall not come except the aforementioned departure (of the Church to heaven) comes first and the man of lawlessness is disclosed (in his true identity). the man of perdition...

The definite article occuring before the word apostasia makes it apply to a particular departure, one known to the writer and the recipients of the letter. John Dawson, A.B., indicates that apostasia means a departure from any place. The following is a list of others who use the word departure:

> Coverdale (1535), Crammer (1539), Beza (1565), the Rev. J. R. Major, M.A. (1831), John James, L.L.D. (1825), Robert Baker, Breechers Bible (1615), John Parkhurst (1851) Lexicon; London—'Properly, a departure,' Robert Scott (1811-1887), Oxford Press—'Second meaning: Departure; disappearance.' James Donnegan, M.D., Greek/English Lexicon, and The Amplified Bible, New Testament footnote.

These excellent Greek scholars and commentators give us sufficient evidence to know of a certainty that this Greek word apostasia can be rightfully translated in more ways than one; 'departure' best fits into this context." (Dr. Roy Hicks: *Another Look at the Rapture*. Harrison House, 1982 Tulsa, pp. 47-49).

Regardless of the correct translation of the word "apostasia" (the concept does not depend on this point), we note that the man of sin cannot be revealed while the restraining force is present. Some have said that the Holy Spirit will be removed and the Church left here. That is monstrous. Jesus said, "And I shall pray the Father, and he shall give you another Comforter, that he may abide with you forever; Even the Spirit of truth" (John 14:16-17).

What then does God use to restrain evil in this present age? Is there sufficient body of Scripture to clearly identify the restraining force?

THE CHURCH AS RESTRAINER

Believers are commanded "Submit yourself therefore to God. *Resist the devil and he will flee from you*" (James 4:7). We wrestle against the dark powers (Ephesians 6:12). Our warfare and weapons are described as being spiritual and "Mighty through God to the pulling down of strongholds." Note *our* warfare. We are commanded to bind the forces of darkness, to make war as "good soldiers of Jesus Christ." Note the following: Ephesians 6:11-17; 2 Corinthians 10:3-6; 1 Timothy 18-20, 6:12; 2 Timothy 2:3-4 4:7, 4:18; Matthew 16:19, 18:18; Philemon 1:2; Philippians 1:27-30 a 1 Peter 5:9.

The Church is the army of God. We are commanded to make war as the powers of hell. We are assured that the gates of hell cannot prevail the Church.

This warrier concept solves the problem of the restrainer being masculine in 2 Thessalonians, chapter two, whereas the Church is generally described as the feminine Bride of Christ (2 Corinthians 11:2, etc.). The Church is indeed a bride in the love relationship with the Lord Jesus Christ. But the Church is masculine in its warring relationship to the God-hating world we live in. We go forth "terrible as an army with banners."

Whatever your position on the Rapture in relation to the Tribulation, let's agree to lay that aside, and join ranks as we battle the powers of Antichrist *as long as we are here*, however long or short a time that may be.

Friends, if the very presence of the Church is the vehicle of restraint used by the Holy Spirit to hinder the appearance of the Antichrist, think of what could be done if we would begin to *consciously* restrain the forces of darkness. What if we truly unite, in the Spirit and in intercession to put the enemy to flight? How would this affect end-time victory? Rather than give in to defeatism and gloom, we will rise up as men and women of God and take a stand for Jesus in the face of the greatest onslaught of evil the world has ever known. We can do it, and we can win the battle of the end times. Don't wait for Armageddon. Do it now.

CHAPTER 28

FROM HERE TO ETERNITY

Planet Earth is under observation. The angelic hosts look on and are interested in the progress of events in this world.

> We have become a spectacle to the world—a show in the world's amphitheatre—with both men and angels as spectators.
>
> 1 Corinthians 4:9, Amplified Translation

> Likewise, I say unto you, there is joy in the presence of the angels of God over one sinner that repenteth.
>
> Luke 15:10

> But ye are come unto Mount Sion, and unto the city of the living God, the heavenly Jerusalem, and to an innumerable company of angels.
>
> Hebrews 12:22

> I charge thee before God, and the Lord Jesus Christ, and the elect angels, that thou observe these things....
>
> 1 Timothy 5:21

The prophet Daniel interpolates an interesting Chaldean word into his prophecies. The angelic beings are called "eer" (Chaldean) and is translated "watchers" in the King James. Watcher or observer is the correct translation. (See Daniel 4:13,17,23.)

Our comprehension of reality, and the scope of the war we are involved in, is enhanced as we read in Ephesians concerning the eternal purposes of God. Paul has been writing of the calling, destiny, mystery, and purpose of the Church when he suddenly looks beyond the immediate sphere of men:

> Also to enlighten all man and made plain to them (regarding the gentiles and providing for the salvation of all men,) of the mystery kept hidden through the ages and concealed until now in (the mind of) God Who created all things by Christ Jesus. (The purpose is) that through the church the complicated, many sided wisdom of God in all its infinite variety and innumerable aspects might now be made known to the angelic rulers and authorities (principalities and powers) in the heavenly sphere. This is in accordance with the terms of the eternal and timeless purpose which He has realized and carried into effect in (the person of) our Lord Jesus Christ.
>
> Ephesians 3:9-11, Amplified New Testament

War rages in our own sphere of perception and also in the supernatural dimension about us. Led by the great angel of God, Michael, heaven's storm troopers do battle with the forces of hell (Revelation 12:7; Daniel 10:12-13).

CALLED TO BE A SOLDIER

We are at war. When you face struggles and hard battles it is not because God doesn't like you or is giving you a bad time. It is because we are at war. The enemy attacks at every opportunity. You are a vital part of the end-time war action. You are called to be a soldier in the army of God. Your only effective defense is to take the offense against the devil and his minions. "Resist the devil and he will flee from you" (James 4:7).

We want the whole Church to be like a mighty army, but when apathy bounds in the churches, the dedicated must act as a guerrilla band— termined to infiltrate every level of the enemy's world structure and win y from him those who will become loyal followers of our King.

sending Jesus to die on the cross and to come forth from the grave, t the lying devil to open shame. God has thus proven the greatness ve and power. He has proven the rightness of His reign. He is going to be justified (show his course of action to be right) when all is said and done. Every knee shall bow to the glory of the Father. "It was to demonstrate and prove at the present time (in the now season) that He himself is righteous" (Romans 3:26, Amplified New Testament).

Even in the midst of the hostile and adverse conditions, God is preparing a people who love Him and who will serve Him eternally. What victory belongs to those who win the overcomer's crown in the agnostic climate of these times when Satan is making his last desperate stand! "Woe to the inhabiters of the earth...for the devil is come down unto you, having great wrath, because he knoweth that he hath but a short time" (Revelation 12:12).

All history approaches its climax. All divine prophecy finds its fulfillment at the return of our Lord Jesus Christ. All profane history finds its end-product in that man of sin, the human Satan who will have a short reign before the righteous Kingdom of our God begins on earth.

There are but two camps today: that of Christ, and that of Antichrist. Where do you stand? Which side are you on in this all-important war? You cannot be neutral, for Jesus said, "He that is not with me is against me" (Matthew 12:30).

For those on God's side, the message of Christ's return is a blessed hope (Titus 2:13). It is not doomsday; it is "hopesday"—for God's intervention is the one hope for the survival of our world now under the attack and raging dominion of Satan.

Where do you stand in the conflict of the ages? Be on God's side—the winning side!

In contemporary Christian literature one finds a strange dichotomy. On one hand, we are inundated with books and articles of an eschatological nature. On the other hand, many fine books on a multitude of subjects concerning life in the now season are being offered. The end-time experts are telling us to get ready to leave this old world behind, or get ready to live under the harsh regime of the Antichrist, depending on whether the writer is pre-, mid- or post-tribulationist in his theology. The two realms of thought seem to be mutually exclusive.

Is there no way to wed the future to the present? Is it possible to live in expectancy of the Second Coming and still have practical concern for the needs of the world today?

We believe that we should be interested in the future. We should be ard students of prophecy. We should study and understand the Book of Revela This understanding of the future should also promote the highest se citizenship responsibility in the life of the one who pursues a know the end times. No escapism or shrugging off of responsiblity ma on anticipation of the rapture of the Church. Prophecy is m intellectual exercise. We are to be doers of the Word and not hearers only.

But what can one *do* about Bible prophecy? That is what this book is about—what you should be *doing* about these end times; how to get involved in the divine plan for today and tomorrow and tomorrow...

In earlier chapters dealing with the "Daniel Factor" we explored some things that are sometimes overlooked in the story of Daniel the Prophet. We believe that this is symptomatic or illustrative of something missing in contemporary emphasis on prophecy. What is missing is a sense of involvement in the purposes of God as revealed in Biblical prophecy.

The New Testament ideal is to maintain a healthy anticipation of the Lord's return, and yet daily be busy with "occupying till he comes." It has been over nineteen centuries since John wrote, "...it is the last time..." The Rapture has not taken place yet. We have good reason to believe we are living in the "last days" but we do not know for sure when Jesus will return. I must pay attention to my Lord's designs for this season, and somehow relate to all that is to come. Here is prophecy set in motion. Here is the secret of moving *with* God through the process of time toward the ultimate fulfillment of the Kingdom:

> "Thy kingdom come — the future
> Thy will be done In earth — now
> As it is in heaven" — now and future

Bible prophecy is not a spectator sport. It is not a game at all. It is the very fabric of present reality. God is not looking for spectators, He is seeking participants in His end-time activities.